CONTENTS

INTRODUCTION

The Associated Board's Diplomas provide an authoritative assessment framework for a wide range of musicians – performers, directors and teachers. Whether you are intending to pursue a career in music, are currently working as a professional and wish to broaden your qualifications, or are purely after the satisfaction of achieving a personal goal, you will find that one of our Diplomas is right for you.

There are three Diploma **subject-lines** – Music Performance, Music Direction, and Instrumental/ Vocal Teaching. Each subject-line has three **levels** of award:

DipABRSM	Diploma of The Associated Board of the Royal Schools of Music
LRSM	Licentiate of the Royal Schools of Music
FRSM	Fellowship of the Royal Schools of Music

The requirements within each subject-line at each level are generally comparable, and the syllabus for each subject-line is published separately.

Encouraging diverse approaches to the performing, directing and teaching of music, the Diplomas stimulate enjoyment and achievement through the progressive acquisition of skills, knowledge and understanding. As a result, their usefulness has been acknowledged by music services and agencies around the world. They are compatible with systems of assessment widely applied in higher education and encourage lifelong learning, without restrictions on length of study or the requirement that you, the candidate, are taught in an institution. In the UK they have been admitted to the National Qualifications Framework and are accredited by the Qualifications and Curriculum Authority (see p. 122).

The **Music Performance Diplomas** are designed to reflect your day-to-day experience as a performer, whether amateur or professional. As well as demonstrating your skills as a soloist, from LRSM level there is the opportunity for you to specialize as an orchestral player, chamber ensemble member or keyboard accompanist. There are also options, at all three levels, to perform on an instrument related to your main instrument for a part of your Recital and to perform repertoire of your own choice. The following tasks are included:

- compiling a balanced recital programme, finding editions that suit your interpretation best, and writing about the music
- talking with confidence about the music and the way you interpret it
- sight-reading at short notice to a reasonable standard (Quick Study)
- putting on the best possible performance on the day.

You will need to satisfy the examiners that you have a command of your chosen instrument in the context of Western art music. (Throughout this syllabus, the term 'instrument' is used to include 'voice'.) As you move up through the Diploma levels you will find that the repertoire becomes more demanding, the Recital time lengthens, and the challenge of the Quick Study, and the scope and length of your written work, increase. At each level you will be assessed according to the overall quality of your performance, as well as your understanding of and sensitivity to the demands of different types of repertoire.

In order to establish basic levels of competence, a specific prerequisite is required before entry can be made to any level. However, in line with our aim to provide open access and to recognize your achievements, we offer a range of substitutions for these prerequisites, including your previous learning and experience. The prerequisites and their substitutions are listed in the tables on pp. 20–21. They are also to be found on our website (www.abrsm.org/exams/diplomas), where any substitutions appearing after the issue of this syllabus will also be listed. We hope that you find the experience of taking one of our Diplomas stimulating, challenging and worthwhile, both during the period of preparation and in the exam itself.

CONTENT OF THE MUSIC PERFORMANCE DIPLOMAS

Overview

The Music Performance Diplomas are available to instrumental and vocal performers. Through live and written components, you, the candidate, will be examined in your command of performance technique and interpretative skill coupled with an appropriate knowledge of the idiom and repertoire of your instrument/voice. The Diplomas are conducted in English (see p. 34) and are assessed wherever possible by two examiners.

Before you can enter for a Music Performance Diploma, you will need to show that you fulfil a specific ABRSM **prerequisite** as evidence that you have reached a required minimum level of competence. The table on pp. 20–21 lists the prerequisites and their possible substitutions.

Each level of Diploma comprises a number of **requirements** that you must satisfy in full. The requirements are divided into two Sections, as outlined below. You must pass all the requirements of both Sections in order for your Diploma to be awarded. The requirements must be met in full within three years.

SECTION 1
- an instrumental or vocal **Recital**.

SECTION 2 Section 2.1

- a **Viva Voce**, entailing a discussion with the examiners.

- a written assignment (relating to your Recital programme) which you should be prepared to discuss as part of your Viva Voce, and which contributes to the Viva Voce mark. At DipABRSM and LRSM levels, this assignment takes the form of **Programme Notes**, which must be presented to the examiners on the day of the exam. At FRSM level, you are required to prepare a **Written Submission**, which you must send to the Board with your entry.

Section 2.2

- a **Quick Study** – performance of a short piece of unaccompanied and previously unseen music.

Full descriptions of each level of Diploma, including preparation guidance, are given on the following pages. All practical information about taking a Diploma is described in Practicalities (pp. 29–34).

Prerequisite ABSRM Grade 8 Practical in the instrument presented or a permitted substitution (see p. 20).

To be submitted on the day of the exam Two copies of **Programme Notes**, written by you and illuminating in your own words the repertoire you have chosen to perform in your Recital, must be presented to the examiners at the start of the exam. Full details regarding the Programme Notes, including length, are given on pp. 24–26.

Timing 60 minutes are allocated to the DipABRSM, of which 35 minutes (± 10%) are devoted to the Recital, up to 12 minutes to the Viva Voce and up to 10 minutes to the Quick Study.

SECTION 1　RECITAL

Duration You should plan your Recital so that it lasts approximately 35 minutes (it may be up to 10% longer or 10% shorter). This total duration includes any breaks between items, as well as one longer pause (of up to 5 minutes) for woodwind, brass and singing candidates. Please note that the examiners reserve the right to stop the Recital if you exceed the prescribed duration.

Programming Your programme should be largely drawn from the prescribed lists of instrumental and vocal works or movements given on pp. 36–98. You may, however, also include in your programme a work or works of your own choice *not* listed on these pages but comparable in standard and lasting no more than 7 minutes in total; prior approval from the Associated Board is not required for any such alternative items. Please note that performing own-choice repertoire gives no advantage over candidates presenting syllabus-listed items only.

In your choice of repertoire, you should aim to present a generalist programme that offers a wide-ranging yet coherent mixture of periods, style, mood and tempo, with no more than one work by any single composer (except where a combination of movements or pieces from a composer's collection is indicated in the prescribed lists). You should be able to demonstrate musical technique and perception at a level worthy of public performance and appreciation.

Examination music The editions quoted in the repertoire lists on pp. 36–98 are recommendations only, and you are free to choose any other editions. All works/movements must be performed complete, although you should use your discretion in matters such as the omission of tutti sections or the inclusion of cadenzas in concerto movements or other works. The observance of repeats and interpretative decisions such as phrasing and the realization of ornaments are also matters in which you are expected to use your discretion to achieve a stylistically appropriate and musically satisfying performance.

Please note that on the day of the exam you will need to provide the examiners with copies of all the music you are performing, ideally in the same editions as those you are using. (If photocopies are to be used for this purpose, it is your responsibility to obtain written permission from the publisher/copyright holder.)

Performing from memory Although there is no specific requirement to perform from memory, you are encouraged to do so if you consider it will enhance your Recital. In particular, singers are advised to perform their programme from memory, with the exception of oratorio items and complex contemporary scores.

Accompanists and page-turners

You must provide your own accompanist, where appropriate. The accompanist may remain in the exam room only while actually engaged in accompanying. Please note that examiners will not act as accompanists under any circumstances. Both you and your accompanist may bring a page-turner, if required. In the case of organ candidates, the page-turner may also act as registrant.

Equipment

You are recommended to bring your own music stand/stool, if required. You may not bring into the exam room any material or equipment unconnected with your exam; any infringement of this rule may lead to disqualification.

Related instrument option

If your instrument is one of those listed under 'Main Instrument' in the table on p. 99, you have the option to play *one* work of your Recital on a related instrument (these are also listed on p. 99), while ensuring that the *majority* of the programme is performed on your main instrument. Please note that there is no advantage to be gained over other candidates by offering a work on a related instrument.

Other requirements

Candidates not meeting the syllabus requirements in any way, such as offering an inappropriate standard of piece, failing to adhere to the minimum/maximum platform times, or not being prepared to perform the minimum number of movements/pieces or the whole of a work if specified in the syllabus, will be liable to penalty.

SECTION 1

PREPARATION GUIDANCE FOR RECITAL

On the day of the exam, establish your stage presence right at the outset. Displaying confidence in entering the exam room, settling in and allowing yourself time to pause and create a space around each item will all increase the impact of your Recital. The marking criteria on p. 112 and the attainment descriptions on pp. 122–124 will help you to understand what qualities the examiners are looking for in your performance. The balance of technical and musical attainment shown through your instrumental ability, and your communication through musicianship, personal insight, interpretative skill and stage presence, are what count. It may help to imagine that the Recital is for performance on the radio or at a public venue.

Although you are not required to perform from memory, you should consider the standard convention for your instrument. For example, solo pianists normally perform recitals from memory (while it is unusual for a pianist playing within a chamber ensemble to do so without the music). In every case, the overriding priority must be the music itself and your communication and interpretation of it in a professional context. For singers, reference to the sheet music in performance may not only be inhibiting but can act as a barrier to the communication and interpretation of the music and the meaning of the text. Singers are therefore advised to use the sheet music only in oratorio items or complex contemporary works, in line with common performance practice.

In preparing for the exam, you may find it helpful to attend recitals on a regular basis in order to learn from approaches taken by professional performers. Critical listening and comparison of interpretations on record, combined with reading about performance techniques and practices, will also be useful. There is a list of recommended texts on the Board's website (www.abrsm.org/exams/diplomas); copies are also available from the Board's office in London. Finally, get to know not only the pieces within your programme but also their general context within each composer's output and the musical era.

SECTION 2.1   VIVA VOCE

The Viva Voce is an opportunity for you to demonstrate your knowledge, approach and understanding to the examiners. Questions will cover your Recital and your Programme Notes, as well as other aspects of performing. The Viva Voce lasts up to 12 minutes.

Typical areas of discussion in the Viva Voce:

- **Musical and instrumental outlook:** questions designed to put you at ease and to lead into the discussion, including: choice of repertoire, the challenges presented and the preparation involved; knowledge of the underlying concepts and principles associated with your instrument.
- **Repertoire and Programme Notes:** knowledge of the repertoire performed, including biographical information about each composer and the context of each work in the composer's life and output; details of commission (if any); the process of composition and first performance; knowledge of the general musical trends of the era and the place of each work in the context of the core repertoire.
- **Musical language and form:** understanding of the structure of each work and the features of its musical language.
- **Style and interpretation:** understanding of style and technique; knowledge of each work in the context of the instrument itself: historical developments, idiom, core repertoire and technical demands; the interpretation of notation and ways to communicate the composer's intentions; performance practices including original instrumentation; approaches to performance, including the use of physical space, memory and communication with an audience.
- **Any further points** you wish to draw to the examiners' attention before the conclusion.

SECTION 2.1   PREPARATION GUIDANCE FOR VIVA VOCE

The tone and manner of the Viva Voce will be as relaxed as possible and the examiners will make every effort to put you at ease. The opening questions will be informal, progressing to topics on which you are likely to be knowledgeable, then on to more challenging questions. All the questions will be clearly and directly expressed by the examiners; some will be open-ended, others will be more specific. You will not be penalized if you ask for clarification of a question, and the examiners will not be concerned by short periods of silence when an answer is being considered.

You may opt not to answer a question because, for example, you feel you might expose an area of fundamental ignorance. If this happens, the examiners will assist you with a number of helpful prompts. They will form a judgement as to whether your incapacity to offer an answer to a particular question or series of questions is a significant factor in the assessment of your overall performance in the exam.

If appropriate, you may demonstrate a particular feature or point by performing it, rather than describing it verbally.

Appendix 1 contains a number of specimen questions and indicative responses, showing the types of question examiners might ask in the Viva Voce and an indication of appropriate responses.

If you are not fluent in English you are strongly advised to bring an interpreter (see Language and interpreters, p. 34).

DIPLOMA CONTENT

SECTION 2.2   QUICK STUDY

In this section of the exam, you are required to perform a short piece of unaccompanied and previously unseen music of a standard similar to ABRSM Grade 6 repertoire.

Before you perform the Quick Study, you will be given five minutes in which to look through the music and to try out any parts of it. During this time the examiners will not be assessing you. Singers may play the key-chord and first note of the Quick Study on the piano before they begin their preparation, and as often as they wish prior to the test itself. During the test, singers who need to relocate their pitch may play a guide note as appropriate. Singers must sing the text, which will always be in English. In total, the Quick Study lasts up to 10 minutes.

SECTION 2.2 | PREPARATION GUIDANCE FOR QUICK STUDY

Many candidates choose to perform the Quick Study after their Viva Voce, but you are at liberty to perform it before or after the Recital, if you prefer. You should inform the examiners of your preferred order at the start of the exam.

The standard of the Quick Study test piece is similar to the demands of the current repertoire lists for the indicated ABRSM grade. You will therefore find it helpful to look at the pieces set for your instrument at this grade. Since the Quick Study tests have all been composed specifically for the Diploma exams, they tend to be in a modern, approachable style, although some of the tests have been written in pastiche styles. For keyboard instruments, guitar and harp, the test will normally be laid out over two pages. For all other instruments, the test will normally occupy one page. The tests for all instruments are unaccompanied.

It is not the length of the test but the technical and musical challenges with which you will be presented that you should concentrate on in preparing for the exam. The marking criteria on p.115 make clear what level of performance is expected for a pass or above in this test. Making it a habit to explore music unknown to you, and treating the exploration as a quick study exercise, will give you useful experience for the exam.

On the day, make sure you have mentally adjusted before you undertake the test; for example, if you have chosen to perform the Quick Study after your Viva Voce, do not allow yourself to think about aspects of the Viva Voce discussion, such as ideas you omitted to mention or might have expressed differently. Using the preparation time to full advantage is vital to your success in the Quick Study. To play through sections that do not need any attention is a waste of valuable time – go straight to the bars that matter. Try to avoid the common mistakes of either playing too slowly in order to get every note correct, or nervously hurrying and tripping over. Getting just the right tempo to allow the music to 'speak' is crucial. And finally, try to project the musical content and style in an expressive way, communicating the music with your best tone quality.

Prerequisite   DipABSRM (Music Performance) in the instrument presented or a permitted substitution (see p. 20).

To be submitted on the day of the exam   Two copies of **Programme Notes**, written by you and illuminating in your own words the repertoire you have chosen to perform in your Recital, must be presented to the examiners at the start of the exam. Full details regarding the Programme Notes, including length, are given on pp. 24–26.

Timing   75 minutes are allocated to the LRSM, of which 40 minutes ($\pm$ 10%) are devoted to the Recital, up to 15 minutes to the Viva Voce and up to 10 minutes to the Quick Study.

SECTION 1   RECITAL

Duration   You should plan your Recital so that it lasts approximately 40 minutes (it may be up to 10% longer or 10% shorter). This total duration includes any breaks between items, as well as one longer pause (of up to 5 minutes) for woodwind, brass and singing candidates. Please note that the examiners reserve the right to stop the Recital if you exceed the prescribed duration.

Programming   Your programme should be largely drawn from the prescribed lists of instrumental and vocal works or movements given on pp. 36–98. You may, however, also include in your programme a work or works of your own choice *not* listed on these pages but comparable in standard and lasting no longer than one third of the total platform time; prior approval from the Associated Board is not required for any such alternative items. Please note that performing own-choice repertoire gives no advantage over candidates· presenting syllabus-listed items only.

In your choice of repertoire, you should aim to present a balanced programme that includes a contrast of repertoire from at least two distinct musical eras. Variety of mood and tempo should also be a guiding factor in the construction of the programme.

Examination music   The editions quoted in the repertoire lists on pp. 36–98 are recommendations only, and you are free to choose any other editions. All works/movements must be performed complete, although you should use your discretion in matters such as the omission of tutti sections or the inclusion of cadenzas in concerto movements or other works. The observance of repeats and interpretative decisions such as phrasing and the realization of ornaments are also matters in which you are expected to use your discretion to achieve a stylistically appropriate and musically satisfying performance.

Please note that on the day of the exam you will need to provide the examiners with copies of all the music you are performing, ideally in the same editions as those you are using. (If photocopies are to be used for this purpose, it is your responsibility to obtain written permission from the publisher/copyright holder.) You should be prepared to discuss your choice of editions with the examiners in the Viva Voce.

Performing from memory   Although there is no specific requirement to perform from memory, you are encouraged to do so if you consider it will enhance your Recital. In particular, singers are advised to perform their programme from memory, with the exception of oratorio items and complex contemporary scores.

Accompanists and page-turners   You must provide your own accompanist, where appropriate. The accompanist may remain in the exam room only while actually engaged in accompanying. Please note that examiners will not act as accompanists under any circumstances. Both you and your accompanist may bring a page-turner, if required. In the case of organ candidates, the page-turner may also act as registrant.

DIPLOMA CONTENT

Equipment You are recommended to bring your own music stand/stool, if required (this also applies to chamber ensemble members: see under Specialist option below). You may not bring into the exam room any material or equipment unconnected with your exam; any infringement of this rule may lead to disqualification.

Related instrument option If your instrument is one of those listed under 'Main Instrument' in the table on p. 99, you have the option to play up to *two* works of your Recital on a related instrument (these are also listed on p. 99), while ensuring that the *majority* of the programme is performed on your main instrument. Please note that there is no advantage to be gained over other candidates by offering a work on a related instrument.

Specialist option As an alternative to performing as a solo recitalist for your entire programme, you may opt to present one third of your Recital within one of the three specialist areas listed below. The choice of repertoire is entirely at your own discretion, although it should be comparable in standard to the items in the lists on pp. 36–98. There is no advantage to be gained over other candidates by offering a specialist option. You must indicate your specialist option on the Entry Form.

- **Orchestral musician:** you are required to present orchestral excerpts, either unaccompanied or accompanied by your pianist. You should anticipate that the examiners will ask for an excerpt (or excerpts) to be repeated and that they may ask for a different tempo or approach to the one presented. Therefore, the total playing time of the excerpts need not be the full one third of the programme.
- **Chamber ensemble member:** you are required to supply your ensemble for the purposes of the exam at your own expense. Groups should normally number between 3 and 9 players (including yourself), with one player to each part.
- **Keyboard accompanist:** you are required to supply your duo partner for the purposes of the exam at your own expense.

Other requirements Candidates not meeting the syllabus requirements in any way, such as offering an inappropriate standard of piece, failing to adhere to the minimum/maximum platform times, or not being prepared to perform the minimum number of movements/pieces or the whole of a work if specified in the syllabus, will be liable to penalty.

SECTION 1 | **PREPARATION GUIDANCE FOR RECITAL**

See guidance on p. 8 which also applies to LRSM candidates.

The following additional guidance is provided for LRSM candidates offering one of the three specialist options. These have been designed for candidates wishing to display their skills in a particular branch of performance activity – orchestral, chamber, or keyboard accompaniment – alongside their skills as a solo recitalist. Should you choose to present orchestral excerpts, you will find that there are numerous published collections of excerpts for your instrument, and it may also be helpful to talk to orchestral musicians about the works that are frequently set at auditions. Although at LRSM level there is an entirely free choice of orchestral repertoire, you may find it useful to refer to the orchestral excerpts set for the FRSM exam (see the lists on pp. 97–98). The chamber option provides an opportunity for you to demonstrate your skills as a member of an ensemble, fulfilling the demands of your own line while contributing to the whole as a team player. Keyboard accompanists, like chamber musicians, will be assessed on their understanding of their part in relation to their duo partner.

SECTION 2.1 VIVA VOCE

The Viva Voce is an opportunity for you to demonstrate your knowledge, approach and understanding to the examiners. Questions will cover your Recital and your Programme Notes, as well as other aspects of performing. The Viva Voce lasts up to 15 minutes.

Typical areas of discussion in the Viva Voce:

- **Musical and instrumental outlook:** questions designed to put you at ease and to lead into the discussion, including choice of repertoire, the challenges presented and the preparation involved.
- **Repertoire and Programme Notes:** detailed knowledge of the repertoire performed, including biographical information about each composer and the context of each work in the composer's life and output; details of commission (if any); the process of composition and first performance; detailed knowledge of the general musical trends of the era and the place of each work in the context of the core repertoire and programme building.
- **Musical language and form:** indepth understanding of the structure of each work and its musical language; influences on the composer; each work's individuality and how far it is representative of the composer and the era.
- **Style and interpretation:** understanding of style, technique and ensemble; knowledge of each work in the context of the instrument itself: historical developments, idiom, core repertoire and technical demands; the interpretation of notation and ways to communicate the composer's intentions; performance practices including original instrumentation; editions; performances and recordings; approaches to performance, including the use of physical space, memory and communication with an audience.
- **Any further points** you wish to draw to the examiners' attention before the conclusion.

SECTION 2.1 | PREPARATION GUIDANCE FOR VIVA VOCE

See guidance on p. 9 which also applies to LRSM candidates.

SECTION 2.2 QUICK STUDY

In this section of the exam, you are required to perform a short piece of unaccompanied and previously unseen music of a standard similar to ABRSM Grade 7 repertoire.

Before you perform the Quick Study, you will be given five minutes in which to look through the music and to try out any parts of it. During this time the examiners will not be assessing you. Singers may play the key-chord and first note of the Quick Study on the piano before they begin their preparation, and as often as they wish prior to the test itself. During the test, singers who need to relocate their pitch may play a guide note as appropriate. Singers must sing the text, which will always be in English. In total, the Quick Study lasts up to 10 minutes.

SECTION 2.2 | PREPARATION GUIDANCE FOR QUICK STUDY

See guidance on p. 10 which also applies to LRSM candidates.

Prerequisite LRSM (Music Performance) in the instrument presented *or* a permitted substitution (see p. 21).

To be submitted with your entry Three copies of a **Written Submission**, which should address idiomatic features and performance issues connected with the Recital, must be submitted when you enter for the Diploma. Full details regarding the Written Submission, including length, are given on pp. 24 and 26–27.

Timing 90 minutes are allocated to the FRSM, of which 50 minutes (± 10%) are devoted to the Recital, up to 20 minutes to the Viva Voce and up to 10 minutes to the Quick Study.

SECTION 1 RECITAL

Duration You should plan your Recital so that it lasts approximately 50 minutes (it may be up to 10% longer or 10% shorter). This total duration includes any breaks between items, as well as one longer pause (of up to 5 minutes) for woodwind, brass and singing candidates. Please note that the examiners reserve the right to stop the Recital if you exceed the prescribed duration.

Programming Your programme should be drawn from the prescribed lists of instrumental and vocal works or movements given on pp. 36–98. You may, however, also include in your programme a work or works of your own choice *not* listed on these pages but comparable in standard and lasting no longer than two thirds of the total platform time; prior approval from the Associated Board is not required for any such alternative items. Please note that performing own-choice repertoire gives no advantage over candidates presenting syllabus-listed items only.

In your choice of repertoire, you should aim to present a specialist programme which may concentrate on one composer or period but should be internally balanced, containing sufficient contrast of mood and style.

Examination music The editions quoted in the repertoire lists on pp. 36–98 are recommendations only, and you are free to choose any other editions. All works/movements must be performed complete, although you should use your discretion in matters such as the omission of tutti sections or the inclusion of cadenzas in concerto movements or other works. The observance of repeats and interpretative decisions such as phrasing and the realization of ornaments are also matters in which you are expected to use your discretion to achieve a stylistically appropriate and musically satisfying performance.

Please note that on the day of the exam you will need to provide the examiners with copies of all the music you are performing, ideally in the same editions as those you are using. (If photocopies are to be used for this purpose, it is your responsibility to obtain written permission from the publisher/copyright holder.) You should be prepared to discuss your choice of editions with the examiners in the Viva Voce.

Performing from memory Although there is no specific requirement to perform from memory, you are encouraged to do so if you consider it will enhance your Recital. In particular, singers are advised to perform their programme from memory, with the exception of oratorio items and complex contemporary scores.

Accompanists and page-turners You must provide your own accompanist, where appropriate. The accompanist may remain in the exam room only while actually engaged in accompanying. Please note that examiners will not act as accompanists under any circumstances. Both you and your accompanist may bring a page-turner, if required. In the case of organ candidates, the page-turner may also act as registrant.

Equipment   You are recommended to bring your own music stand/stool, if required (this also applies to chamber ensemble members: see under Specialist option below). You may not bring into the exam room any material or equipment unconnected with your exam; any infringement of this rule may lead to disqualification.

Related instrument option   If your instrument is one of those listed under 'Main Instrument' in the table on p. 99, you have the option to play up to *two* works of your Recital on a related instrument (these are also listed on p. 99), while ensuring that the *majority* of the programme is performed on your main instrument. Please note that there is no advantage to be gained over other candidates by offering a work on a related instrument.

Specialist option   As an alternative to performing as a solo recitalist for your entire programme, you may opt to present at least half, and no more than two thirds, of your Recital within one of the three specialist areas listed below. The choice of repertoire can be at your own discretion, although it should be comparable in standard to the items in the lists on pp. 36–98. There is no advantage to be gained over other candidates by offering a specialist option. You must indicate your specialist option on the Entry Form.

- **Orchestral musician:** you are required to present orchestral excerpts, either unaccompanied or accompanied by your pianist, *including* those listed on pp. 97–98. You should anticipate that the examiners will ask for an excerpt (or excerpts) to be repeated and that they may ask for a different tempo or approach to the one presented. Therefore, the total playing time of the excerpts need not meet the minimum time specification.
- **Chamber ensemble member:** you are required to supply your ensemble for the purposes of the exam at your own expense. Groups should normally number between 3 and 9 players (including yourself), with one player to each part.
- **Keyboard accompanist:** you are required to supply your duo partner for the purposes of the exam at your own expense.

Other requirements   Candidates not meeting the syllabus requirements in any way, such as offering an inappropriate standard of piece, failing to adhere to the minimum/maximum platform times, or not being prepared to perform the minimum number of movements/pieces or the whole of a work if specified in the syllabus, will be liable to penalty.

SECTION 1 | PREPARATION GUIDANCE FOR RECITAL

See guidance on p. 8 which also applies to FRSM candidates.

The following additional guidance is provided for FRSM candidates offering one of the three specialist options. These have been designed for candidates wishing to display their skills in a particular branch of performance activity – orchestral, chamber, or keyboard accompaniment – alongside their skills as a solo recitalist. Should you choose to present orchestral excerpts, you will find that there are numerous published collections of excerpts for your instrument, and it may also be helpful to talk to orchestral musicians about the works that are frequently set at auditions. Please note that you *must* include those orchestral excerpts listed for your instrument on pp. 97–98. The chamber option provides an opportunity for you to demonstrate your skills as a member of an ensemble, fulfilling the demands of your own line while contributing to the whole as a team player. Keyboard accompanists, like chamber musicians, will be assessed on their understanding of their part in relation to their duo partner.

SECTION 2.1 VIVA VOCE

The Viva Voce is an opportunity for you to demonstrate your knowledge, approach and understanding to the examiners. Questions will cover your Recital and your Written Submission, as well as other aspects of performing. The Viva Voce lasts up to 20 minutes.

Typical areas of discussion in the Viva Voce:

- **Musical and instrumental outlook:** questions designed to put you at ease and to lead into the discussion, including choice of repertoire, the challenges presented and the preparation involved.
- **Repertoire and Written Submission:** comprehensive knowledge of the repertoire performed, including biographical information about each composer and the context of each work in the composer's life and output; familiarity with significant contemporaries; knowledge of the standard repertoire and programme building; points of clarification in the Written Submission; questions prompting expansion, analysis and evaluation of particularly interesting or original points; ability to deal with complex issues and to communicate conclusions clearly to a specialist and non-specialist audience.
- **Musical language and form:** perceptive insights into the structure of each work and its musical language; influences on the composer; each work's degree of innovation and personal style as opposed to conformity with contemporary trends and received or traditional style, and the level of success achieved.
- **Style and interpretation:** understanding of style, technique and ensemble; knowledge of each work in the context of the instrument itself: historical developments, idiom, technical demands, the composer's use of the instrument in relation to standard practice; design history, leading makers, major developments in technical approaches; the developing role of the instrument in either solo, chamber or orchestral music and the associated repertoire (*depending on specialist option, if chosen*); core didactic material; the interpretation of notation and ways to communicate the composer's intentions; performance practices including original instrumentation; sources, editions and the editorial apparatus (logic and consistency of approach and faithfulness to the original source) and any alternatively viable solutions; the most important exponents and their influence on performing conventions now in common usage; seminal performances and recordings; approaches to performance and performance preparation, including psychology, nerves and tension, the use of physical space, memory and communication with an audience.
- **Any further points** you wish to draw to the examiners' attention before the conclusion.

SECTION 2.1 | PREPARATION GUIDANCE FOR VIVA VOCE

See guidance on p. 9 which also applies to FRSM candidates.

SECTION 2.2 QUICK STUDY

In this section of the exam, you are required to perform a short piece of unaccompanied and previously unseen music of a standard similar to ABRSM Grade 8 repertoire.

Before you perform the Quick Study, you will be given five minutes in which to look through the music and to try out any parts of it. During this time the examiners will not be assessing you. Singers may play the key-chord and first note of the Quick Study on the piano before they begin their preparation, and as often as they wish prior to the test itself. During the test, singers who need to relocate their pitch may play a guide note as appropriate. Singers must sing the text, which will always be in English. In total, the Quick Study lasts up to 10 minutes.

SECTION 2.2 | PREPARATION GUIDANCE FOR QUICK STUDY

See guidance on p. 10 which also applies to FRSM candidates.

DIPLOMA CONTENT

Summary of skills, knowledge and understanding at all levels

At **DipABRSM** and **LRSM** levels, successful candidates will have demonstrated:

- Performance skills covering a range of styles, including technical competence and musical understanding.

- Knowledge and understanding of the repertoire performed, including its idiom, form, style and interpretation.

- Knowledge and understanding of the instrument/voice, its idiom and repertoire.

- Communication skills and ability to articulate knowledge and understanding through musical performance, orally and in writing.

- Research skills.

- Musical literacy and musicianship skills, including the ability to perform previously unseen music.

In addition, successful **FRSM** candidates will have demonstrated:

- Ability to deal with complex issues and to communicate conclusions clearly to a specialist and non-specialist audience.

- Ability to make critical evaluations of sources.

PREREQUISITES AND SUBSTITUTIONS

Prerequisites and substitutions

To be eligible to enter for a Diploma, you will need to show that you fulfil a specific ABRSM **prerequisite** as evidence that you have reached a required minimum level of competence. However, reflecting our aim to provide open access and to recognize candidates' achievements, we offer a range of possible **substitutions** or alternatives for these prerequisites. The substitutions are given in the table below alongside the prerequisites.

	Prerequisite	Substitutions
DipABRSM	ABRSM Grade 8 Practical in the instrument presented	• Appropriate professional experience (see p. 22) • Grade 8 Practical from Guildhall School of Music & Drama, London College of Music & Media, Dublin Institute of Technology, Australian Music Examination Board or University of South Africa; Grade 9 Practical from Royal Conservatory of Music, Toronto • Grade 8 Practical from Trinity College London or Royal Irish Academy of Music (with ABRSM Grade 5 Theory or equivalent from any of the boards listed in this table) • ATCL or ALCM Performer's Certificates from Trinity College London or Guildhall School of Music & Drama (with ABRSM Grade 5 Theory or equivalent from any of the boards listed in this table) • CPD Training Strategy, Module 1, from Royal Air Force Music Services • TEQA 1 from Royal Military School of Music, Kneller Hall • M2 from Royal Marines School of Music • BMus (Hons) from Royal Academy of Music or Royal College of Music (successful completion of all course units for the first year) • BMus (Hons) or BA (Music) from Royal Northern College of Music (successful completion of all course units for the first year) • BEd (Music), BA (Musical Studies) or BMus (Performance) from Royal Scottish Academy of Music & Drama (successful completion of the first year)
LRSM	DipABRSM (Music Performance) in the instrument presented	• Appropriate professional experience (see p. 22) • A university music degree with verified performance modules, such as final-year recital (required: copy of degree certificate, breakdown of results, and reference from course tutor/ instrumental teacher affiliated with university) • Advanced Certificate from ABRSM • DipABRSM (Music Direction) (with ABRSM Grade 8 Practical in the instrument presented) • LGSMD (Performing) from Guildhall School of Music & Drama • LLCM (Performing) from London College of Music & Media • LTCL (Performing) from Trinity College London • ARCT from Royal Conservatory of Music, Toronto • CPD Training Strategy, Module 3, from Royal Air Force Music Services • Band Sergeant Course or Band Sergeant Major Course from Royal Military School of Music, Kneller Hall • BMus (Hons), GRSM (Hons) or MMus (Performance Studies) from Royal Academy of Music • BMus (Hons) or GRSM (Hons) from Royal College of Music • BSc (Physics with Studies in Musical Performance) from Imperial College London and Royal College of Music

FRSM	LRSM (Music Performance) in the instrument presented	• Appropriate professional experience (see p. 22) • A university master's degree in Performance with verified performance components (required: copy of degree certificate, breakdown of results, and reference from course tutor/instrumental teacher affiliated with university) • LRAM (Performing) or Performer's Certificate from Royal Academy of Music • ARCM (Performing) or DipRCM (Performing) from Royal College of Music • FGSMD (Performing) from Guildhall School of Music & Drama • FLCM (Performing) from London College of Music & Media • FTCL (Performing) from Trinity College London • PGDip (Performance) from Royal Academy of Music • PGDip (Performance or Advanced Performance) or MMus (Performance Studies) from Royal College of Music • BMus (Hons), BA (Music), PPRNCM, PGDipRNCM or MMus (Performance) from Royal Northern College of Music • BA (Musical Studies), BMus (Performance), PGDipMus (Performance) or MMus (Performance) from Royal Scottish Academy of Music & Drama

PREREQUISITES

NB
- Any additions to the above list of substitutions will be posted on the Associated Board's website (www.abrsm.org/exams/diplomas).
- If you have a qualification that you consider to be at a higher level than those specified in the table above, you may apply for it to be accepted as a substitution for the listed prerequisite.
- There are no time limits on the validity of prerequisites.

Supporting documentation

If you are fulfilling the prerequisite through one of the listed substitutions, you will need to enclose supporting documentation with your Entry Form. In the case of qualifications, you should enclose a photocopy of the relevant certificate. For courses (or parts of courses), a signed declaration from the institution concerned is acceptable (standard wording for this declaration is given on p. 117).

For candidates offering the standard ABRSM prerequisite:

UK & Republic of Ireland: a photocopy of the certificate (or mark form) should be enclosed *only* if the exam was taken before 1994 or in a centre outside the UK/Republic of Ireland.

All other countries: a photocopy of the certificate (or mark form) should be enclosed in all cases.

Appropriate professional experience

At all three levels you may apply to offer **appropriate professional experience** as a substitution for the standard ABRSM prerequisite. This is done by filling in the application form on p. 116 and sending it to the Director of Examinations for consideration. The form must reach the Board at least six weeks before the published closing date for the session in which you wish to be examined. It is important to note that applying for this substitution is a *separate* procedure from sending in your Entry Form, and that approval of your professional experience must already have been given *before* you can enter for the Diploma. When you are ready to enter, you must enclose the Associated Board's approval letter with your completed Entry Form.

Please note the following points:

- The professional experience that you cite on your application form must be comparable in both subject and level to the prerequisite you are applying to substitute. This experience should consist of some or all of the following: full-time music courses other than those listed in the table on pp. 20–21; qualifications gained in areas specifically relating to the prerequisite; and relevant practical experience (for example, regular (semi-)professional appearances as a performer). These should have been undertaken or completed within the preceding five years.

- Your professional experience must be supported by a signed declaration from an independent person of appropriate standing (for example, a course director/ supervisor/tutor, a musical director, orchestral manager, head teacher or other education professional). Standard wording for this declaration is given on p.117.

- Wherever possible, your application form should be supported by documentary evidence, such as copies of certificates, details of module/course content, samples of marked work, concert programmes and reviews, or publicly available recordings.

SUBMISSIONS

General information regarding submissions

In this syllabus, the word **submission** refers to:

- the **Programme Notes** (DipABRSM and LRSM only)
- the **Written Submission** (FRSM only)

These are pieces of **prepared work** that you will be expected to discuss with the examiners as part of your Viva Voce and which contribute to the Viva Voce (Section 2.1) mark.

Declaration of genuine work

All submissions must genuinely be your own work and you are accordingly required to complete a candidate declaration form substantiating each submission. This form is to be found on the Entry Form as well as on our website (www.abrsm.org/exams/diplomas).

In the case of the Written Submission, the declaration form must be submitted with your entry. For Programme Notes, you must present the examiners with your declaration form on the day of the exam, along with the Programme Notes themselves.

If the examiners perceive a significant discrepancy between the level of authority of a submission and your performance in the Viva Voce (allowing for the fact that you may be nervous), it may be necessary to probe deeper to establish that the work is genuinely your own.

Plagiarism

The Associated Board defines plagiarism as an attempt to pass off the work of others as one's own. Thus, copying from a published or unpublished source without acknowledging it, or constructing a précis of someone else's writing or ideas without citing that writer, constitutes plagiarism. The Director of Examinations will consider all suspected cases and candidates will be penalized or disqualified if a charge of plagiarism is upheld. Candidates will have a right of appeal and representation if such a charge is made.

Other points

- For quality-assurance purposes, you should not identify your name on or inside any submission. Instead, the Associated Board will attach a Candidate Number to each submission before passing it on to the examiners.
- Permission to use copyright extracts from musical scores is not usually required for examination submissions. You must ensure, however, that you quote the appropriate publisher credit. If in any doubt, you should contact the publisher concerned.
- A submission may not be drawn upon for future use at a higher level of Associated Board Diploma, although reference to it may be cited.
- A failed submission may form the basis of a resubmission at the same level.
- A submission must neither have been previously published nor submitted to any institution or agency for another academic award.
- The Associated Board reserves the right to refuse examination of any submission if, in its view, it contains material of an unsuitable, unseemly or libellous nature.
- The Associated Board regrets that it cannot return any submissions, so you are advised to keep a copy for your records.

Specific details regarding the Programme Notes and Written Submission are given on the following pages.

Programme Notes (DipABRSM and LRSM)

You must present two identical copies of your **Programme Notes** to the examiners at the start of the exam. (If your Programme Notes are in a language other than English, one copy of the original should be submitted together with two copies of an independently verified translation into English.) The Notes should discuss and illuminate in your own words the works you have chosen to perform in your Recital, and they must be authenticated as your own work by a declaration form (see p. 24). Remember that you should be prepared to discuss your Programme Notes in your Viva Voce.

Required length
- DipABRSM   1,100 words (± 10%)
- LRSM   1,800 words (± 10%)

NB   If your Programme Notes fall outside these limits, you will be penalized.

Format   Your Programme Notes must be typed or printed in black, and the title page must contain the following information:

- the full title of the Diploma and your instrument
- the date of the exam
- the word count (excluding title page)
- the works in your programme in the order in which you are to perform them (excepting orchestral excerpts, if offered as a specialist option at LRSM level)

In addition, all the pages must be consecutively numbered. Please remember that you must not identify your name anywhere on or inside your Programme Notes.

SUBMISSIONS

PREPARATION GUIDANCE FOR PROGRAMME NOTES

At both DipABRSM and LRSM levels, your Programme Notes should illuminate the content of your Recital programme in an interesting and relevant way.

At **DipABRSM** level, you should write your Programme Notes as if for a general concert audience – that is, an audience of non-musicians who are interested in music and are relatively knowledgeable. If your programme contains standard repertoire works, the generalist audience will probably already know something about them and may have heard either live or recorded performances of them before. Writing about very well-known pieces may initially seem a daunting task (what more can there be left to say about Bach's Cello Suites or Beethoven's 'Moonlight' Sonata?). But the audience will still appreciate being reminded, or told for the first time, of the background to the pieces, the composers' intentions, and other relevant information about the works and what makes them popular. Some technical but universally common language may be helpful and necessary, but its meaning should always be clear. The following examples show the style of writing you are aiming for at DipABRSM level:

- The defining features of the chaconne are a triple metre and an ostinato (repeating) bass line, which often begins with a descending scale. The repeated bass line of this chaconne is simply a series of four descending notes, which can be heard very clearly in the piano introduction.

- Like the majority of Scarlatti's arias, 'Ergiti, amor' uses the 'da capo' aria form that dominated eighteenth-century Italian opera. It consists of three sections (ABA), in which the repeated A section is usually sung with additional ornamentation.

- Towards the end of the movement there is the conventional cadenza passage which provides an opportunity for the performer to improvise using themes from the movement. The cadenza played today is not an improvisation, but has been written by the performer in a Mozartian style.

SUBMISSIONS

At **LRSM** level, you need to discuss the musical content in more detail and with more technical language. Write as though your Programme Notes are going to be read by an intelligent, informed reader. Here are some examples:

● In the Adagio, effective use is made of many of the violin's tone colours, for example through the use of the mute and harmonics at the end of the piece which produce a pure and ringing sound. This contributes to one of the essential features of the composer's style – his unique adaptation of French impressionism. The oriental-influenced harmonic and melodic language is in complete contrast to the previous movement, with its emphasis on tonal melody and conventional triadic harmony.

● The third variation combines the characteristic dotted rhythm of the main theme with a revision of the original melodic contour, now based on the dissonant interval of an augmented fourth – the 'diabolus in musica' (devil in music) of medieval music theory. While the basic binary (AB) structure of the theme is maintained, the second section is much extended with contrapuntal elaborations of the melodic material.

● The serene rondo theme of the finale is anchored to a deep pedal note and has the character of a folksong. The spacious layout of the movement allows for two episodes – easily discernible since the tension increases as each plunges into strident and energetic octave passages in minor keys – as well as for a good deal of development besides. The rondo theme becomes the focus of the brilliant *prestissimo* coda in which long trills decorate the penultimate appearance, anticipating Beethoven's most mature style of piano writing.

Further guidance on writing programme notes is contained in *Writing Programme Notes: A guide for diploma candidates* by Nigel Scaife, published on the Associated Board's website (www.abrsm.org/exams/diplomas). For those without internet access, this text is available free of charge from the Board's office in London. It clearly shows the expectations at DipABRSM and LRSM levels and discusses in detail aspects such as the use of descriptive language, prose style, format and the use of technical terms. Clear guidance is also given regarding the degree of analysis and evaluation required, particularly through the provision of examples.

Written Submission (FRSM)

You must send three identical copies of your **Written Submission** with your entry. (If your Written Submission is in a language other than English, one copy of the original should be submitted together with three copies of an independently verified translation into English.) The Written Submission should address idiomatic features and performance issues connected with your Recital, and it must be authenticated as your own work by a declaration form (see p. 24). Remember that you should be prepared to discuss your Written Submission in your Viva Voce.

Required length   4,500 words (± 10%)

NB   If your Written Submission falls outside these limits, you will be penalized.

Format   Your Written Submission must be in the following format:

- typed or printed in black on good-quality white paper of international A4 (297mm x 210mm) or US Legal size
- the margins should be of the following minimum widths:
      inside margin: 45mm
      top and outside margins: 15mm
      bottom margin: 20mm
- only one side of each sheet should be used
- each copy must be securely bound, with all pages consecutively numbered
- the title page must contain the following information:
      the full title of the Diploma and your instrument; the date of submission;
      the word count (excluding title page, endnotes/footnotes, bibliography/ discography)
- the title page must be followed by an outline or précis of your Submission of about 150–250 words and a contents page
- references to either endnotes or footnotes, if used, must be clearly inserted in the text
- the Submission must be consistent in its presentation and approach to the citation of sources
- a bibliography and, where appropriate a discography, must be included, citing all works used in the preparation of the Submission.

Please remember that you must not identify your name anywhere on or inside your Written Submission.

SUBMISSIONS

PREPARATION GUIDANCE FOR WRITTEN SUBMISSION

In your Written Submission you are required to explore some of the content of your Recital programme and to focus in detail on a particular aspect or aspects surrounding the composition and performance history of one or more items of the chosen repertoire. You do *not* need to make reference to the whole programme.

Appropriate areas for discussion might include issues about period and style or analytical approaches that illuminate interpretation. Other possible topics include issues of authenticity, reception history, the influence of wider cultural developments, the study of manuscript sources, the history of critical thought in relation to the repertoire, and the relationship between each work and its composer's output. You might also wish to research the historical context of the chosen repertoire or the way in which a work exploits the particular idiom of the instrument/voice.

The Submission should include personal insights and contain substantial evidence of critical evaluation and appropriate research. It should also reflect the preoccupations relevant to you as a performer as well as any issues that you take into account in your work. Above all, the Associated Board would like to encourage candidates to think creatively about their Submission and to research a topic that focuses on an area of personal interest, i.e. not necessarily one covered in the suggestions given above.

Trevor Herbert's *Music in Words* (London: ABRSM, 2001) defines presentational conventions for written work, while also providing a basis for researching and writing at higher educational levels.

PRACTICALITIES

PRACTICALITIES

Before the exam (Entry)

Entry Forms

There are separate Diploma **Entry Forms** for candidates in the UK/Republic of Ireland, and for candidates in all other countries. Each Diploma Entry Form is accompanied by a **Supplementary Information** leaflet, which contains clear step-by-step instructions to help you fill in your Entry Form.

In the **UK and Republic of Ireland**, Diploma Entry Forms can be obtained from the Associated Board's Diplomas Office or from our website. In **all other countries**, Entry Forms can be obtained through local Representatives, from the Board's International Department or from our website. (See syllabus back cover for contact details.)

Payment and fees

Payment must be made at the time of entry and your fee is dependent on the level of Diploma and whether you are making a substitution.

For candidates in the **UK and Republic of Ireland**, the fees for all three levels of Diploma are given on the Entry Form, which is issued annually with updated fee details. Candidates **in all other countries** should refer to the separate Dates and Fees leaflet for their country, which is available from the local Representative or Contact, or from the Board's International Department.

Submissions and supporting documentation

When returning your Entry Form and fee, please ensure that you carefully complete the Checklist (on the Entry Form), enclosing any of the following required documentation and submissions:
- documentation supporting your prerequisite or substitution for a prerequisite (see p. 21)
- your Written Submission (FRSM only) with authenticating declaration form (see p. 24)
- the Associated Board's letter approving appropriate professional experience (see p. 22).

Where to send your entry

In the **UK and Republic of Ireland**, completed Entry Forms, together with fees, submissions and any supporting documents, should be sent to the address indicated on the Entry Form, and must be received by the closing date published in the Supplementary Information leaflet. In **all other countries**, completed Entry Forms etc. should be returned to the local Representative or, where there is no Representative, direct to the Board's International Department, by the last date of entry published in the appropriate Dates and Fees leaflet as well as in the current *Examination Regulations & Information* booklet (international edition).

Other points
- We regret that we cannot accept responsibility for the loss of any documents in the post, and we recommend you use a guaranteed postal delivery method.
- Entries for Diplomas can be accepted by the Associated Board only in accordance with the regulations given in this syllabus and on the understanding that in all matters our decision must be accepted as final. We reserve the right to refuse or cancel any entry, in which case the examination fee will be returned.

On the day of the exam

Places of examination

Music Performance Diploma exams are held in regional centres in the UK and Ireland (at the discretion of the Associated Board and subject to the availability of examiners and the suitability of venues) and in the main centres of all countries listed in the current *Examination Regulations & Information* booklet (international edition).

You will normally be greeted by a steward and, where a practice room is available, allowed a short time to warm up prior to entering the exam room. If you are an organ, harpsichord or percussion candidate, the exam venue must be organized by you, at no cost to the Board. It should be quiet and well-lit and should contain a writing table and chairs for the examiners. Someone should be provided to act as steward outside the exam room. If necessary, you must arrange transport for the examiners, to enable the exam timetable to be completed within the most suitable itinerary. An invoice for transport provided may be sent to the Board.

Dates of examination

In the UK and Republic of Ireland, Diploma exams are held on the dates specified in the Supplementary Information leaflet. In all other countries, exams are held on the dates given in the Dates and Fees leaflet for each country.

Examiners

Number of examiners

Wherever possible, two examiners will be present at each Diploma exam. When only one examiner can be present, the documentation and recorded evidence will be carefully monitored after their return to London in accordance with the Board's standard quality-assurance procedures (see Results, p. 32). At the Board's discretion, an additional person appointed by the Board may also be in attendance for monitoring purposes.

The examiners and you

Where two examiners are present, one examiner will, wherever possible, be a specialist in your discipline, and the other will be a generalist. In these cases, you will be welcomed into the exam room by the specialist examiner who will introduce the generalist examiner. Both will have been fully trained by the Associated Board. Each examiner will mark you independently. Their combined judgement ensures that you are assessed not only by someone with an intimate knowledge of your discipline, but also by another musician who is there to place your attainments within a broader musical setting.

Monitoring

For monitoring and moderation purposes, the live aspects of your Diploma will normally be audio-recorded by the examiners and returned to London for use by the Diploma Board (see p. 33). By submitting your entry you agree to your exam being recorded and to the recording becoming the property of the Associated Board (no copy will be made available to you). The recording may be used anonymously for training purposes. These procedures are detailed in the Diploma Board Code of Practice, available upon request from the office of the Director of Examinations.

Feedback

The Associated Board invites feedback from all Diploma candidates, for use by the Diploma Board. A feedback form is provided for this purpose, and we would be grateful if you could complete it and ensure that it is returned to the Board.

PRACTICALITIES

After the exam

Marking The marking process is designed to be fair and open. All candidates are assessed according to a two-Section examination structure, amounting to a total of 100 marks. Section 1 accounts for 60 of the total marks, with the two components of Section 2 accounting for the remaining 40 marks. All components of both Sections must be passed in order for a Diploma to be awarded. The pass mark is 40% – this applies to each component and Section as well as to the overall result. Candidates who pass with an overall mark of 70% or more are awarded the Diploma with Distinction.

0	10	20	30	40	50	60	70	80	90	100 %

Section 1
Recital

Section 2.1
Viva Voce

Section 2.2
Quick Study

24					60	10		25	6	15
pass mark					maximum mark	pass mark		maximum mark	pass mark	maximum mark

Viva Voce marks

Please note that your Programme Notes/Written Submission do not receive a separate mark but contribute to the overall mark of Section 2.1, whereas the Quick Study is marked separately, as Section 2.2.

The examiners review Programme Notes during the exam, whereas the Written Submission is assessed before the exam and given a guideline mark, which is then confirmed or adjusted on the basis of your responses in the Viva Voce.

Tables outlining the **marking criteria** for all components of the Music Performance Diplomas are given in Appendix 2 on pp. 112–115.

Results On the day of your exam, the examiners will not give any indication of your result. After the examiners have returned the mark form and recorded evidence to the Associated Board, they are placed before the Diploma Board (see p. 33) as part of our rigorous quality-assurance procedures. This means that you are likely to wait approximately eight weeks for your result.

All results – your certificate (if successful) and the examiners' mark form – will be despatched by post. We regret that we are not able to give any results by telephone, fax or e-mail, nor can we accept responsibility for the loss of results in the post.

Retakes If you are unsuccessful in any part of your Diploma, you may wish to consider a retake. Please bear in mind, however, that your Diploma must be completed within three years from your first attempt.

You may choose to retake the entire exam in order to aim for higher marks. Alternatively, you are entitled to carry credit forward from any component (Recital, Viva Voce or Quick Study) from your previous attempt. The examiners will be aware of any credit carried forward, but this will in no way affect the objectivity of the assessment process.

Details of retake options are included in the letter accompanying results. This letter also covers the options for Programme Notes/Written Submission for candidates wishing to retake their Diploma.

PRACTICALITIES

Quality assurance and Diploma Board

For the purposes of quality assurance there is a Diploma Board which oversees all matters relating to Diplomas. As well as ratifying procedures and monitoring decisions taken by its committees, the Diploma Board advises on standards and considers all matters of quality assurance, including the training and professional development of examiners and the handling of appeals.

Membership of the Diploma Board comprises a Chairman (currently a Principal of one of the UK's Royal Schools of Music), Heads of Studies from the Royal Schools, three Independent Verifiers, three Diploma examiners (one of whom is the Associated Board's Chief Examiner), and the Director of Examinations of the Associated Board. Further information regarding the Diploma Board, its terms of reference and modes of operation, is contained in the Diploma Board Code of Practice, available upon request from the office of the Director of Examinations.

Appeals

An appeals procedure exists for candidates who feel they have been dealt with unfairly or inefficiently by the Associated Board or its examiners on a matter of procedure. Appeals on purely academic grounds (e.g. if a candidate is disappointed by his/her result) are not permitted. An appeal, if upheld, could lead to a re-examination, a review of the result, or some other course of action beneficial to the candidate. Before the Associated Board embarks upon the formal appeals procedure, it would need to be convinced that there is a *prima facie* case for an appeal, on the grounds that some aspect of the examination process has been handled other than in accordance with syllabus regulations, and that this is likely to have affected the candidate's result.

Candidates wishing to appeal against the procedure of a Diploma assessment should write to the Director of Examinations within 14 days of the issue of the result. They should clearly state the grounds for appeal and how these are felt to have affected the result; evidence supporting the claim must be given. A copy of the mark form should be enclosed. The Director of Examinations will then review the appeal, taking advice where necessary. Should there be further dispute, the case will be referred directly to the Diploma Board, which may then appoint a panel to consider the appeal. The decision of this panel shall be final.

Other matters

Absence

If you are unable to be present for your exam, you should notify the Board immediately, giving an explanation of your inability to attend. Provided your withdrawal is made necessary by an unavoidable event (such as illness or bereavement), part of the entry fee may be refunded at the discretion of the Board. (In the case of illness, a medical certificate is required.) Alternatively, in all countries other than the UK and Republic of Ireland, and at the Associated Board's discretion, a voucher may be issued entitling the candidate to re-enter the exam within one year of the original exam date. Such a voucher cannot subsequently be exchanged for cash. A candidate re-entered on a voucher and again absent is not entitled to any further concession.

Access (for candidates with special needs)

Standard arrangements exist for candidates who have a visual or hearing impairment, or learning difficulties such as dyslexia or autistic spectrum disorders. Details of these arrangements are given in the Supplementary Information leaflet accompanying the Entry Form. In addition, the Board publishes guidelines for candidates with visual impairments, hearing impairments, dyslexia and autistic spectrum disorders; these separate documents are available from the office of the Director of Examinations.

Candidates with other sensory impairments or learning difficulties must tick the relevant box on the Entry Form and also attach a statement from either a general practitioner, specialist, educational psychologist or other similarly qualified person, outlining the particular difficulties the candidate experiences and the likely impact upon his/her performance in an exam setting.

PRACTICALITIES

Candidates whose requirements are not covered above, or who have particular physical access requirements, are requested to write to the Director of Examinations with full details. The Board will then liaise with the relevant exam venue to ensure that all feasible arrangements are made.

The Board's policy does not make any concessions in terms of marking standards; rather, we try to alter the administration of our exams or, occasionally, to provide an alternative test or mode of assessment, in line with the particular needs of the candidate.

Language and interpreters

All examinations are conducted in English. If you are not comfortable using English, you are strongly advised to bring an independent person (who is neither your teacher nor a relative) to act as interpreter in the exam room. (Please tick the relevant box on the Entry Form.) Extra time will be allowed in such cases. Any costs incurred are the responsibility of the candidate. Candidates may make use of the Associated Board's interpreter service, where available (for details, contact your local Representative), on payment of an additional fee. Candidates should bear in mind that exams are normally recorded (see Monitoring, p. 31) and that translations will be checked for accuracy, as necessary.

Replacement certificates

A duplicate of a certificate can usually be provided on payment of a search fee of £10 (candidates outside the UK/Republic of Ireland should pay by banker's draft). Applications should state the country and year the exam took place in, the name of the candidate and his/her Candidate Number. A further fee may be required if information is inaccurate.

Academic recognition and dress

Each Diploma entitles the successful candidate to append the appropriate letters after his/her name. Academic dress for holders of the Associated Board's Diplomas may be obtained from William Northam & Co Ltd, P.O. Box 367, Waterbeach, Cambridge CB5 9QY (*telephone* 0870 2401852; *e-mail* enquiries@wmnortham.co.uk), to whom all enquiries should be made.

REPERTOIRE LISTS

Requirements concerning programming and examination music, as well as other performance details, are given on pp. 7–8 (DipABRSM), pp. 11–12 (LRSM) and pp. 14–15 (FRSM). Candidates are advised to study these requirements carefully when planning their Recital programmes. For contact details of publishers and distributors referred to in the following repertoire lists, see pp. 118–121.

A brace is used in the repertoire lists to indicate instances where two or more items appear in the same volume, e.g.:

Toccata no.3 in D, BWV 912: complete
Toccata no.5 in E minor, BWV 914: complete ⎰ *Bach 7 Toccatas (Henle or Henle – Schott/M.D.S.)*

Piano: DipABRSM

J.S. Bach   Any *one* of the following 48 Preludes and Fugues from 'The Well-Tempered Clavier'
Part 1: no.12 in F minor, BWV 857;
     no.14 in F♯ minor, BWV 859; no.16 in G minor, BWV 861 ⎤ (*Associated Board*)
Part 2: no.5 in D, BWV 874;
     no.9 in E, BWV 878; no.11 in F, BWV 880;   ⎫ (*Associated Board*)
     no.16 in G minor, BWV 885; no.17 in A♭, BWV 886 ⎭
Toccata no.3 in D, BWV 912: complete   ⎫ *Bach 7 Toccatas* (*Henle* or *Henle – Schott/M.D.S.*)
Toccata no.5 in E minor, BWV 914: complete ⎭

Bartók   Any *two or more* of the '6 Dances in Bulgarian Rhythm', from 'Mikrokosmos', Vol.6 (*Boosey & Hawkes*)

Beethoven   Sonata in F minor, Op.2 no.1: complete (*Associated Board*)
Sonata in C minor, Op.10 no.1: complete (*Associated Board*)
Sonata in F, Op.10 no.2: complete (*Associated Board*)
Sonata in C minor ('Pathétique'), Op.13: complete (*Associated Board*)
Sonata in E, Op.14 no.1: complete (*Associated Board*)
Sonata in G, Op.14 no.2: complete (*Associated Board*)
Sonata in A♭, Op.26: complete (*Associated Board*)
Sonata in C♯ minor ('Moonlight'), Op.27 no.2: complete (*Associated Board*)
Sonata in F, Op.54: complete (*Associated Board*)
Sonata in E minor, Op.90: complete (*Associated Board*)
6 Variations in F, Op.34   ⎫ *Beethoven Variations, Vol.1* (*Wiener Urtext/M.D.S*)
32 Variations in C minor, WoO 80 ⎭

L. Berkeley   Concert Study in E♭, Op.48 no.2 (*Chester/Music Sales*)

Howard Blake   Chaconne *and* Toccatina: nos.5 *and* 6 from '8 Character Pieces' (*Highbridge Music*)

Brahms   Capriccio in F♯ minor, Op.76 no.1. *Brahms 8 Piano Pieces, Op.76* (*Associated Board*)
Rhapsody in G minor, Op.79 no.2. *Brahms 2 Rhapsodies, Op.79* (*Associated Board*)
Intermezzo in A minor, Op.116 no.2. *Brahms 7 Fantasies, Op.116* (*Associated Board*)
Intermezzo in A, Op.118 no.2   ⎫
Ballade in G minor, Op.118 no.3 ⎬ *Brahms 6 Piano Pieces, Op.118* (*Associated Board*)
Romance in F, Op.118 no.5   ⎭

Diana Burrell   Constellations I and II. *Spectrum* (*20 Contemporary Works for Solo Piano*) (*Associated Board*)

Chopin   Berceuse in D♭, Op.57. *Chopin Complete Piano Works, Vol.11* (*P.W.M./M.D.S.*)
Impromptu no.3 in G♭, Op.51 (*Henle or Henle – Schott/M.D.S.*)
Introduction and Variations in B♭ on a theme from Hérold's 'Ludovic', Op.12. *Chopin Complete Piano Works, Vol.13* (*P.W.M./M.D.S.*)
Mazurka in C♯ minor, Op.50 no.3 (*Henle or Henle – Schott/M.D.S.*)
Nocturne in E, Op.62 no.2. *Chopin Nocturnes* (*Associated Board* or *Wiener Urtext/M.D.S.*)
Any *two* of the 3 Nouvelles Études (*Wiener Urtext/M.D.S.*)

Copland   Scherzo Humoristique 'The Cat and the Mouse' (*Durand/U.M.P.*)

Debussy   La plus que lente: Valse (*U.M.P.*)
Any *one* of the following Préludes:
Book 1: no.4 'Les sons et les parfums tournent dans l'air du soir', no.10 'La Cathédrale engloutie' (*U.M.P.* or *Wiener Urtext/M.D.S.*)
Book 2: no.3 'La Puerta del Vino' (*U.M.P.* or *Wiener Urtext/M.D.S.*)
Suite 'Pour le Piano': 2nd movt, *Sarabande* (*Henle* or *Henle – Schott/M.D.S.* or *U.M.P.*)

Fauré   Barcarolle no.1 in A minor, Op.26   ⎫ *Fauré Piano Works, Vol.2* (*Peters EP 9560b*)
Barcarolle no.6 in E♭, Op.70   ⎭
Impromptu no.2 in F minor, Op.31. *Fauré Piano Works, Vol.1* (*Peters EP 9560a*)

Gershwin   'The Man I Love' *and* 'I Got Rhythm'. *Meet George Gershwin at the Keyboard* (*Warner/I.M.P.*)

Haydn   Andante con Variazioni in F minor, Hob.XVII/6 (*Wiener Urtext/M.D.S.*)
Sonata in A♭, Hob.XVI/46: complete. *Haydn Selected Keyboard Sonatas, Book 4* (*Associated Board*)
Sonata in C, Hob.XVI/48: complete ⎫ *Haydn Complete Keyboard Sonatas, Vol.3*
Sonata in E♭, Hob.XVI/49: complete ⎭ (*Wiener Urtext/M.D.S.*)

Hindemith   Interludium (p.12) and Fuga no.3, from 'Ludus Tonalis' (*Schott ED 3964/M.D.S.*)

Janáček   Any *two* of the 4 pieces from 'In the Mists' (*Bärenreiter*)

Liszt   Liebestraum no.2 ('Seliger Tod'). *Liszt Liebesträume: 3 Notturnos* (*Henle* or *Henle – Schott/M.D.S.*)
Sonetto 123 del Petrarca: no.6 from 'Anneés de Pèlerinage, 2ème Anneé, Italie' (*Henle* or *Henle – Schott/M.D.S.*)

John McCabe   5 Bagatelles: complete (*Novello/Music Sales*)

Joseph Makholm   Any *two* of the '3 Impressions' (*Billaudot/U.M.P.*)

Mendelssohn   Prelude and Fugue in F minor: no.5 from '6 Preludes and Fugues', Op.35 (*Associated Board*)

Piano: DipABRSM

Messiaen	Regard de l'Étoile: no.2 Regard de la Vierge: no.4 $\Big\}$ from $\Big|$ 'Vingt Regards sur l'Enfant Jésus' (*Durand/U.M.P.*) Rondeau (*Leduc/U.M.P.*)
Mozart	Adagio in B minor, K.540. *Mozart Miscellaneous Pieces* (*Associated Board*) Sonata in D, K.284: complete (*Associated Board*) Sonata in C, K.309: complete (*Associated Board*) Sonata in D, K.311: complete (*Associated Board*) Sonata in Bb, K.570: complete (*Associated Board*) 10 Variations on 'Les hommes pieusement' ('Unser dummer Pöbel meint'), K.455 (*Associated Board*) 9 Variations on a Minuet by Duport, K.573 (*Associated Board*)
Poulenc	Toccata: no.3 from 'Trois Pièces' (*Heugel/U.M.P.*)
Prokofiev	Visions Fugitives nos.8, 14, 19 *and* 20, from 'Visions Fugitives', Op.22 (*Boosey & Hawkes*)
Rachmaninov	Any *one* of the following Preludes: Prelude in Eb, Op.23 no.6 Prelude in C minor, Op.23 no.7 $\Big\}$ *Rachmaninov Complete Preludes* (*Boosey & Hawkes*) Prelude in G, Op.32 no.5 Prelude in G♯ minor, Op.32 no.12
Ravel	Sonatine: complete (*Peters EP 7375*)
Edwin Roxburgh	Moonscape. *Spectrum* (*20 Contemporary Works for Solo Piano*) (*Associated Board*)
Scarlatti	Any *one* of the following *pairs* of Sonatas: 2 Sonatas in A, Kp.208 (L.238) *and* Kp.209 (L.428) $\Big\}$ *Scarlatti 60 Sonatas, Vol.1* 2 Sonatas in G, Kp.259 (L.103) *and* Kp.260 (L.124) (*Schirmer/Music Sales*) Sonata in E minor, Kp.263 (L.321) *and* Sonata in E, Kp.264 (L.466) $\Big\}$ *Scarlatti 60 Sonatas, Vol.2* 2 Sonatas in C, Kp.308 (L.359) *and* Kp.309 (L.454) (*Schirmer/Music Sales*)
Schoenberg	6 Little Pieces, Op.19: complete (*Universal 5069/M.D.S.*)
Schubert	Impromptu in Gb, Op.90 no.3, D899/3. *Schubert 4 Impromptus, D.899* (*Associated Board*) Sonata in A minor, Op.164, D.537: complete. *Schubert Sonatas, Vol.1* (*Associated Board*) Sonata in A, Op.120, D.664: complete. *Schubert Sonatas, Vol.2* (*Associated Board*)
Schumann	Des Abends (At Evening) *and* Aufschwung (Soaring): nos.1 *and* 2 from 'Phantasiestücke', Op.12 (*Associated Board*) Novellette in F: no.1 from '8 Novelletten', Op.21 (*Henle* or *Henle – Schott/M.D.S.*) Romanze in B: no.3 from '3 Romanzen', Op.28 (*Associated Board*)
Scriabin	Impromptu in Bb, Op.12 no.2 (*Belaieff 150/Peters*) Any *two* of the '24 Preludes', Op.11 (*Henle* or *Henle – Schott/M.D.S.*)
Peter Sculthorpe	Night Pieces: complete (*Faber*)
Shostakovich	Preludes nos.3 in G *and* 11 in B, from '24 Preludes', Op.34 (*Boosey & Hawkes*) Preludes nos.5 in D *and* 19 in Eb, from '24 Preludes', Op.34 (*Boosey & Hawkes*)
Stravinsky	Tango (*Schott ED 4917/M.D.S.*)
Szymanowski	Etude in Bb minor, no.3 from '4 Etudes', Op.4 (*Universal 03855/M.D.S.*)

Piano: LRSM

Albéniz	Any *one* of the 12 pieces from 'Iberia', *except* no.1 'Evocación' (*4 Vols: U.M.E./Music Sales*)
J.S. Bach	Chromatic Fantasia and Fugue in D minor, BWV 903 (*Henle* or *Henle – Schott/M.D.S.*) Partita no.2 in C minor, BWV 826: complete. *Bach Partitas 1–3* (*Associated Board*) Partita no.5 in G, BWV 829: complete. *Bach Partitas 4–6* (*Associated Board*) Any *one or two* of the following 48 Preludes and Fugues from 'The Well-Tempered Clavier': *Part 1:* no.3 in C♯, BWV 848; no.4 in C♯ minor, BWV 849; no.7 in Eb, BWV 852; no.8 in Eb minor, BWV 853; $\Big\}$ (*Associated Board*) no.20 in A minor, BWV 865; no.24 in B minor, BWV 869 *Part 2:* no.3 in C♯, BWV 872; no.4 in C♯ minor, BWV 873; no.10 in E minor, BWV 879; no.14 in F♯ minor, BWV 883; no.16 in G minor, BWV 885; no.18 in G♯ minor, BWV 887; $\Big\}$ (*Associated Board*) no.21 in Bb, BWV 890; no.22 in Bb minor, BWV 891; no.23 in B, BWV 892; no.24 in B minor, BWV 893
Bartók	Suite, Op.14: complete (*Universal 5891/M.D.S.*)
Beethoven	Sonata in C, Op.2 no.3: complete (*Associated Board*) Sonata in Eb, Op.7: complete (*Associated Board*) Sonata in D, Op.10 no.3: complete (*Associated Board*) Sonata in G, Op.31 no.1: complete (*Associated Board*) Sonata in D minor ('Tempest'), Op.31 no.2: complete (*Associated Board*) Sonata in Eb, Op.31 no.3: complete (*Associated Board*) Sonata in Eb ('Les Adieux'), Op.81a: complete (*Associated Board*)

Piano: LRSM

Richard Rodney Bennett	Any *two* of the '5 Studies' (*Universal 12995K/M.D.S.*)
Berg	Sonata, Op.1: complete (*Universal 8812/M.D.S.*)
Brahms	Capriccio in B minor, Op.76 no.2
	Capriccio in C# minor, Op.76 no.5 } *Brahms 8 Piano Pieces, Op.76* (*Associated Board*)
	Capriccio in C, Op.76 no.8
	Capriccio in D minor, Op.116 no.1
	Capriccio in G minor, Op.116 no.3 } *Brahms 7 Fantasies, Op.116* (*Associated Board*)
	Capriccio in D minor, Op.116 no.7
	Intermezzo in E♭ minor, Op.118 no.6. *Brahms 6 Piano Pieces, Op.118* (*Associated Board*)
	Rhapsody in B minor, Op.79 no.1. *Brahms 2 Rhapsodies, Op.79* (*Associated Board*)
	Rhapsody in E♭, Op.119 no.4. *Brahms 4 Piano Pieces, Op.119* (*Associated Board*)
Casella	Toccata, Op.6 (*Ricordi/U.M.P.*)
Chopin	Any *one* of the 4 Ballades: G minor Op.23, F Op.38, A♭ Op.47, F minor Op.52 (*Wiener Urtext/M.D.S.*)
	Barcarolle in F#, Op.60. *Chopin Piano Pieces* (*Henle* or *Henle – Schott/M.D.S.*)
	Any *two* contrasted Études from the '12 Études', Op.10 *or* the '12 Études', Op.25 (*Wiener Urtext/M.D.S.*)
	Fantaisie in F minor, Op.49 (*Henle* or *Henle – Schott/M.D.S.*)
	Polonaise-Fantaisie in A♭, Op.61. *Chopin Polonaises* (*Henle* or *Henle – Schott/M.D.S.*)
	Any *one* of the 4 Scherzi: B minor Op.20, B♭ minor Op.31, C# minor Op.39, E Op.54 (*Wiener Urtext/M.D.S.*)
Copland	Sonata: complete (*Boosey & Hawkes*)
Dallapiccola	Sonatina Canonica in E♭: complete (*Suvini Zerboni/William Elkin*)
Debussy	Any *one or more* of the 3 pieces from 'Estampes': Pagodes, La soirée dans Grenade, Jardins sous la pluie (*Henle* or *Henle – Schott/M.D.S.* or *U.M.P.*)
	Any *one, two or three* of the '12 Études' (*Henle* or *Henle – Schott/M.D.S.*)
	Any *one, two or three* of the 6 pieces from 'Images', 1st and 2nd Sets: Reflets dans l'eau, Hommage à Rameau, Mouvement, Cloche à travers les feuilles, Et la lune descend sur le temple qui fût, Poissons d'or (*2 vols: Henle* or *Henle – Schott/M.D.S.* or *U.M.P.*)
	L'Isle joyeuse (*Henle* or *Henle – Schott/M.D.S.* or *U.M.P.*)
	Any *two* of the following Préludes:
	Book 1: no.3 'Le vent dans la plaine', no.5 'Les collines d'Anacapri', no.7 'Ce qu'a vu le vent d'ouest', no.11 'La danse de Puck' (*U.M.P.* or *Wiener Urtext/M.D.S.*)
	Book 2: no.4 'Les feés sont d'exquises danseuses', no.7 'La terrasse des audiences du clair de lune', no.8 'Ondine', no.11 'Les tierces alterneés', no.12 'Feux d'artifice' (*U.M.P.* or *Wiener Urtext/M.D.S.*)
Dohnányi	Rhapsody in C, Op.11 no.3 (*Weinberger/William Elkin*)
Fauré	Barcarolle no.5 in F# minor, Op.66. *Fauré Piano Works, Vol.2* (*Peters EP 9560b*)
	Impromptu no.3 in A♭, Op.34. *Fauré Piano Works, Vol.1* (*Peters EP 9560a*)
	Nocturne no.4 in E♭, Op.36. *Fauré Piano Works, Vol.3* (*Peters EP 9560c*)
Ferguson	Sonata in F minor, Op.8: complete (*Boosey & Hawkes*)
Michael Finnissy	Yvaropera 5. *Spectrum* (*20 Contemporary Works for Solo Piano*) (*Associated Board*)
Fricker	Studies nos.2 *and* 4 from '12 Studies', Op.38 (*Schott ED 10804/M.D.S.*)
Ginastera	Any *one or more* of the '3 Danzas Argentinas' (*Durand/U.M.P.*)
	Sonata no.1, Op.22: complete (*Boosey & Hawkes*)
Granados	Any *one* of the 6 pieces from 'Goyescas', Vols.1 and 2 (*U.M.E./Music Sales*)
Haydn	Sonata in C, Hob.XVI/50: complete. *Haydn Selected Keyboard Sonatas, Book 4* (*Associated Board*)
	Sonata in E♭, Hob.XVI/52: complete. *Haydn Complete Keyboard Sonatas, Vol.3* (*Wiener Urtext/M.D.S.*)
Hindemith	Any *one or two* of the following Interludes and Fugues from 'Ludus Tonalis': Interludium p.7 *and* Fuga secunda in G, Interludium p.20 *and* Fuga quinta in E, Interludium p.38 *and* Fuga nona in B♭ (*Schott ED 3964/M.D.S.*)
	Sonata no.2 in G: complete (*Schott ED 2519/M.D.S.*)
	Sonata no.3 in B♭: complete (*Schott ED 2521/M.D.S.*)
Ireland	Amberley Wild Brooks (*Stainer & Bell*)
	April (*Stainer & Bell*)
	Chelsea Reach (*Stainer & Bell*)
	Ragamuffin (*Stainer & Bell*)
Kabalevsky	Sonata no.3 in F, Op.46: complete. *Kabalevsky 3 Sonatas* (*Boosey & Hawkes*)
Bryan Kelly	Sonata: complete (*Novello/Music Sales*)
Oliver Knussen	Sonya's Lullaby, Op.16 (*Faber*)
Kenneth Leighton	Conflicts (Fantasy on Two Themes), Op.51 (*Novello/Music Sales*)

Liszt Any *one* of the '5 Concert Studies' ⎫ *Liszt Piano Works, Vol.4 (Peters EP 3600d)*
Any *one* of the '6 Paganini Studies' ⎭
Any *one* of the '12 Études d'exécution transcendante', *except* no.1. *Liszt Piano Works, Vol.3*
  (*Peters EP 3600c*)
Either or *both* of the '2 Légendes' (St François d'Assise; St François de Paule) (*Peters EP 7202*)
Les jeux d'eaux à la Villa d'Este: no.4 from 'Années de Pèlerinage, 3ème Année' (*Henle* or *Henle –
  Schott/M.D.S.* or *publ. separately: Schott ED 06297/M.D.S.*)

Mendelssohn Andante and Rondo Capriccioso, Op.14 (*Henle* or *Henle – Schott/M.D.S.*)
Any *one or two* of the following from '6 Preludes and Fugues', Op.35: no.1 in E minor, no.3 in
  B minor, no.5 in F minor (*Associated Board*)
Variations Sérieuses, Op.54 (*Henle or Henle – Schott/M.D.S.*)

Messiaen Any *one* of the following from '8 Préludes': no.3 'Le Nombre léger', no.4 'Instants défunts'
  (*Durand/U.M.P.*)
Any *one* of the following pieces from 'Vingt Regards sur l'Enfant Jésus': no.8 'Regard des hauteurs',
  no.11 'Première communion de la Vierge', no.14 'Regard des Anges', no.15 'Le baiser de l'Enfant-
  Jésus', no.16 'Regard des prophètes, des bergers et des Mages' (*Durand/U.M.P.*)

Mozart Rondo in A minor, K.511 (*Associated Board*)
Sonata in A minor, K.310: complete (*Associated Board*)
Sonata in C minor, K.457: complete (*Associated Board*)
Sonata in F, K.533: complete (*Associated Board*)
Sonata in D, K.576: complete (*Associated Board*)

Poulenc 'Napoli' Suite: complete (*Salabert/U.M.P.*)

Prokofiev Sonata no.2 in D minor, Op.14: complete (*Boosey & Hawkes*)
Sonata no.3 in A minor, Op.28 (*Boosey & Hawkes*)
Sonata no.4 in C minor, Op.29: complete (*Boosey & Hawkes*)
Sonata no.5 in C, Op.38: complete (*Boosey & Hawkes*)

Rachmaninov Any *one* of the 9 'Etudes-tableaux', Op.39. *Rachmaninov Etudes-tableaux* (*Boosey & Hawkes*)
Any *one* of the following Preludes:
Op.23: no.3 in D minor, no.4 in D, no.5 in G minor, no.10 in G♭, ⎫ *Rachmaninov*
Op.32: no.1 in C, no.2 in B♭ minor, no.3 in E, no.4 in E minor, ⎬ *Complete Preludes*
no.6 in F minor, no.8 in A minor, no.9 in A, no.10 in B minor, no.13 in D♭ ⎭ (*Boosey & Hawkes*)

Ravel Jeux d'eau (*Peters EP 7373*)
Any *one* of the following pieces from 'Miroirs': no.1 'Noctuelles', no.3 'Une Barque sur l'Océan',
  no.4 'Alborada del gracioso' (*Peters EP 7374*)
Ondine: no.1 from 'Gaspard de la Nuit' (*Peters EP 7378*)
Toccata: no.6 from 'Le Tombeau de Couperin' (*Peters EP 7376*)

Roger Redgate trace. *Spectrum* (*20 Contemporary Works for Solo Piano*) (*Associated Board*)

Scarlatti Any *one or two* of the following *pairs* of Sonatas:
Sonata in D minor, Kp.52 (L.267) *and* Sonata in D, Kp.96 (L.465) ⎫ *Scarlatti 60 Sonatas, Vol.1*
2 Sonatas in C minor, Kp.115 (L.407) *and* Kp.116 (L.452) ⎭ (*Schirmer/Music Sales*)
Sonata in G minor, Kp.426 (L.128) *and* Sonata in G, Kp.427 (L.286) ⎫ *Scarlatti 60 Sonatas, Vol.2*
2 Sonatas in B♭, Kp.544 (L.497) *and* Kp.545 (L.500) ⎭ (*Schirmer/Music Sales*)
2 Sonatas in G, Kp.424 (L.289) *and* Kp.425 (L.333). *Scarlatti 11 Sonatas* (*Associated Board*)

Schoenberg Any *two* of the '5 Pieces', Op.23 (*Hansen/Music Sales*)
Suite, Op.25: any *two* movts (*Universal 07627/M.D.S.*)

Schubert Sonata in A minor, Op.143, D.784: complete. *Schubert Sonatas, Vol.2* (*Associated Board*)
Sonata in C minor, D.958: complete ⎫ *Schubert Sonatas, Vol.3* (*Associated Board*)
Sonata in A, D.959: complete ⎭

Schumann Any *one* of the following from 'Novelletten', Op.21: no.2 in D, no.8 in F♯ minor (*Henle* or *Henle –
  Schott/M.D.S.*)
Sonata in G minor, Op.22: complete (*Henle* or *Henle – Schott/M.D.S.*)
Variations on the name 'Abegg', Op.1 (*Henle* or *Henle – Schott/M.D.S.*)

Scriabin *Either or both* of the following from '12 Etudes', Op.8: no.10 in D♭, no.12 in D♯ minor (*Belaieff
  145/Peters*)
Sonata no.4 in F♯, Op.30: complete (*Belaieff 159/Peters*)
Sonata no.5 in F♯, Op.53 (*Boosey & Hawkes*)

Seiber Scherzando capriccioso (*Schott ED 10247/M.D.S.*)

Shostakovich Any *one or two* of the following from '24 Preludes and Fugues', Op.87:
Vol. 1: no.4 in E minor, no.7 in A (*Boosey & Hawkes*)
Vol. 2: no.15 in D♭, no.17 in A♭ (*Boosey & Hawkes*)

Tippett Sonata no.2 (*Schott ED 10815/M.D.S.*)

Webern Variations, Op.27: complete (*Universal 10881/M.D.S.*)

Piano: FRSM

J.S. Bach	Partita no.6 in E minor, BWV 830: complete. *Bach Partitas 4–6* (*Associated Board*)
J.S. Bach/Busoni	Chaconne in D minor (from Partita no.2 for solo violin) (*Peters EP 7436*)
Barber	Sonata in E♭, Op.26: complete (*Schirmer/Music Sales*)
Bartók	Sonata (1926): complete (*Universal 8772/M.D.S.*)
Bax	Sonata no.3 in G♯ minor: complete (*Studio Music*)
Beethoven	Sonata in C ('Waldstein'), Op.53: complete (*Associated Board*)
	Sonata in F minor ('Appassionata'), Op.57: complete (*Associated Board*)
	Sonata in E♭ ('Les Adieux'), Op.81a: complete (*Associated Board*)
	Sonata in A, Op.101: complete (*Associated Board*)
	Sonata in E, Op.109: complete (*Associated Board*)
	Sonata in A♭, Op.110: complete (*Associated Board*)
	Sonata in C minor, Op.111: complete (*Associated Board*)
	15 Variations and Fugue in E♭, Op.35 ('Eroica Variations') (*Wiener Urtext/M.D.S.*)
Pierre Boulez	Sonata no.1: complete (*Amphion/U.M.P.*)
Brahms	Sonata in C, Op.1: complete (*Wiener Urtext/M.D.S.*)
	Sonata in F♯ minor, Op.2: complete (*Wiener Urtext/M.D.S.*)
	Sonata in F minor, Op.5: complete (*Wiener Urtext/M.D.S.*)
	11 Variations in D on an Original Theme, Op.21 no.1. *Brahms Variations, Op.21* (*Henle* or *Henle – Schott/M.D.S.*)
	25 Variations and Fugue on a Theme by Handel, Op.24 (*Henle* or *Henle – Schott/M.D.S.*)
	28 Variations on a Theme by Paganini, Op.35 (*Henle* or *Henle – Schott/M.D.S.*)
Bridge	Sonata: complete (*Stainer & Bell*)
Chopin	Sonata in B♭ minor, Op.35: complete (*Henle* or *Henle – Schott/M.D.S.*)
	Sonata in B minor, Op.58: complete (*Henle* or *Henle – Schott/M.D.S.*)
Fauré	Theme and Variations in C♯ minor, Op.73 (*Hamelle/U.M.P.*)
Franck	Prélude, Aria et Final, Op.23 (*Peters EP 3740b*)
	Prélude, Choral et Fugue, Op.21 (*Peters EP 3740a*)
Grainger	In Dahomey ('Cakewalk Smasher') (*Peters EP 66950*)
Hindemith	Sonata no.3 in B♭: complete (*Schott ED 2521/M.D.S.*)
Liszt	Après une Lecture de Dante (Fantasia quasi Sonata): no.7 from 'Anneés de Pèlerinage, 2ème Anneé, Italie' (*Henle* or *Henle – Schott/M.D.S.*)
	Funérailles (*Henle or Henle – Schott/M.D.S.*)
	Mazeppa *and/or* Feux follets: no.4 *and/or* no.5 from '12 Études d'exécution transcendante'. *Liszt Piano Works, Vol.3* (*Peters EP 3600c*)
	Sonata in B minor: complete (*Henle* or *Henle – Schott/M.D.S.*)
James MacMillan	Sonata: complete (*Boosey & Hawkes*)
Martinů	Sonata no.1: complete (*Eschig/U.M.P.*)
Medtner	Sonata tragica, Op.39 no.5: complete. *Medtner Complete Piano Sonatas, Series 2* (*Dover*)
Mendelssohn	Sonata in B♭, Op.106: complete. *Mendelssohn Complete Piano Works, Vol.5* (*Peters EP 1704e*)
Messiaen	Île de feu 1 *and* 2 (*U.M.P.*)
Prokofiev	Sonata no.6 in A, Op.82: complete (*Boosey & Hawkes*)
	Sonata no.7 in B♭, Op.83: complete (*Boosey & Hawkes*)
	Sonata no.8 in B♭, Op.84: complete. *Prokofiev Sonatas for Piano, Vol.2* (*Boosey & Hawkes*)
	Sonata no.9 in C, Op.103: complete (*Boosey & Hawkes*)
Rachmaninov	Sonata no.2 in B♭ minor, Op.36 (*revised version 1931*): complete (*Boosey & Hawkes*)
	Variations on a Theme of Corelli, Op.42 (*Belwin Mills/Maecenas Europe*)
Ravel	Gaspard de la Nuit: complete (*Peters EP 7378*)
Schubert	Fantasy in C ('The Wanderer'), Op.15, D.760 (*Associated Board*)
	Sonata in C minor, D.958: complete ⎤
	Sonata in A, D.959: complete *Schubert Sonatas, Vol.3* (*Associated Board*)
	Sonata in B♭, D.960: complete ⎦
Schubert/Liszt	Erlkönig *and* Gretchen am Spinnrade. *Liszt Piano Works, Vol.9* (*Peters EP 3602a*)
Schumann	Carnaval, Op.9: complete (*Henle* or *Henle – Schott/M.D.S.*)
	Fantasy in C, Op.17 (*Henle* or *Henle – Schott/M.D.S.*)
	Kreisleriana, Op.16: complete (*Henle* or *Henle – Schott/M.D.S.*)
	Symphonische Etüden (12 Études Symphoniques), Op.13: complete (*Henle* or *Henle Schott/M.D.S.*)
	Toccata in C, Op.7 (*Henle or Henle – Schott/M.D.S.*)
Stravinsky	Serenade in A: complete (*Boosey & Hawkes*)

Piano: FRSM

Szymanowski	Masques, Op.34: complete (*Universal 05858/M.D.S.*)
	Metopes, Op.29: complete (*Universal 06997/M.D.S.*)
Tippett	Sonata no.3: complete (*Schott ED 11162/M.D.S.*)
	Sonata no.4: complete (*Schott ED 12250/M.D.S.*)

Harpsichord: DipABRSM

Pieces which require a two-manual harpsichord are indicated by an asterisk following the title.

C.P.E. Bach	Sonata in A minor, Wq.49/1: complete*. *C.P.E. Bach 6 Württenberg Sonatas* (*Bärenreiter BA 6498*)
J.S. Bach	French Suite no.5 in G, BWV 816: complete. *J.S. Bach 6 French Suites* (*Associated Board*)
	Italian Concerto in F, BWV 971: complete*. *J.S. Bach Clavierübung, Part 2* (*Associated Board*) or (*separately: Wiener Urtext/M.D.S.*)
	Prelude and Fugue no.24 in B minor, BWV 869, from 'The Well-Tempered Clavier', Part 1 (*Associated Board*)
Blow	Ground in E minor. *John Blow's Anthology* (*Stainer & Bell*)
Böhm	Prelude, Fugue and Postlude in G minor. *Böhm Complete Works for Harpsichord* (*Breitkopf & Härtel 8086*)
Bull	Pavana *and* Galiard to the Pavan (Fantastic Pavan *and* Galliard). *Nos.34* and *35 from The Fitzwilliam Virginal Book, Vol.1* (*Dover/Music Sales*)
Byrd	Walsingham. *No.68 from The Fitzwilliam Virginal Book, Vol.1* (*Dover/Music Sales*)
F. Couperin	Ordre no.26 in F♯ minor: complete. *F. Couperin Pièces de Clavecin, Vol.4* (*Heugel/U.M.P.*)
L. Couperin	Suite no.15 in G minor: 7th *and* 8th movts, *Passacaille* and *Chaconne*. *L. Couperin Pièces de Clavecin, Vol.2* (*Heugel/U.M.P.*)
Frescobaldi	Partite 11 sopra l'Aria di Monicha in G minor: complete. *Frescobaldi Complete Organ and Keyboard Works, Vol.3* (*Bärenreiter BA 2203*)
	Toccata Nona in F. *Frescobaldi Complete Organ and Keyboard Works, Vol.4* (*Bärenreiter BA 2204*)
Handel	Chaconne in G and 21 Variations (no.2 from 1727/1733 Collection), HWV 435. *Handel Keyboard Works, Vol.2* (*Bärenreiter BA 4221*)
	Suite no.2 in F (no.2 from 1720 Collection): HWV 427: complete. *Handel 8 Great Suites, Book 1* (*Associated Board*)
Haydn	Sonata in D, Hob.XVI/37: complete*. *Haydn Selected Keyboard Sonatas, Book 3* (*Associated Board*)
György Ligeti	Hungarian Rock (Chaconne)* (*Schott ED 6805/M.D.S.*)
Persichetti	Harpsichord Sonata no.10, Op.167*: complete (*Elkan-Vogel/U.M.P.*)
Rameau	La Joyeuse, L'entretien des Muses, Les Tourbillons *and* Les Cyclopes. *Rameau Pièces de Clavecin* (*Bärenreiter BA 3800*)
Scarlatti	Any *one* of the following *pairs* of Sonatas:
	2 Sonatas in C, Kp.460 (L.324) *and* Kp.461 (L.8) *Scarlatti 60 Sonatas, Vol.2*
	2 Sonatas in B♭, Kp.544 (L.497) *and* Kp.545 (L.500) (*Schirmer/Music Sales*)
Sweelinck	Ut, re, mi, fa, sol, la, a 4 voci (Hexachord Fantasia). *No.118 from The Fitzwilliam Virginal Book, Vol.2* (*Dover/Music Sales*)

Harpsichord: LRSM

Pieces which require a two-manual harpsichord are indicated by an asterisk following the title.

C.P.E. Bach	Sonata in E minor, Wq.49/3: complete*. *C.P.E. Bach 6 Württenberg Sonatas* (*Bärenreiter BA 6498*)
J.S. Bach	English Suite no.6 in D minor, BWV 811: complete. *J.S. Bach English Suites 4–6* (*Associated Board*)
	Prelude and Fugue no.20 in A minor, BWV 865, from 'The Well-Tempered Clavier', Part 1 (*Associated Board*)
	Toccata no.3 in D, BWV 912 complete. *J.S. Bach 7 Toccatas* (*Henle* or *Henle – Schott/M.D.S.*)
Blow	Suite no.1 in D minor, from 'A Choice Collection of Lessons': complete. *Blow 6 Suites* (*Stainer & Bell*)
Böhm	Prelude, Fugue and Postlude in G minor. *Böhm Complete Works for Harpsichord* (*Breitkopf & Härtel 8086*)
Byrd	Sellinger's Round. *No.64 from The Fitzwilliam Virginal Book, Vol.1* (*Dover/Music Sales*)
F. Couperin	Ordre no.23 in F: complete. *F. Couperin Pièces de Clavecin, Vol.4* (*Heugel/U.M.P.*)
L. Couperin	Suite no.14 in G: complete. *L. Couperin Pièces de Clavecin, Vol.2* (*Heugel/U.M.P.*)
Frescobaldi	Partite 14 sopra l'Aria della Romanesca in G minor: complete. *Frescobaldi Complete Organ and Keyboard Works, Vol.3* (*Bärenreiter BA 2203*)
	Toccata Prima in G minor. *Frescobaldi Complete Organ and Keyboard Works, Vol.3* (*Bärenreiter BA 2203*)
Handel	Chaconne in G and 21 Variations (no.2 from 1727/1733 Collection), HWV 435. *Handel Keyboard Works, Vol.2* (*Bärenreiter BA 4221*)
	Suite no.6 in F♯ minor (no.6 from 1720 Collection): HWV 431: complete. *Handel 8 Great Suites, Book 2* (*Associated Board*)

REPERTOIRE LISTS

Harpsichord: LRSM

Haydn Sonata in G, Hob.XVI/39: complete*. *Haydn Complete Keyboard Sonatas, Vol.2* (*Wiener Urtext/M.D.S.*)

György Ligeti Hungarian Rock (Chaconne)* (*Schott ED 6805/M.D.S.*)

Muffat Passacaglia in G minor. *Baroque Keyboard Pieces, Book 5, ed. Jones* (*Associated Board*)

Rameau Les Trois Mains, Fanfarinette and La Triomphante. *Rameau Pièces de Clavecin* (*Bärenreiter BA 3800*)

Scarlatti Any *one or two* of the following *pairs* of Sonatas:
Sonata in D minor, Kp.52 (L.267) *and* Sonata in D, Kp.96 (L.465) | *Scarlatti 60 Sonatas, Vol.1*
2 Sonatas in C minor, Kp.115 (L.407) *and* Kp.116 (L.452) | (*Schirmer/Music Sales*)
2 Sonatas in C, Kp.132 (L.457) *and* Kp.133 (L.282). *Baroque Keyboard Pieces, Book 5, ed. Jones*
  (*Associated Board*)
Sonata in E minor, Kp.263 (L.321) *and* Sonata in E, Kp.264 (L.466) | *Scarlatti 60 Sonatas, Vol.2*
2 Sonatas in F, Kp.366 (L.119) *and* Kp.367 (L.172) | (*Schirmer/Music Sales*)
2 Sonatas in D, Kp.490 (L.206) *and* Kp.491 (L.164) |

Soler 2 Sonatas in C minor, R.100 *and* 19. *Early Spanish Keyboard Music, Vol.3* (*O.U.P.*)

Sweelinck 6 Variations on 'Mein junges Leben hat ein End'. *Sweelinck Song Variations for Keyboard* (*Schott ED 2482/M.D.S.*)

Tōru Takemitsu Rain Dreaming (*Schott SJ 1032/M.D.S.*)

Thomas Tomkins Pavan *and* Galliard 'Earl Strafford' (*short versions, and with editorial repeats*). *Tomkins 15 Dances* (*Stainer & Bell*)

Harpsichord: FRSM

Pieces which require a two-manual harpsichord are indicated by an asterisk following the title.

C.P.E. Bach Sonata in A♭, Wq.49/2: complete*. *C.P.E. Bach 6 Württenberg Sonatas* (*Bärenreiter BA 6498*)

J.S. Bach Chromatic Fantasia and Fugue in D minor, BWV 903 (*Henle* or *Henle – Schott/M.D.S.*)
Partita no.4 in D, BWV 828: complete. *Bach Partitas 4–6* (*Associated Board*)
Toccata no.6 in G minor, BWV 915: complete. *Bach 7 Toccatas* (*Henle* or *Henle – Schott/M.D.S.*)

Bull In Nomine. *No.119 from The Fitzwilliam Virginal Book, Vol.2* (*Dover/Music Sales*)
The Quadran Pavan *and* Galiard to the Quadran Pavan. *No.31* and *no.33 from The Fitzwilliam Virginal Book, Vol.1* (*Dover/Music Sales*)

Byrd Passamezzo Pavana *and* Galiardas Passamezzo. *Nos.56* and *57 from The Fitzwilliam Virginal Book, Vol.1* (*Dover/Music Sales*)

F. Couperin Ordre no.8 in B minor: complete. *F. Couperin Pièces de Clavecin, Vol.2* (*Heugel/U.M.P.*)

James Dillon Birl (*Peters EP 7353*)

Frescobaldi Cento Partite sopra Passacagli: complete. *Frescobaldi Complete Organ and Keyboard Works, Vol.3* (*Bärenreiter BA 2203*)

Froberger Toccata II in D minor, FbWV 102 *and* Canzon I in D minor, FbWV 301. *Froberger Complete Keyboard and Organ Works, Vol.1* (*Bärenreiter BA 8063*)

Gibbons Peascod Time (or The Hunt's Up). *Gibbons 8 Keyboard Pieces* (*Stainer & Bell*)

Handel Suite no.7 in G minor (no.7 from 1720 Collection): HWV 432: complete. *Handel 8 Great Suites, Book 2* (*Associated Board*)

Haydn Sonata in A♭, Hob.XVI/46: complete*. *Haydn Selected Keyboard Sonatas, Book 4* (*Associated Board*)

Betsy Jolas Autour (*Heugel/U.M.P.*)

György Ligeti Continuum* (*Schott ED 6111/M.D.S.*)

Michael Nyman The Convertibility of Lute Strings (*Chester/Music Sales*)

Poglietti Il Rossignolo: Aria Allemagna con 20 Varazioni. *Poglietti Compositions for the Keyboard* (*Ricordi/ U.M.P.*)

Rameau Allemande, Courante, Sarabande, Gavotte *and* 6 Doubles de la Gavotte in A minor/major, from 'Nouvelles Suites de Pièces de Clavecin'. *Rameau Pièces de Clavecin* (*Bärenreiter BA 3800*)

Scarlatti Any *one or two* of the following *pairs* of Sonatas:
2 Sonatas in G, Kp.493 (L.S.24) *and* Kp.494 (L.287). *Scarlatti 60 Sonatas, Vol.2* (*Schirmer/Music Sales*)
2 Sonatas in C, Kp.548 (L.404) *and* Kp.549 (L.S.1). *Scarlatti Sonatas, Vol.11* (*Heugel/U.M.P.*)

Soler 2 Sonatas in C♯ minor, R.20 *and* 21. *Soler 14 Sonatas from the Fitzwilliam Collection* (*Faber*)

Sweelinck Fantasia. *No.217 from The Fitzwilliam Virginal Book, Vol.2* (*Dover/Music Sales*)
Poolsche Dans. *Sweelinck Works for Organ and Keyboard* (*Dover/Music Sales*)

Organ. DipADRCM

J.A. Alain   Le Jardin suspendu. *Alain 3 Pieces* (*Leduc/U.M.P.*) or *Alain Organ Works, Vol.2* (*Leduc/U.M.P.*)

J.S. Bach   Chorale Prelude 'Wachet auf, ruft uns die Stimme', BWV 645   ] *Bach Organ Works* (*Bärenreiter*
Chorale Prelude 'Wer nur den lieben Gott lässt walten', BWV 647] *Vol.1; Novello Book 16; Peters Vol.7*)
Chorale Prelude: Fugue on the Magnificat 'Meine Seele erhebet den Herren', BWV 733. *Bach Organ Works* (*Bärenreiter Vol.3; Novello Book 18; Peters Vol.7*)
Fantasia in G, BWV 572. *Bach Organ Works* (*Bärenreiter Vol.7; Novello Book 9; Peters Vol.4*)
Fugue in G minor, BWV 578. *Bach Organ Works* (*Bärenreiter Vol.6; Novello Book 3; Peters Vol.4*)
Prelude and Fugue in A, BWV 536   ] *Bach Organ Works* (*Bärenreiter Vol.5; Novello Book 3;*
Prelude and Fugue in C, BWV 545   ] *Peters Vol.2*)
Trio Sonata no.1 in E♭, BWV 525: complete. *Bach Organ Works* (*Bärenreiter Vol.7; Novello Book 5; Peters Vol.1*)

Brahms   Chorale Prelude 'Herzlich tut mich erfreuen': no.4 from 11 Chorale Preludes, Op.122. *Brahms Works for Organ* (*Henle* or *Henle – Schott/M.D.S.*)

Buxtehude   Passacaglia in D minor, BuxWV 161. *Buxtehude Organ Works* (*Bärenreiter Vol.1; Hansen Vol.1/Music Sales*)
Praeludium and Fugue in D, BuxWV 139. *Buxtehude Organ Works* (*Bärenreiter Vol.1; Hansen Vol.2/Music Sales*)
Praeludium and Fugue in G minor, BuxWV 148. *Buxtehude Organ Works* (*Bärenreiter Vol.3; Hansen Vol.2 p.122/Music Sales*)

F. Couperin   Offertoire sur les Grands jeux: no.15 from 'Messe pour les Paroisses' (*Edwin Kalmus 3315/Maecenas Europe*)

Clérambault   Suite du Deuxième Ton: complete, from 'Premier Livre d'Orgue' (*Schola Cantorum/U.M.P.*)

Petr Eben   A Festive Voluntary (*U.M.P.*)

Franck   Cantabile in B: no.2 from '3 Pièces'. *Franck Complete Organ Works, Vol.3* (*Wiener Urtext/M.D.S.*)
Choral in A minor: no.3 from '3 Chorals'. *Franck Complete Organ Works, Vol.4* (*Wiener Urtext/M.D.S.*)
Prélude, Fugue et Variation in B minor, Op.18: no.3 from '6 Pièces'. *Franck Complete Organ Works, Vol.1* (*Wiener Urtext/M.D.S.*)

Frescobaldi   Toccata Quinta **and/or** Toccata Sesta, from '2nd Book of Toccatas, Canzoni etc.'. *Frescobaldi Complete Organ and Keyboard Works, Vol.4* (*Bärenreiter BA 2204*)

Jongen   Petit Prélude. *Jongen Organ Album* (*O.U.P.*)

Langlais   Suite Brève: 2nd movt *Cantilène* (*Bornemann/U.M.P.*)

Mendelssohn   Prelude and Fugue in C minor, Op.37 no.1. *Mendelssohn Complete Organ Works* (*Bärenreiter Vol.1; Novello Vol.1/Music Sales*)

Messiaen   Les Enfants de Dieu: no.5 from 'La Nativité du Seigneur', Vol.2 (*Leduc/U.M.P.*)

Parry   Chorale Prelude on 'Christe, Redemptor omnium': no.6 *from* '7 Chorale Preludes', Set 1 (*Novello/Music Sales*)
Chorale Prelude on 'Croft's 136th': no.1 from '7 Chorale Preludes', Set 2 (*Novello/Music Sales*)

Reger   Benedictus, Op.59 no.9 (*Peters EP 3114*)

Saint-Saëns   Fantaisie no.1 in E♭ ('Echo-Fantaisie') (*Billaudot/U.M.P.*)

S. Scheidt   Variations on a Galliard of John Dowland. *Scheidt Tabulatura Nova and other Compositions* (*Peters EP 4393b*)

Stanford   Postlude in D minor: no.6 from '6 Short Preludes and Postludes', 2nd Set, Op.105 (*Stainer & Bell*)

Vierne   Symphonie no.1 in D minor, Op.14: 6th movt, *Final* (*movt. publ. separately: U.M.P.*)

Widor   Symphonie no.6 in G, Op.42 no.2: 5th movt, *Finale: Vivace* (*Hamelle/U.M.P.*)

Arthur Wills   Variations on 'Amazing Grace' (*Novello/Music Sales*)

Organ: LRSM

J.A. Alain Litanies ⎤ *Alain 3 Pieces* (*Leduc/U.M.P.*) or *Alain Organ*
Variations sur un Thème de Clément Jannequin ⎦ *Works, Vol.2* (*Leduc/U.M.P.*)

J.S. Bach Chorale Prelude: Fantasia on 'Komm, heiliger Geist, Herre Gott', BWV 651. *Bach Organ Works* (*Bärenreiter Vol.2; Novello Book 17; Peters Vol.7*)
Chorale Prelude 'An Wasserflüssen Babylon', BWV 653. *Bach Organ Works* (*Bärenreiter Vol.2; Novello Book 17; Peters Vol.6*)
Chorale Prelude 'Schmücke dich, O liebe Seele', BWV 654. *Bach Organ Works* (*Bärenreiter Vol.2; Novello Book 17; Peters Vol.7*)
Chorale Prelude: Trio on 'Herr Jesu Christ, dich zu uns wend', BWV 655. *Bach Organ Works* (*Bärenreiter Vol.2; Novello Book 17; Peters Vol.6*)
Chorale Prelude 'O Lamm Gottes, unschuldig', BWV 656. *Bach Organ Works* (*Bärenreiter Vol.2; Novello Book 17; Peters Vol.7*)
Chorale Prelude 'Dies sind die heil'gen zehn Gebot', BWV 678. *Bach Organ Works* (*Bärenreiter Vol.4; Novello Book 16; Peters Vol.6*)
Chorale Prelude 'Christ, unser Herr, zum Jordan kam', BWV 684. *Bach Organ Works* (*Bärenreiter Vol.4; Novello Book 16; Peters Vol.6*)
Concerto in A minor (after Vivaldi, Op.3 no.8), BWV 593: complete. *Bach Organ Works* (*Bärenreiter Vol.8; Novello Book 11; Peters Vol.8*)
Prelude and Fugue in G, BWV 541. *Bach Organ Works* (*Bärenreiter Vol.5; Novello Book 8; Peters Vol.2*)
Prelude and Fugue in A minor, BWV 543. *Bach Organ Works* (*Bärenreiter Vol.5; Novello Book 7; Peters Vol.2*)
Prelude and Fugue in C minor, BWV 546. *Bach Organ Works* (*Bärenreiter Vol.5; Novello Book 7; Peters Vol.2*)
Prelude and Fugue in C, BWV 547. *Bach Organ Works* (*Bärenreiter Vol.5; Novello Book 9; Peters Vol.3*)
Prelude and Fugue in G, BWV 550. *Bach Organ Works* (*Bärenreiter Vol.5; Novello Book 7; Peters Vol.4*)
Toccata, Adagio and Fugue in C, BWV 564. *Bach Organ Works* (*Bärenreiter Vol.6; Novello Book 9; Peters Vol.3*)
Trio Sonata no.3 in D minor, BWV 527: complete. *Bach Organ Works* (*Bärenreiter Vol.7; Novello Book 4; Peters Vol.1*)
Trio Sonata no.4 in E minor, BWV 528: complete. *Bach Organ Works* (*Bärenreiter Vol.7; Novello Book 5; Peters Vol.1*)
Trio Sonata no.6 in G, BWV 530: complete. *Bach Organ Works* (*Bärenreiter Vol.7; Novello Book 5; Peters Vol.1*)

Buxtehude Ciacona in E minor, BuxWV 160. *Buxtehude Organ Works* (*Bärenreiter Vol.2; Hansen Vol.1/Music Sales*)
Praeludium and Fugue in G minor, BuxWV 150. *Buxtehude Organ Works* (*Bärenreiter Vol.3; Hansen Vol.2 p.128/Music Sales*)

M. Dupré Cortège et Litanie, Op.19 (*Leduc/U.M.P.*)
Final in G minor: no.7 from '7 Pièces', Op.27 (*Bornemann/U.M.P.*)

Petr Eben Hommage à Dietrich Buxtehude (Toccatenfuge) (*Schott ED 7543/M.D.S.*)

Elgar Sonata in G, Op.28: 1st movt, *Allegro maestoso* (*Breitkopf & Härtel 3404*)

Franck Final in B♭, Op.21: no.6 from '6 Pièces' ⎤ *Franck Complete Organ Works, Vol.2*
Pastorale in E, Op.19: no.4 from '6 Pièces' ⎦ (*Wiener Urtext/M.D.S.*)

Hindemith Sonata no.2: complete (*Schott ED 2558/M.D.S.*)
Sonata no.3 on Old Folksongs: complete (*Schott ED 3736/M.D.S.*)

Honegger Fugue: no.1 from '2 Pieces' (*Chester/Music Sales*)

Howells Saraband (For the morning of Easter): no.2 from '6 Pieces' ⎤ (*Novello/Music Sales*)
Master Tallis's Testament: no.3 from '6 Pieces' ⎦

Lübeck Prelude and Fugue in E. *Lübeck Organ Works* (*Peters EP 4437*)

John McCabe Elegy (*Novello/Music Sales*)

Mendelssohn Any of the '6 Sonatas', Op.65. *Mendelssohn Complete Organ Works* (*Bärenreiter Vol.2; Novello Vol.4/Music Sales*)

Reger Toccata and Fugue in D minor, Op.59 nos.5 **and** 6 (*Peters EP 3008g*)

Rheinberger Sonata no.1 in C minor, Op.27: complete ⎤
Sonata no.2 in A♭ ('Fantasia Sonata'), Op.65: complete ⎟ (*Novello 010152/Music Sales*)
Sonata no.3 in G ('Pastoral'), Op.88: complete ⎦
Sonata no.4 in A minor, Op.98: complete ⎤ (*Novello 010143/Music Sales*)
Sonata no.5 in F♯, Op.111: complete ⎦
Sonata no.8 in E minor, Op.132: complete ⎤ (*Novello 010146/Music Sales*)
Sonata no.9 in B♭ minor, Op.142: complete ⎦

REPERTOIRE LISTS

Organ: FR3M

J.A. Alain 3 Danses: Joies, Deuils *and* Luttes. *Alain Organ Works, Vol.1* (*Leduc/U.M.P.*)
2e Fantaisie. *Alain Organ Works, Vol.3* (*Leduc/U.M.P.*)

J.S. Bach 2 Chorale Preludes on 'Allein Gott in der Höh' sei Ehr', BWV 662 *and* 663. *Bach Organ Works* (*Bärenreiter Vol.2; Novello Book 17; Peters Vol.6*)
Chorale Prelude 'Kyrie, Gott Vater in Ewigkeit', BWV 669 ⎤ *Bach Organ Works*
Chorale Prelude 'Christe, aller Welt Trost', BWV 670 ⎥ (*Bärenreiter Vol.4; Novello Book 16;*
Chorale Prelude 'Kyrie, Gott heiliger Geist', BWV 671 ⎥ *Peters Vol.7* (*BWV 670 in Vol.6*))
Chorale Prelude 'Vater unser im Himmelreich', BWV 682 ⎦
Chorale Variations on 'Sei gegrüsset, Jesu gütig', BWV 768. *Bach Organ Works* (*Bärenreiter Vol.1; Novello Book 19; Peters Vol.5*)
Fantasia and Fugue in G minor, BWV 542. *Bach Organ Works* (*Bärenreiter Vol.5; Novello Book 8; Peters Vol.2*)
Passacaglia and Fugue in C minor, BWV 582. *Bach Organ Works* (*Bärenreiter Vol.7; Novello Book 10; Peters Vol.1*)
Prelude and Fugue in E♭ ('St Anne'), BWV 552. *Bach Organ Works* (*Bärenreiter Vol.4; Novello Book 6; Peters Vol.3*)
Prelude and Fugue in E minor, BWV 548. *Bach Organ Works* (*Bärenreiter Vol.5; Novello Book 17; Peters Vol.2*)
Trio Sonata no.2 in C minor, BWV 526: complete. *Bach Organ Works* (*Bärenreiter Vol.7; Novello Book 4; Peters Vol.1*)
Trio Sonata no.5 in C, BWV 529: complete. *Bach Organ Works* (*Bärenreiter Vol.7; Novello Book 5; Peters Vol.1*)

Brahms Fugue in A♭ minor, WoO 8 ⎤ *Brahms Works for Organ* (*Henle or Henle – Schott/M.D.S.*)
Prelude and Fugue in G minor, WoO 10 ⎦

Buxtehude Praeludium and Fugue in F♯ minor, BuxWV 146. (*Bärenreiter Vol.2; Hansen Vol.2/Music Sales*)

Demessieux Te Deum, Op.11 (*Durand/U.M.P.*)

M. Dupré Prelude and Fugue in B, Op.7 no.1 ⎤ *Dupré 3 Preludes and Fugues, Op.7* (*Leduc/U.M.P.*)
Prelude and Fugue in F minor, Op.7 no.2 ⎦
Variations sur un vieux Noël, Op.20 (*Leduc/U.M.P.*)

Duruflé Prélude et Fugue sur le nom d'Alain, Op.7 (*Durand/U.M.P.*)
Suite, Op.5: 3rd movt, *Toccata* (*Durand/U.M.P.*)

Petr Eben Molto Ostinato, from 'Sunday Music' (*Bärenreiter*)

Franck Choral no.2 in B minor, from '3 Chorals'. *Franck Complete Organ Works, Vol.4* (*Wiener Urtext/M.D.S.*)
Pièce héroïque. *Franck Complete Organ Works, Vol.3* (*Wiener Urtext/M.D.S.*)

Hindemith Sonata no.1: complete (*Schott ED 2557/M.D.S.*)

Jongen Sonata Eroïca, Op.94: complete (*Leduc/U.M.P.*)

Langlais La Nativité: no.2 from '3 Poèmes Evangéliques' (*Consortium/U.M.P.*)
Triptyque: 3rd movt, *Final* (*Novello/Music Sales*)

Kenneth Leighton Et Resurrexit (Theme, Fantasy and Fugue) (*Novello/Music Sales*)

Liszt Prelude and Fugue on B-A-C-H. *Liszt Complete Organ Works, Vol.2* (*Peters EP 3628b*)

Frank Martin Passacaille (1944) (*Universal 17479/M.D.S.*)

Messiaen Diptyque (Essai sur la vie terrestre et l'éternité bien heureux) (*Durand/U.M.P.*)
Verset pour le Fête de la Dédicace (*Leduc/U.M.P.*)

Mozart Fantasia (Allegro *and* Andante) in F minor, K.608 (*Novello/Music Sales*)

Parry Fantasia and Fugue in G. *Parry Organ Album, Book 1* (*Novello/Music Sales*)

Reger Introduction and Passacaglia in D minor (*Breitkopf & Härtel 8513*)
Toccata and Fugue in A minor: nos.11 *and* 12 from '12 Pieces', Op.80 Vol.2 (*Peters EP 3064b*)

Saint-Saëns Prelude and Fugue in E, Op.90 no.1 ⎤ *Saint-Saëns 6 Preludes and Fugues, Vol.1* (*Durand/U.M.P.*)
Prelude and Fugue in B, Op.90 no.2 ⎦

Schumann Fugue in B♭, Op.60 no.2 ⎤ *Schumann 6 Fugues on B-A-C-H, Op.60* (*Peters EP 2382*)
Fugue in B♭, Op.60 no.6 ⎦

Richard Stoker Partita: complete (*Boosey & Hawkes*)

Sweelinck Fantasia chromatica. *Sweelinck Selected Organ Works, Vol.1* (*Peters EP 4645a*)

Vierne Any *one or more* of the following pieces from 'Pièces de Fantaisie: Suite no.2', Op.53: no.4 'Feux Follets', no.5 'Clair de Lune', no.6 'Toccata in B♭ minor' (*Lemoine/U.M.P.*)
Impromptu: no.2 from 'Pièces de Fantaisie: Suite no.3', Op.54 (*Lemoine/U.M.P.*)
Naïades: no.4 from 'Pièces de Fantaisie: Suite no.4', Op.55 (*Lemoine/U.M.P.*)
Symphonie no.2, Op.20: 3rd movt, *Scherzo in E* (*Hamelle/U.M.P.*)

Whitlock	Divertimento: no.2 from '4 Extemporisations'. *Whitlock Complete Shorter Organ Music* (*O.U.P.*)
Widor	Symphonie no.5 in F, Op.42 no.1: 1st movt, *Allegro vivace* (*Hamelle/U.M.P.*)
	Symphonie no.6 in G, Op.42 no.2: 1st movt, *Allegro* (*Hamelle/U.M.P.*)

Violin: DipABRSM

J.S. Bach Concerto in E, BWV 1042: 1st movt (*Bärenreiter BA 5190a*)
Partita for solo violin no.2 in D minor, BWV 1004:
   3rd *and* 4th movts, *Sarabanda* and *Giga*
Partita for solo violin no.3 in E, BWV 1006:
   2nd *and* 3rd movts, *Loure* and *Gavotte en Rondeau*
       } *Bach 3 Sonatas and 3 Partitas for solo violin* (*Bärenreiter BA 5116*)
Sonata in E minor, BWV 1023: complete. *Bach 2 Sonatas for Violin and Continuo* (*Wiener Urtext/M.D.S.*)

Barber Concerto, Op.14: 1st movt (*Schirmer/Music Sales*)

Beethoven Romance in F, Op.50. *Beethoven 2 Romances* (*Henle* or *Henle – Schott/M.D.S.*)
1st movement from any *one* of the following Sonatas:
   Op.12 no.2 in A, Op.12 no.3 in E♭, Op.23 in A minor, Op.24 in F ('Spring'), Op.30 no.1 in A, Op.30 no.2 in C minor, Op.30 no.3 in G. *Beethoven Sonatas for Piano and Violin* (*2 volumes: Henle* or *Henle – Schott/M.D.S.*)

Bloch Nigun (Improvisation) (no.2 from 'Baal Shem' Suite) (*Carl Fischer/Boosey & Hawkes* or *Carl Fischer – Schott/M.D.S.*)
Simchas Torah (no.3 from 'Baal Shem' Suite) (*Carl Fischer/Boosey & Hawkes* or *Carl Fischer – Schott/M.D.S.*)

Brahms Sonata in G, Op.78: 1st movt (*Wiener Urtext/M.D.S.*)
Sonata in A, Op.100: 1st movt (*Wiener Urtext/M.D.S.*)
Sonata Movement (Scherzo) in C minor (*Breitkopf & Härtel 6049*)

Bridge Moto Perpetuo (*Stainer & Bell*)

Delius Sonata no.3: 3rd movt (*Boosey & Hawkes*)

Dvořák 4 Romantic Pieces, Op.75: complete (*Bärenreiter Praha H 1903*)

Elgar Sonata in E minor, Op.82: 1st movt (*Novello/Music Sales*)

Falla Danse Espagnole (from 'La Vida Breve'), arr. Kreisler (*Schott BSS 31837/M.D.S.*)
Pantomime (from 'El Amor Brujo'), arr. Kochański (*Chester/Music Sales*)

Fauré Romance in B♭, Op.28 (*Hamelle/U.M.P.*)

Françaix Sonatine: complete (*Schott ED 2451/M.D.S.*)

Geminiani Sonata in C minor: complete. *18th Century Violin Sonatas, Book 2* (*Associated Board*)

Grieg Sonata no.3 in C minor, Op.45: 1st movt (*Peters EP 2414*)

Haydn Concerto in C, Hob.VIIa/1: 1st movt (*Henle* or *Henle – Schott/M.D.S.*)

Hindemith Sonata in E♭, Op.11 no.1: any movt or movts (*Schott ED 1918/M.D.S.*)

Kabalevsky Concerto in C, Op.48: 1st movt (*Boosey & Hawkes*)

Khachaturian Chant-Poème (*Boosey & Hawkes*)

Kreisler Variations on a theme of Corelli in the style of Tartini (*Schott BSS 29027/M.D.S.*)

R. Kreutzer 42 Études or Caprices: no.35 in E♭ *and/or* no.42 in D minor (*Peters EP 284*)

Lalo Symphonie Espagnole, Op.21: 2nd movt (*Peters EP 3797a*)

Leclair Sonata in D, Op.9 no.3: complete (*Schott VLB 15/M.D.S.*)

Kenneth Leighton Metamorphoses, Op.48 (*Novello/Music Sales*)

Messiaen Thème et Variations (*Leduc/U.M.P.*)

Mozart Concerto no.3 in G, K.216: 1st movt (*Bärenreiter BA 4865a*)
Concerto no.4 in D, K.218: 1st movt (*Bärenreiter BA 4866a*)
1st movement from any *one* of the following Sonatas: K.296 in C, K.376 in F, K.378 in B♭. *Mozart Sonatas for Piano and Violin, Vol.2* (*Henle* or *Henle – Schott/M.D.S.* or *Wiener Urtext/M.D.S.*)

Paul Patterson Luslawice Variations for solo violin (*Universal 21005/M.D.S.*)

Ravel Pièce en Forme de Habanera, trans. Catherine (*Leduc/U.M.P.*)

Saint-Saëns Concerto no.3 in B minor, Op.61: 1st movt (*Durand/U.M.P.*)

Schumann 3 Fantasiestücke, Op.73: complete (*Henle* or *Henle – Schott/M.D.S.*)
Sonata no.3 in A minor WoO 27: 1st movt (*Schott ED 10505/M.D.S.*)

Smetana From My Native Country: nos.1 *and* 2 (*Peters EP 2634*)

Stravinsky Chanson Russe (Russian Maiden's Song from 'Mavra'), arr. Dushkin (*Boosey & Hawkes*)
Suite Italienne: any *two* movts (*Boosey & Hawkes*)

Szymanowski Chant de Roxanne (from 'King Roger'), arr. Kochański (*Universal 8694/M.D.S.*)

Violin: DipABRSM

Tartini	Sonata in G minor ('Didone abbandonata'), Op.1 no.10: 1st *and* 2nd movts (*Schott VLB 31/M.D.S.*)
Telemann	Any *one* Fantasia complete from '12 Fantasias for Violin without Bass' (*Bärenreiter BA 2972*)
Walton	2 Pieces: Canzonetta *and* Scherzetto (*O.U.P.*)

Violin: LRSM

J.S. Bach	Partita for solo violin no.1 in B minor, BWV 1002:
	    7th *and* 8th movts, *Tempo di Borea* **and** *Double*
	Sonata for solo violin no.1 in G minor, BWV 1001:
	    3rd *and* 4th movts, *Siciliana* and *Presto*
	Sonata for solo violin no.2 in A minor, BWV 1003:
	    3rd *and* 4th movts, *Andante* and *Allegro*
	Sonata for solo violin no.3 in C, BWV 1005:
	    3rd *and* 4th movts, *Largo* and *Allegro assai* 〕 *Bach 3 Sonatas and 3 Partitas for solo violin* (*Bärenreiter BA 5116*)

Bartók	Rhapsody no.1: complete (*Boosey & Hawkes*)

Beethoven	Any *two* contrasting movements from any *one* of the following Sonatas:
	    Op.12 no.1 in D, Op.12 no.2 in A, Op.12 no.3 in E♭, Op.23 in A minor, Op.24 in F ('Spring'),
	    Op.30 no.1 in A, Op.30 no.2 in C minor, Op.30 no.3 in G. *Beethoven Sonatas for Piano and Violin*
	    (*2 volumes: Henle* or *Henle – Schott/M.D.S.*)

L. Berkeley	Introduction and Allegro for solo violin, Op.24. *Berkeley 2 Pieces for Solo Violin* (*Chester/Music Sales*)
Brahms	Sonata in G, Op.78: any *two* movts (*Wiener Urtext/M.D.S.*) Sonata in A, Op.100: any *two* movts (*Wiener Urtext/M.D.S.*)
Bruch	Concerto no.1 in G minor, Op.26: 1st movt (*Peters EP 4590*)
Debussy	Sonata: complete (*Henle* or *Henle – Schott/M.D.S.*)
Delius	Légende in E♭ (*Forsyth*)
Dvořák	Sonata in F, Op.57: 1st movt (*Bärenreiter Praha H 2178*)
Elgar	Sonata in E minor, Op.82: 2nd *and* 3rd movts (*Novello/Music Sales*)
Fauré	Sonata in A, Op.13: 1st movt (*Peters EP 7487*)
Franck	Sonata in A: 3rd *and* 4th movts (*Henle* or *Henle – Schott/M.D.S.* or *Wiener Urtext/M.D.S.*)
Grieg	Sonata no.2 in G, Op.13: 2nd *and* 3rd movts (*Peters EP 2279*)
Khachaturian	Concerto in D minor: 1st movt (*Boosey & Hawkes*)
Lalo	Symphonie Espagnole, Op.21: 1st movt (*Peters EP 3797a*)
Lutosławski	Partita: 1st movt (*Chester/Music Sales*)
Mendelssohn	Concerto in E minor, Op.64: 1st movt (*Peters EP 1731a*)
Mozart	Concerto no.5 in A, K.219: 1st movt (*with cadenza*) (*Bärenreiter BA 4712a*) Sonata in B♭, K.454: 1st *and* 2nd movts 〕 *Mozart Sonatas for Piano and Violin, Vol.3* Sonata in E♭, K.481: 1st *and* 2nd movts 〕 (*Henle* or *Henle – Schott/M.D.S.*)
Arvo Pärt	Fratres (*Universal 17274/M.D.S.*)
Prokofiev	Any *three* of the '5 Mélodies', Op.35b (*Boosey & Hawkes*) Sonata no.2 in D, Op.94b: 1st *and* 2nd movts (*Boosey & Hawkes*)
Ravel	Sonata: any *one or two* movts (*Durand/U.M.P.*) Tzigane (Rapsodie de Concert) (*Durand/U.M.P.*)
Rodrigo	Concierto de Estío: 1st *and* 2nd movts (*Ediciones Joaquín Rodrigo/U.M.P.*)
Saint-Saëns	Havanaise, Op.83 (*Durand/U.M.P.*)
Schubert	Sonata (Duo) in A, Op.162, D.574: 3rd *and* 4th movts (*Bärenreiter BA 5605*)
Schumann	Sonata no.1 in A minor, Op.105: 1st *and* 2nd movts (*Henle* or *Henle – Schott/M.D.S.*)
Seiber	Concert Piece (*Schott ED 10429/M.D.S.*)
Shostakovich	Concerto no.1 in A minor, Op.77: 1st movt (*Boosey & Hawkes*)
Suk	Any *two* of the '4 Pieces', Op.17 (2 Vols: *Simrock/Boosey & Hawkes*)
Vaughan Williams	Concerto 'Accademico' in D minor: 1st movt (*O.U.P. archive/Allegro*) Sonata in A minor: 3rd movt, *Tema con Variazioni* (*O.U.P.*)
Vieuxtemps	Concerto no.5 in A minor, Op.37: 1st movt (*Peters EP 3323*)

Violin: FRSM

J.S. Bach	Partita for solo violin no.3 in E, BWV 1006:
	  1st *and* 2nd movts, *Preludio* **and** *Loure* — *Bach 3 Sonatas and 3 Partitas for solo violin*
	Sonata for solo violin no.1 in G minor, BWV 1001: (*Bärenreiter BA 5116*)
	  1st *and* 2nd movts, *Adagio* **and** *Fuga: Allegro*

Bartók	Concerto no.2 in B minor: 1st movt (*Boosey & Hawkes*)

Beethoven	Concerto in D, Op.61: 1st movt (*with cadenza*) (*Henle* or *Henle – Schott/M.D.S.*)
	Any *two* contrasting movements from *one* of the following Sonatas:
	  Op.47 in A ('Kreutzer'), Op.96 in G. *Beethoven Sonatas for Piano and Violin, Vol.2* (*Henle* or
	  Henle – Schott/M.D.S.)

Berg	Concerto: 1st *or* 2nd movt (*Universal 10903/M.D.S.*)
Brahms	Concerto in D, Op.77: 1st movt (*with cadenza by Joachim*) (*International 1502/M.D.S.*) Sonata in D minor, Op.108: any *two* movts (*Wiener Urtext/M.D.S.*)
Bruch	Concerto no.1 in G minor, Op.26: 3rd movt (*Peters EP 4590*)
Chausson	Poème, Op.25 (*Schott ED 1532/M.D.S.*)
Dvořák	Concerto in A minor, Op.53: 1st movt (*Bärenreiter*)
Elgar	Concerto in B minor, Op.61: 1st movt (*Novello/Music Sales*)
Franck	Sonata in A: 1st *and* 2nd movts (*Henle* or *Henle – Schott/M.D.S.* or *Wiener Urtext/M.D.S.*)
Lutosławski	Subito (*Chester/Music Sales*)
Mendelssohn	Concerto in E minor, Op.64: 1st *and* 2nd movts, *or* 2nd *and* 3rd movts (*Peters EP 1731a*)

Mozart	Any *two* movements (*with cadenzas where appropriate*) from *one* of the 5 Concertos:
	  no.1 in B♭, K.207 (*Bärenreiter BA 4863a*), no.2 in D, K.211 (*Bärenreiter BA 4864a*), no.3 in G,
	  K.216 (*Bärenreiter BA 4865a*), no.4 in D, K.218 (*Bärenreiter BA 4866a*), no.5 in A, K.219
	  (*Bärenreiter BA 4712a*)

Paganini	Any of the '24 Capricci', Op.1 (*Henle* or *Henle – Schott/M.D.S.*)
Krzysztof Penderecki	Cadenza for solo violin (*Schott ED 7649/M.D.S.*)
Prokofiev	Concerto no.2 in G minor, Op.63: 1st movt (*Boosey & Hawkes*)
Ravel	Sonata: 1st *and* 2nd movts, *or* 2nd *and* 3rd movts (*Durand/U.M.P.*)
Rubbra	Sonata no.2, Op.31: 1st *and* 3rd movts (*O.U.P. archive/Allegro*)
Saint-Saëns	Concerto no.3 in B minor, Op.61: any *two* movts (*Durand/U.M.P.*) Introduction et Rondo Capriccioso in A minor, Op.28, trans. Bizet (*Durand/U.M.P.*)
Sarasate	Any *two* of the following 'Danzas Españolas': Malagueña: no.1 from 'Spanish Dances', Book 1, Op.21 (*Simrock/Boosey & Hawkes*) Romanza Andaluza: no.3 from 'Spanish Dances', Book 2, Op.22 (*Simrock/Boosey & Hawkes*) Zapateado: no.6 from 'Spanish Dances', Book 3, Op.23 (*Simrock/Boosey & Hawkes*)
Schoenberg	Phantasy, Op.47 (*Peters EP 6060*)
Schubert	Rondo in A, D.438 (*Schott ED 5290/M.D.S.*)
Schumann	Sonata no.2 in D minor, Op.121: 1st *and* 3rd movts. *Schumann 2 Violin Sonatas* (*Peters EP 2367*)
Sibelius	Concerto in D minor, Op.47: 1st movt (*Peters D 2420*)
B. Stevens	Sonata in A minor in one movement (*Bardic Edition – Schott/M.D.S.*)
Stravinsky	Elegie for solo violin (*Schott VLB 47/M.D.S.*)
Szymanowski	Any *two* of the '3 Myths', Op.30 (*Universal 06836, 06837 and 06838/M.D.S.*)
Tōru Takemitsu	From far beyond Chrysanthemums and November Fog (*Schott SJ 1014/M.D.S.*)
Tartini	Sonata in G minor ('Devil's Trill'): complete (*Bärenreiter HM 278*)
Tchaikovsky	Concerto in D, Op.35: 1st movt, *or* 2nd *and* 3rd movts (*Peters EP 3019b*)
Turina	Sonate Espagnole: 1st movt (*Schott VLB 85/M.D.S.*)
Vaughan Williams	The Lark Ascending (*O.U.P.*)
Walton	Concerto: 1st movt (*O.U.P.*) Sonata: *either* movt *or* complete (*O.U.P. archive/Allegro*)
Wieniawski	Concerto no.2 in D minor, Op.22: 1st movt (*Peters EP 3296*) Polonaise de Concert in D, Op.4 (*International 2627/M.D.S.*) Polonaise Brillante in A, Op.21 (*International 2628/M.D.S.*) Scherzo-Tarantelle in G minor, Op.16 (*Peters EP 3292*)

The Associated Board of
the Royal Schools of Music
(Publishing) Limited

ACHIEVING SUCCESS

Preparing for your
Diploma in Music Performance

Clara Taylor
Chief Examiner – Associated Board

D 399 4   DVD
D 540 7   VHS

An invaluable guide for anyone
preparing for the Associated Board's
Diploma in Music Performance

- demonstrates the standards required at each diploma level – DipABRSM, LRSM, and FRSM

- 33 performance extracts on piano, violin, clarinet, oboe and voice

- advice on how to make the exam day go smoothly, including choosing repertoire, writing programme notes and preparing for the Quick Study test and *viva voce*

- interviews with successful candidates and with a diploma examiner, offering tips on preparing for the exam and what the examiners will be looking for

- commentary by the Associated Board's Chief Examiner, Clara Taylor

- available in DVD and VHS video formats

- optional Chinese subtitles and Cantonese voice-over (DVD only)

- 92 minutes running time

Available from all good music retailers worldwide

24 Portland Place   London W1B 1LU   United Kingdom   publishing@abrsm.ac.uk   www.abrsmpublishing.com

PUBLISHING

The Associated Board of
the Royal Schools of Music
(Publishing) Limited

Music in Words

A Guide to Researching and Writing about Music

This book's straightforward approach makes it a much-needed support and reference tool for students preparing for the Associated Board's diplomas

- addresses issues encountered when undertaking a written task, from programme notes for a Diploma to dissertations

- *two-part format*: 'how to' section on researching and writing about music, on citation and on using illustrations, and a quick-reference compendium of information

- includes an introduction to the strategic use of the internet and details of useful websites

Sample pages and a list of useful internet resources can be viewed on
www.abrsmpublishing.com/musicinwords

D 236 X

Performer's Guides

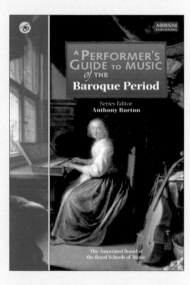

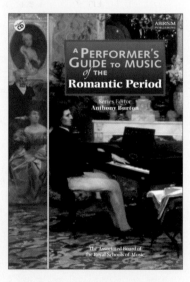

A Performer's Guide to Music of the Baroque Period
D 192 4

A Performer's Guide to Music of the Classical Period
D 193 2

A Performer's Guide to Music of the Romantic Period
D 194 0

These stimulating guides offer much-needed support to students writing programme notes for the Associated Board's Diploma exams and will help students achieve stylistic performances of music of the Baroque, Classical and Romantic periods.

All three guides:

- help students to write programme notes for Diplomas

- discuss the latest thinking on stylish performance in a clear, helpful and practical way

- feature chapters from experts on historical background, notation and interpretation, and on sources and editions

- include specialist advice for keyboard, string and wind players, and for singers

- are fully illustrated with many music examples, facsimiles and pictures

- include a full-length CD of excerpts from authoritative recordings

Available from all good music retailers worldwide

24 Portland Place   London W1B 1LU   United Kingdom   publishing@abrsm.ac.uk   www.abrsmpublishing.com

Viola: DipABRSM

Malcolm Arnold	Sonata: 2nd *and* 3rd movts (*Lengnick/Faber*)

J.S. Bach	Cello Suite no.1 in G, BWV 1007:
	    2nd, 4th *and* 7th movts, *Allemande, Sarabande* **and** *Gigue*
	Cello Suite no.3 in C, BWV 1009:
	    3rd *and* 4th movts, *Courante* **and** *Sarabande*
	Cello Suite no.5 in C minor, BWV 1011:
	    3rd, 4th *and* 7th movts, *Courante, Sarabande* **and** *Gigue* *Bach 6 Suites for Solo Cello, trans. Forbes* (*Chester/Music Sales*)
	Any *three* movements from *one* of the 3 Viola da Gamba Sonatas: no.1 in G, BWV 1027, no.2 in D, BWV 1028, no.3 in G minor, BWV 1029. *Bach 3 Sonatas for Viola da Gamba* (*Bärenreiter BA 5186*)

L. Berkeley	Sonata in D minor, Op.22: 1st movt (*Chester/Music Sales*)
Howard Blake	Prelude for solo viola (from 'Benedictus') (*Highbridge Music*)
Bloch	Suite (1919): 1st movt (*Schirmer/Music Sales*)
Brahms	Sonata in F minor, Op.120 no.1: any *two* movts (*Wiener Urtext/M.D.S.*) Sonata in E♭, Op.120 no.2: any *two* movts (*Wiener Urtext/M.D.S.*)
Britten	Elegy for solo viola (*Faber*) Lachrymae, Op.48 (Reflections on a Song by John Dowland) (*Boosey & Hawkes*)
F.X. Brixi	Concerto in C: 1st movt (*Schott VAB 5/M.D.S.*)
Bruch	Kol Nidrei, Op.47, arr. de Smet (*Peters EP 7177a*)
Campagnoli	Any of the following from '41 Caprices' for solo viola, Op.22: nos.1, 9, 12, 15, 17, 36 (*Peters EP 2548*)
Dittersdorf	Sonata in E♭: complete (*International 2211/M.D.S.*)
Handel	Sonata in G minor, Op.1 no.6, HWV 364b, arr. Pilkington: complete (*Stainer & Bell*)
Hindemith	Kammermusik no.5, Op.36 no.4: 1st movt (*Schott ED 1977/M.D.S.*) Sonata in F, Op.11 no.4: 1st *and* 2nd movts (*Schott ED 1976/M.D.S.*)
Hoffmeister	Concerto in D: 1st movt (*Peters EP 9857*)
Holst	Lyric Movement (*O.U.P. archive/Allegro*)
Hummel	Sonata in E♭, Op.5 no.3: complete (*Schott VAB 16/M.D.S.*)
G. Jacob	Air and Dance (*O.U.P.*) Concerto no.2 in G: 1st *and* 2nd movts (*Simrock/Boosey & Hawkes*) Sonatina: 1st movt (*Novello/Music Sales*)
Kodály	Adagio (*Editio Musica/Faber*)
R. Kreutzer	Any *one* of the following from '42 Studies', trans. Pagels: nos.9, 12, 26, 27, 29 (*International 0976/M.D.S.*)
Maconchy	Any *two* of the '5 Sketches' for solo viola (*Chester/Music Sales*)
Mazas	Études Speciales, Op.36 Book 1: no.18 *or* no.23 (*International 1091/M.D.S.*)
Milhaud	La Californienne *and* The Wisconsonian, *or* La Bruxelloise *and* La Parisienne (nos.1 *and* 2, *or* nos.3 *and* 4 of 'Quatre Visages', Op.238) (*all publ. separately: Heugel/U.M.P.*) Sonata no.2, Op.244: any *two* movts (*Heugel/U.M.P.*)
Rawsthorne	Sonata: 1st movt (*O.U.P. archive/Allegro*)

Reger	Any *one* of the following movements from the '3 Suites for solo viola', Op.131d:
	    Suite no.1 in G minor: 1st *or* 2nd movt
	    Suite no.2 in D: 1st *or* 4th movt (*Peters EP 3971*)
	    Suite no.3 in E minor: 2nd *or* 4th movt

Rivier	Concertino: 1st movt (*Salabert/U.M.P.*)
Schubert	Sonata in A minor ('Arpeggione'), D.821, arr. Wrochem: 1st movt (*Bärenreiter BA 5683*)
Schumann	Märchenbilder, Op.113: nos.1 *and* 3, *or* nos.2 *and* 4 (*Peters EP 2372*)
C. Stamitz	Concerto in D, Op.1: 3rd movt (*Peters EP 3816a*)
Roger Steptoe	Narration, Burlesque *and* Elegy from '3 Pieces' (*Stainer & Bell*)
Telemann	Concerto in G, TWV 51:G9: complete (*Bärenreiter BA 3712*) Any *one* Fantasia complete from *Telemann 12 Fantasias for Unaccompanied Viola, arr. Rood* (*2 Vols: McGinnis & Marx*)
Vaughan Williams	Romance (*O.U.P.*) Suite for Viola: Group 1 complete (*O.U.P.*)
Vivaldi	Concerto in G for Viola d'Amore (RV 392): complete (*Edwin Kalmus/Maecenas Europe*)
Weber	Andante e Rondo ungarese, Op.35 (*Schott VAB 36/M.D.S.*) Variations in C (*Peters EP 8321*)

Viola: LRSM

J.C. Bach Concerto in C minor, arr. Casadesus: 2nd *and* 3rd movts (*Salabert/U.M.P.*)

J.S. Bach Any *one* of the following combinations of movements from *one* of the *Bach 6 Suites for Solo Cello*, trans. Forbes (*Chester/Music Sales*):
Cello Suite no.1 in G, BWV 1007: 1st, 2nd *and* 3rd movts, *Prélude, Allemande* and *Courante*
Cello Suite no.2 in D minor, BWV 1008: 1st *and* 2nd movts, *Prélude* and *Allemande, or* 4th *and* 7th movts, *Sarabande* and *Gigue*
Cello Suite no.3 in C, BWV 1009: 1st *and* 2nd movts, *Prélude* and *Allemande, or* 3rd, 4th, 5th *and* 6th movts, *Courante, Sarabande* and *Bourrée I and II*
Cello Suite no.4 in E♭, BWV 1010: 4th, 5th *and* 6th movts, *Sarabande* and *Bourrée I and II*
Cello Suite no.5 in C minor, BWV 1011: 4th, 5th *and* 6th movts, *Sarabande* and *Gavotte I and II*

Bartók Concerto: 1st movt (*Boosey & Hawkes*)

Bax Legend (*Studio Music*)
Sonata (1922): 1st movt (*Studio Music*)

L. Berkeley Sonata in D minor, Op.22: complete (*Chester/Music Sales*)

Bliss Sonata (1933): complete (*O.U.P. archive/Allegro*)

Bloch Suite (1919): complete (*Schirmer/Music Sales*)

Brahms Sonata in F minor, Op.120 no.1: complete (*Wiener Urtext/M.D.S.*)
Sonata in E♭, Op.120 no.2: complete (*Wiener Urtext/M.D.S.*)

Britten Elegy for solo viola (*Faber*)

Hindemith Der Schwanendreher: 1st movt (*Schott ED 2517/M.D.S.*)
Sonata in F, Op.11 no.4: complete (*Schott ED 1976/M.D.S.*)

Hoffmeister Concerto in B♭: 1st movt (*Schott ED 11247/M.D.S.*)

G. Jacob Concerto no.1 in C minor: complete (*Simrock/Boosey & Hawkes*)
Concerto no.2 in G: complete (*Simrock/Boosey & Hawkes*)

Maconchy Any *three* of the '5 Sketches' for solo viola (*Chester/Music Sales*)

Martinů Rhapsody Concerto: 1st *or* 2nd movt (*Bärenreiter BA 4316a*)

Milhaud Sonata no.1, Op.240: complete (*Heugel/U.M.P.*)
Sonata no.2, Op.244: complete (*Heugel/U.M.P.*)

Paul Patterson 'Tides of Mananan' for solo viola (*Weinberger/William Elkin*)

Rawsthorne Sonata: complete (*O.U.P. archive/Allegro*)

Reger Any *two* contrasting movements from *one* of the '3 Suites for solo viola', Op.131d :
no.1 in G minor, no.2 in D, no.3 in E minor (*Peters EP 3971*)

J. Reicha Concerto in E♭, Op.2 no.1: 1st movt (*Simrock/Boosey & Hawkes*)

Rivier Concertino: 1st *and* 2nd movts (*Salabert/U.M.P.*)

Rubbra Concerto in A, Op.75: 1st movt (*Lengnick/Faber*)

Schubert Sonata in A minor ('Arpeggione'), D.821, arr. Wrochem: complete (*Bärenreiter BA 5683*)

Shostakovich Sonata, Op.147: 1st *and* 2nd movts (*Boosey & Hawkes*)

C. Stamitz Concerto in D, Op.1: 1st movt (*Peters EP 3816a*)

Vaughan Williams Suite for Viola: Group 2 complete (*O.U.P.*)
Suite for Viola: Group 3 complete (*O.U.P.*)

Walton Concerto: any *two* movts (*O.U.P.*)

Hugh Wood Variations, Op.1 (*Chester/Music Sales*)

Viola: FRSM

J.S. Bach Cello Suite no.3 in C, BWV 1009: complete
Cello Suite no.5 in C minor, BWV 1011: complete   *Bach 6 Suites for Solo Cello, trans. Forbes*
Cello Suite no.6 in G, BWV 1012: complete   (*Chester/Music Sales*)

Brahms Sonata in F minor, Op.120 no.1: complete (*Wiener Urtext/M.D.S.*)
Sonata in E♭, Op.120 no.2: complete (*Wiener Urtext/M.D.S.*)

Glinka Sonata in D minor: complete (*Musica Rara 1034/Breitkopf & Härtel*)

Hindemith Sonata for solo viola, Op.11 no.5: complete (*Schott ED 1968/M.D.S.*)
Sonata for solo viola, Op.25 no.1: complete (*Schott ED 1969/M.D.S.*)
Sonata for solo viola, Op.31 no.4: complete (*Schott ED 8278/M.D.S.*)
Sonata for solo viola (1937): complete (*Schott ED 8279/M.D.S.*)

Hoffmeister Concerto in B♭: complete (*with cadenza*) (*Schott ED 11247/M.D.S.*)

Maconchy 5 Sketches for solo viola: complete (*Chester/Music Sales*)

Martinů Rhapsody Concerto: complete (*Bärenreiter BA 4316a*)

Milhaud Concerto no.2, Op.340: complete (*Heugel/U.M.P.*)

Viola: FRSM

Paul Patterson	'Tides of Mananan' for solo viola (*Weinberger/William Elkin*)
Krzysztof Penderecki	Cadenza for solo viola (*Schott VAB 52/M.D.S.*)
Rainier	Sonata: complete (*Schott ED 10410/M.D.S.*)
Reger	Suite in G minor: complete: no.1 from '3 Suites for solo viola', Op.131d (*Peters EP 3971*)
Schubert	Sonata in A minor ('Arpeggione'), D.821, arr. Wrochem: complete (*Bärenreiter BA 5683*)
Seiber	Elegie (*Schott ED 10422/M.D.S.*)
Shostakovich	Sonata, Op.147: complete (*Boosey & Hawkes*)
C. Stamitz	Concerto in D, Op.1: any *two* movts (*with cadenza where appropriate*) (*Peters EP 3816a*)
Vaughan Williams	Suite for Viola: Group 2 complete (*O.U.P.*)
	Suite for Viola: Group 3 complete (*O.U.P.*)
Walton	Concerto: complete (*O.U.P.*)

Cello: DipABRSM

J.S. Bach	Suite no.3 in C, BWV 1009: 3rd, 4th *and* 7th movts, *Courante, Sarabande* and *Gigue* — Suite no.4 in E♭, BWV 1010: 1st movt, *Prélude* — *Bach 6 Suites for Violoncello solo (Bärenreiter BA 320)*
Beethoven	Sonata in A, Op.69: 1st movt. *Beethoven Sonatas for Piano and Violoncello* (*Henle* or *Henle – Schott/M.D.S.*)
	7 Variations on a Theme 'Bei Männern' from Mozart's 'Magic Flute', WoO 46 (*Peters EP 7048*)
Bridge	Sonata: 1st movt (*Boosey & Hawkes*)
Chopin	Sonata in G minor, Op.65; 1st movt (*Henle* or *Henle – Schott/M.D.S.*)
George Crumb	Sonata for solo cello: 1st *and* 2nd movts (*Peters EP 6056*)
Delius	Sonata: complete. *Delius Works for Cello and Piano* (*Boosey & Hawkes*)
Dvořák	Rondo in G minor, Op.94 (*Henle* or *Henle – Schott/M.D.S.*)
Elgar	Concerto in E minor, Op.85: 1st *and* 2nd movts (*Novello/Music Sales*)
Fauré	Sonata no.2 in G minor, Op.117: 1st movt (*Durand/U.M.P.*)
Francoeur	Sonata in F: 1st *and* 2nd movts (*Schott CB 74/M.D.S.*)
Haydn	Concerto in C, Hob.VIIb/1: 1st movt (*Henle* or *Henle – Schott/M.D.S.*)
Hindemith	'A Frog he went a-courting': Variations on an old English nursery song (*Schott ED 4276/M.D.S.*)
Holst	Invocation, Op.19 no.2 (*Faber*)
Ireland	Sonata in G minor: 1st movt (*Stainer & Bell*)
Kenneth Leighton	Elegy (*Lengnick/Faber*)
Martinů	Variations on a Theme of Rossini (*Boosey & Hawkes*)
Aaron Minsky	Laid-back Devil, Like Crazy *and* The Crack of Dawn: nos.4, 8 *and* 9 from '10 American Cello Etudes' for solo cello (*O.U.P.*)
Saint-Saëns	Concerto no.1 in A minor, Op.33: 1st *and* 2nd movts (*Durand/U.M.P.*)
Schumann	Adagio and Allegro in A♭, Op.70 (*Peters EP 2386*)
Vivaldi	Concerto in G minor, RV 417: complete (*International 3073/M.D.S.*)
Walton	Passcaglia for unaccompanied cello (*O.U.P. archive/Allegro*)

Cello: LRSM

J.S. Bach	Any *three* contrasting movements from *one* of the 6 Suites for Violoncello solo, BWV 1007–1012 (*Bärenreiter BA 320*)
Bloch	Nigun (Improvisation), arr. Schuster (from 'Baal Shem' Suite) (*Carl Fischer/Boosey & Hawkes* or *Carl Fischer – Schott/M.D.S.*)
Boccherini	Concerto in B♭: 1st movt (*Peters EP 8780*)
	Sonata no.2 in C: complete (*International 1202/M.D.S.*)
Brahms	Sonata in E minor, Op.38: complete (*Wiener Urtext/M.D.S.*)
Caporale	Sonata in D minor: complete (*Schott CB 100/M.D.S.*)
Danzi	Variations on a Theme from Mozart's 'Don Giovanni' (*Breitkopf & Härtel 6522*)
Davidov	At the Fountain, Op.20 no.2 (*International 1672/M.D.S.*)
Debussy	Sonata in D minor: complete (*Henle* or *Henle – Schott/M.D.S.*)
Dvořák	Concerto in B minor, Op.104: 2nd movt (*Peters EP 9362*)
Fauré	Papillon, Op.77 (*International 0652/M.D.S.*)
Frescobaldi	Toccata, arr. Cassadó (*Universal 08282/M.D.S.*)
Grieg	Sonata in A minor, Op.36: complete (*Peters EP 2157*)

Cello: LRSM

Hans Werner Henze	Serenade (1949) for solo cello: any *five* movts (*Schott ED 4330/M.D.S.*)
Hindemith	Sonata for solo cello, Op.25 no.3: any *two* movts (*Schott ED 1979/M.D.S.*)
Kabalevsky	Concerto no.1 in G minor, Op.49: 1st movt (*Peters EP 4779*)
Khachaturian	Concerto (1946): 1st movt (*Boosey & Hawkes*)
Lalo	Concerto in D minor: 3rd movt (*Peters EP 3799*)
Lutosławski	Grave (*Chester/Music Sales*)
Mendelssohn	Variations Concertantes, Op.17. *Mendelssohn Original Cello Compositions* (*Peters EP 1735*)
Martinů	Variations on a Slovakian Theme (*Bärenreiter BA 3969*)
Paganini	Variations on One String on a Theme from Rossini's 'Moses' (*International 2344/M.D.S.*)
Popper	Spinning Song, Op.55 no.1 (*International 0684/M.D.S.*)
Prokofiev	Sonata in C, Op.119: 1st movt (*Boosey & Hawkes*)
Rachmaninov	Sonata in G minor, Op.19: 1st *and* 2nd movts (*Boosey & Hawkes*)
Rawsthorne	Sonata (1948): complete (*O.U.P. archive/Allegro*)
Schumann	3 Fantasiestücke, Op.73: complete (*cello version: Henle* or *Henle – Schott/M.D.S.*)
Shostakovich	Sonata in D minor, Op.40: 1st *and* 3rd movts (*Boosey & Hawkes*)
Telemann	Sonata in D (from 'Der getreue Musikmeister'), TWV 41:D6 (*Bärenreiter HM 13*)
Tchaikovsky	Pezzo Capriccioso, Op.62 (*International 0667/M.D.S.*)
Walton	Concerto: 1st *and* 2nd movts, *or* 1st *and* 3rd movts (*O.U.P.*)

Cello: FRSM

J.S. Bach	Suite no.4 in E♭, BWV 1010: complete Suite no.6 in D, BWV 1012: complete } *Bach 6 Suites for Violoncello solo* (*Bärenreiter BA 320*)
Beethoven	Sonata in A, Op.69: complete Sonata in D, Op.102 no.2: complete } *Beethoven Sonatas for Piano and Violoncello* (*Henle* or *Henle – Schott/M.D.S.*)
Bloch	Schelomo (*Schirmer/Music Sales*)
Boccherini	Sonata no.6 in A: complete (*International 0653/M.D.S.*)
Brahms	Sonata in F, Op.99: complete (*Wiener Urtext/M.D.S.*)
Britten	Suite no.1, Op.72: complete Suite no.2, Op.80: complete } *Britten 3 Suites for Cello solo* (*Faber*) Suite no.3, Op.87: complete
Chopin	Polonaise Brillante, Op.3 (*International 1971/M.D.S.*) Sonata in G minor, Op.65: complete (*Henle* or *Henle – Schott/M.D.S.*)
Dohnányi	Konzertstück in D, Op.12 (*Weinberger/William Elkin*)
Dvořák	Concerto in B minor, Op.104: 1st *or* 3rd movt (*Peters EP 9362*)
Haydn	Concerto in D, Op.101, Hob.VIIb/2: 1st movt (*with cadenza*) (*Henle* or *Henle – Schott/M.D.S.*)
Kodály	Sonata, Op.4: complete (*Universal 07130/M.D.S.*)
Popper	Dance of the Elves (Elfentanz), Op.39 (*International 2520/M.D.S.*)
Schubert	Sonata in A minor ('Arpeggione'), D.821, arr. Storck: complete (*Bärenreiter BA 6970*)
Schumann	Concerto in A minor, Op.129: 1st movt (*Breitkopf & Härtel 8597*)
Shostakovich	Concerto no.1 in E♭, Op.107: 1st movt (*Boosey & Hawkes*)
Stravinsky	Suite Italienne, arr. Piatigorsky: complete (*Boosey & Hawkes*)
Tchaikovsky	Variations on a Rococo Theme, Op.33 (*International 1263/M.D.S.*)

Double Bass: DipABRSM

Candidates may choose to play any of the following works using editions published for either solo scordatura or orchestral tuning, provided the piano part is suitably transposed wherever necessary.

J.S. Bach	Any *two* movements from *one* of the 6 Solo Violoncello Suites, trans. Sterling (*3 Vols: Peters EP 238b, c and d*)
L. Berkeley	Introduction and Allegro, Op.80 (*Yorke/Spartan Press*)
Capuzzi	Concerto in D: any *two* movts (*Yorke/Spartan Press*)
Cimador	Concerto in G: 1st *and* 2nd movts (*Yorke/Spartan Press*)
Dragonetti	Solo in E minor (*Yorke/Spartan Press*)
Fauré	Après un Rêve, Op.7 no.1, arr. Zimmermann (*International 1740/M.D.S.*) Sicilienne, Op.78, arr. Zimmermann (*International 0919/M.D.S.*)
Franz Keyper	Romance and Rondo (*Yorke/Spartan Press*)
Kohaut	Concerto in D: 1st *and* 2nd movts, *or* 2nd *and* 3rd movts (*Yorke/Spartan Press*)

Double Bass: DipABRSM

Vojta Kuchynka	Humoreska à la Mazurka for solo double bass (*Recital Music*)
B. Marcello	Sonata in D (Op.1 no.1), trans Zimmermann: 1st *and* 2nd movts (*International 2488/M.D.S.*) Sonata in E minor (Op.2 no.2): complete (*International 1050/M.D.S.*) Sonata in G (Op.2 no.6): complete (*International 1159/M.D.S.*)
Massenet	Meditation (from 'Thaïs'), arr. Drew (*Belwin/Maecenas Europe*)
Sperger	Sonata in D: 1st *and* 2nd movts (*Hofmeister 7511/William Elkin*)
Telemann	Sonata in A minor, arr. Sankey: 3rd *and* 4th movts (*International 2308/M.D.S.*)

Double Bass: LRSM

Candidates may choose to play any of the following works using editions published for either solo scordatura or orchestral tuning, provided the piano part is suitably transposed wherever necessary.

J. S. Bach	Any *Prélude and one* other movement from *one* of the 6 Solo Violoncello Suites, trans. Sterling (*3 Vols: Peters EP 238b, c* and *d*)
Bottesini	Bolero Gavotta ⎤ *Yorke Complete Bottesini, Vol.1* Romanza Patetica (Melodie) ⎟ (*Yorke/Spartan Press*) Tema con Variazioni on Paisiello's 'Nel cor più non mi sento' ⎦ Concerto no.2 in B minor: 1st *and* 2nd movts (*scordatura edn: International 2301/M.D.S.*) or (*orchestral tuning edn. in A minor: Yorke/Spartan Press*) Elegia in D (*Recital Music* or *Ricordi/U.M.P.*) Fantasia on a Theme from Bellini's 'La Sonnambula' (*International 3263/M.D.S.*) Tarantella in A minor (*International 1707/M.D.S.*)
Derek Bourgeois	Romance, Op.64 (*Yorke/Spartan Press*)
Dittersdorf	Concerto no.1 in E♭: 1st *and* 2nd movts (*with cadenzas*), *or* 2nd *and* 3rd movts (*with cadenzas*) (*scordatura edn: Schott ED 2449/M.D.S.*) or *Dittersdorf 2 Double Bass Concertos* (*orchestral tuning edn. in D: Yorke/Spartan Press*) Concerto no.2 in E: 1st *and* 2nd movts (*with cadenzas*) (*scordatura edn: Schott ED 2473/M.D.S.*) or *Dittersdorf 2 Double Bass Concertos* (*orchestral tuning edn. in D: Yorke/Spartan Press*)
Dragonetti	Concerto in A: any *two* movts (*International 2098/M.D.S.*)
attrib. H. Eccles	Sonata in G minor, arr. Zimmermann: complete (*International 1712/M.D.S.*)
David Ellis	Sonata for solo double bass, Op.42: complete (*Yorke/Spartan Press*)
Hans Fryba	Suite in Olden Style: any *three* movts (*Weinberger/William Elkin*)
Hindemith	Sonata (1949): complete (*Schott ED 4043/M.D.S.*)
G. Jacob	A Little Concerto: 1st *and* 2nd movts (*Yorke/Spartan Press*)
Koussevitzky	Chanson Triste, Op.2 (*Forberg F-231/Peters*) Valse Miniature, Op.1 no.2 (*Forberg F-241/Peters*)
Mišek	Sonata no.1 in A, Op.5: complete (*Hofmeister/William Elkin*)
Pichl	Concerto in D: 1st *or* 3rd movt (*Hofmeister/William Elkin*)
Miloslav Raisigl	Suite no.1 for solo double bass: complete (*Recital Music*)
Vivaldi	Any *one* of the 6 Cello Sonatas, RV 40–1, 43, 45–7, trans. Zimmermann (*publ. separately: International/M.D.S.*)
Julien-François Zbinden	Hommage à J. S. Bach, Op.44, for solo double bass (*Breitkopf & Härtel 6554*)

Double Bass: FRSM

Candidates may choose to play any of the following works using editions published for either solo scordatura or orchestral tuning, provided the piano part is suitably transposed wherever necessary.

Bottesini	Concerto no.2 in B minor: complete (*scordatura edn: International 2301/M.D.S.*) or (*orchestral tuning edn. in A minor: Yorke/Spartan Press*)
Bucchi	Concerto Grottesco: complete (*Suvini Zerboni/William Elkin*)
Peter Maxwell Davies	Strathclyde Concerto no.7: complete (*Boosey & Hawkes*)
Dittersdorf	Concerto no.2 in E: complete (*with cadenza*) (*scordatura edn: Schott ED 2473/M.D.S.*) or *Dittersdorf 2 Double Bass Concertos* (*orchestral tuning edn. in D: Yorke/Spartan Press*)
Françaix	Concerto: complete (*Schott ED 6653/M.D.S.*)
Hans Fryba	Suite in Olden Style: complete (*Weinberger/William Elkin*)
Glière	Intermezzo, Op.9 no.1 *and* Tarantella, Op.9 no.2 (*Forberg F-194* and *F-258/Peters*) Prélude, Op.32 no.1 *and* Scherzo, Op.32 no.2 (*Forberg F-259* and *F-260/Peters*)
Hoffmeister	Concerto no.1 in C: complete (*Hofmeister/William Elkin*)
Koussevitzky	Concerto, Op.3: complete (*Forberg F-24/Peters*)

Double Bass: FRSM

Nicholas Maw	'The Old King's Lament' for solo double bass (*Yorke/Spartan Press*)
Annibale Mengoli	20 Concert Studies: no.1 *or* no.2 *or* no.5 (*Theodore Presser 2042/U.M.P.*)
Vilmos Montag	Sonata in E minor: complete (*Hofmeister/William Elkin*)
Paganini	Variations on One String on a Theme from Rossini's 'Moses' (*International 2340/M.D.S.*)
Vanhal	Concerto in E: any *two* movts (*scordatura edn.* or *orchestral tuning edn. in D: Hofmeister/William Elkin*)

Guitar: DipABRSM

* *Works available for guitar and piano reduction to be performed with a keyboard accompaniment.*

Asencio	Suite Valenciana: 1st movt, *Preludi* (*Bèrben/De Haske*)
J.S. Bach	Any *one* of the following movements or combinations of movements from *one* of the following works included in *Bach Lute Suites for Guitar, ed. Willard* (*Ariel Publications/Music Sales*) or *Bach Solo Lute Works for Guitar, ed. Koonce* (*Neil Kjos Music/Music Sales*):
	Prelude, Fugue and Allegro (in D), BWV 998: *Prelude* only
	Suite no.1 in E minor, BWV 996: 1st movt, *Praeludio – Presto, or* 3rd *and* 4th movts, *Courante* and *Sarabande*
	Suite no.2 (in A minor), BWV 997: 1st movt, *Preludio, or* 3rd *and* 4th movts, *Sarabande* and *Gigue*
	Suite no.3 (in A minor), BWV 995: 1st movt, *Prelude – Presto, or* 2nd *and* 7th movts, *Allemande* and *Gigue*
	Suite no.4 in E, BWV 1006a: 1st movt, *Prelude, or* 2nd *and* 3rd movts, *Loure* and *Gavotte en Rondeau*
Barrios	La Catedral / Vals, Op.8 no.4 } *Barrios 18 Concert Pieces, Vol.1, ed. Burley* (*Schott ED 12370/M.D.S.*)
L. Berkeley *	Concerto, Op.88: 2nd movt (*Chester/Music Sales*)
	Theme and Variations, Op.77 (*Chester/Music Sales*)
Léo Brouwer	Canticum (*Schott GA 424/M.D.S.*)
	Elogio de la Danza (*Schott GA 425/M.D.S.*)
*	Retrats Catalans: no.1, Mompou *or* no.2, Gaudí (*Eschig/U.M.P.*)
F. Burkhart	Passacaglia (*Universal 11959/M.D.S.*)
Castelnuovo-Tedesco	Aranci in Fiore, Op.87b (*Ricordi/U.M.P.*)
*	Concerto in D, Op.99: 2nd movt (*Schott GA 166/M.D.S.*)
	Tarantella, Op.87a (*Ricordi/U.M.P.*)
Coste	La Source du Lyson, Op.47. *Coste Collected Guitar Works, Vol.5* (*Chanterelle 405/Guitarnotes*)
Stephen Dodgson *	Concerto no.1: 2nd movt (*Bèrben/De Haske*)
	Merlin (*Moeck 7016*)
Dowland	The Right Honourable Robert, Earl of Essex, His Galliard. *Dowland Anthology of Selected Pieces, trans. Burley* (*Schott ED 12393/M.D.S.*)
	Fantasia no.5 *or* Fantasia no.11. *Dowland 12 Fantasias for Guitar, trans. Ruhe* (*Moeck 7006*)
Falla	Homenaje: Le Tombeau de Claude Debussy (*Chester/Music Sales* or *Ricordi/U.M.P.*)
Francesco da Milano	Fantasia no.6 *and* Ricercare no.3, *or* Fantasias nos.10 *and* 18. *F. da Milano Complete Lute Works, Vol.1, trans. Chiesa* (*Suvini Zerboni/William Elkin*)
M. Giuliani *	Concerto no.1 in A, Op.30: 3rd movt (*Suvini Zerboni/William Elkin*)
	Sonata in C, Op.15: 1st movt (*Suvini Zerboni/William Elkin* or *Universal 11320/M.D.S.*)
	Variations on a Theme of Handel, Op.107 (*Suvini Zerboni/William Elkin* or *Universal 16713/M.D.S.*)
Guerau	Gallardas *and* Canario. *Guerau 5 Pieces from 'Poemo Harmónico', trans. Duarte* (*Universal 29161/M.D.S.*)
Hans Werner Henze	Royal Winter Music: 2nd Sonata on Shakespearean Characters: 1st movt, *Sir Andrew Aguecheek* (*Schott GA 473/M.D.S.*)
Frank Martin	Prelude *and* Plaint: nos.1 *and* 3 from '4 Pièces Brèves' (*Universal 12711/M.D.S.*)
John McCabe	Canto (*Novello/Music Sales*)
Milán	Fantasia no.22 *and/or* Fantasia no.31, from 'Libro de Musica de Vihuela', Vols.2 and 3, trans. Monkemeyer (*Hofmeister/William Elkin*)
Mompou	Suite Compostelana: *Preludio* and *Canción* (*Salabert/U.M.P.*)
Moreno Torroba	Madroños. *20th Century Guitar Music* (*Schirmer/Music Sales*)
	Nocturno (*Schott GA 103/M.D.S.*)
	Suite Castellana: 1st *and* 2nd movts, *Fandanguillo* and *Arada* (*Schott GA 104/M.D.S.*)
Ohana	Tiento (*Billaudot/U.M.P.*)
Piazzolla	Any *two* of '5 Pieces' (*Bèrben/De Haske*)

Guitar: DipABRSM

Ponce *	Concierto del Sur: 2nd *or* 3rd movt (*Peermusic Classical/William Elkin*)
	Sonata Romántica (Hommage à Schubert): 1st movt (*Schott GA 123/M.D.S.*)
	Sonatina Meridonal: 1st movt, *or* 2nd **and** 3rd movts (*Schott GA 151/M.D.S.*)
Rodrigo	En los trigales: no.1 from 'Por los campos de España' (*Ediciones Joaquín Rodrigo/Guitarnotes* or
	Ediciones Joaquín Rodrigo/U.M.P.)
Roussel	Ségovia, Op.29 (*Durand/U.M.P.*)
Scarlatti	2 Sonatas in D, Kp.335 *and* 336. *Scarlatti 4 Sonatas, trans. Tanenbaum* (*Guitar Solo Publications/*
	Ashley Mark Publishing)
	Sonata in E minor, L.352 *and* Sonata in A, L.483. *Scarlatti 9 Sonatas, Vol.1, trans. Barbosa-Lima*
	(*Columbia Music/M.D.S.*)
Reginald Smith Brindle	El Polifemo de Oro (*Schott ED 11846/M.D.S.*)
Soler	Sonata in E minor, R.118. *Anthology of Baroque Sonatas, trans. Burley* (*Schott ED 12481/M.D.S.*)
Sor	Fantasia no.6 ('Les Adieux'), Op.21. *Sor Fantasias, Vol.2* (*Peters EP 7339*) or *publ. separately* (*Schott*
	GA 350/M.D.S.)
	Variations on 'Les Folies d'Espagne' **and** a Minuet, Op.15a (*Universal 16709/M.D.S.*)
Tōru Takemitsu	Equinox (*Schott SJ 1090/M.D.S.*)
	Any of the 3 pieces from 'In The Woods' (*Schott SJ 1099/M.D.S.*)
Tárrega	Estudio sobre la Sonatina de Delfin Alard (*Ricordi/U.M.P.*)
	Recuerdos de la Alhambra (*Universal 14427/M.D.S.*)
Turina	Hommage à Tárrega, Op.69: complete (*Schott GA 136/M.D.S.*)
Villa-Lobos	12 Études: no.1 in E minor *and* no.5 in C, *or* no.2 in A *and* no.9 in F♯ minor, *or* no.3 in D *and* no.4
	in G (*Eschig/U.M.P.*)
	Gavotta-Chôro (Suite Populaire Brésilienne: no.4) (*Eschig/U.M.P.*)
	Valsa-Chôro (Suite Populaire Brésilienne: no.3) (*Eschig/U.M.P.*)
Walton	Bagatelles nos.2 *and* 3, from '5 Bagatelles' (*O.U.P.*)
S.L. Weiss	Capricio in D │ *Weiss Anthology of Selected Pieces, trans. Burley*
	Tombeau sur la Mort de Mr. Comte de Logy │ (*Schott ED 12320/M.D.S.*)
	Suite in E minor: 1st *and* 6th movts, *Allemande* **and** *Gigue*. *Weiss 2 Suites, trans. Biberian*
	(*Peters EP 7336*)
Arthur Wills	Pavane *and* Galliard (*Ricordi/U.M.P.*)

Guitar: LRSM

* **Works available for guitar and piano reduction to be performed with a keyboard accompaniment.**

Aguado	Rondo in A minor: no.2 from '3 Rondo Brillanti', Op.2 (*Suvini Zerboni/William Elkin*)
Albéniz	Suite Española, Op.47, trans. Barrueco: any *four* movts (*Belwin/Maecenas Europe*)
Malcolm Arnold *	Concerto, Op.67: 1st movt (*Paterson/Music Sales*)
	Fantasy, Op.107 (*Faber*)
J.S. Bach	Fugue (in A minor), BWV 1000 │ *Bach Lute Suites for Guitar, ed. Willard* (*Ariel Publications/*
	Prelude, Fugue and Allegro (in D), │ *Music Sales*) or *Bach Solo Lute Works for Guitar,*
	BWV 998: complete │ *ed. Koonce* (*Neil Kjos Music/Music Sales*)
	Any *one* of the following combinations of movements from *one* of the following Suites included in
	Bach Lute Suites for Guitar, ed. Willard (*Ariel Publications/Music Sales*) or *Bach Solo Lute Works for*
	Guitar, ed. Koonce (*Neil Kjos Music/Music Sales*):
	Suite no.1 in E minor, BWV 996: 1st, 4th *and* 6th movts, *Praeludio – Presto, Sarabande* **and** *Gigue*
	Suite no.2 (in A minor), BWV 997: 1st *and* 2nd movts, *Preludio* **and** *Fuga*
	Suite no.3 (in A minor), BWV 995: 1st, 5th *and* 6th movts, *Prelude – Presto, Gavotte I* **and** *Gavotte II*
	en Rondeau
	Suite no.4 in E, BWV 1006a: 1st, 2nd *and* 7th movts, *Prelude, Loure* **and** *Gigue*
Batchelar	Mounsieurs Almaine, trans. Hinojosa (*Transatlantiques/U.M.P.*)
Richard Rodney Bennett	5 Impromptus: complete (*Universal 14433/M.D.S.*)
L. Berkeley *	Concerto, Op.88: 1st movt (*Chester/Music Sales*)
M. Berkeley	Sonata in One Movement (*O.U.P.*)
Léo Brouwer *	Concerto no.3 ('Elegiaco'): 1st movt (*Eschig/U.M.P.*)
	El Decameron Negro: complete (*Transatlantiques/U.M.P.*)
Castelnuovo-Tedesco	Capriccio Diabolico (Omaggio a Paganini), Op.85 (*Ricordi/U.M.P.*)
Peter Maxwell Davies	Hill Runes (*Boosey & Hawkes*)
Diabelli	Sonata in A, arr. Bream: complete. *The Julian Bream Guitar Library, Vol.2* (*Faber*)
Stephen Dodgson *	Concerto no.1: complete (*Bèrben/De Haske*)
	Fantasy-Divisions (*Bèrben/De Haske*)

Guitar: LRSM

Dowland	Lachrimae Pavan *and* Fantasia (P.1), trans. Scheit (*Universal 14480/M.D.S.*)
Francesco da Milano	Fantasia no.39 *and* Ricercare no.57. *F. da Milano Complete Lute Works, Vol.1, trans. Chiesa* (*Suvini Zerboni/William Elkin*)
R. Gerhard	Fantasia (*Belwin/I.M.P. Express Print*)
Ginastera	Sonata, Op.47: 1st *and* 2nd movts (*Boosey & Hawkes*)
M. Giuliani *	Concerto no.1 in A, Op.30: 1st movt (*Suvini Zerboni/William Elkin*)
	Gran Sonata Eroica, Op.150: complete (*Suvini Zerboni/William Elkin* or *Tecla Editions/William Elkin*)
Granados	Danza Española no.10 'Melancólica' *and* Tonadilla 'La Maja de Goya', trans. Llobet. *Llobet Guitar Works, Vol.3* (*Chanterelle 893/Guitarnotes*) or *publ. separately* (*U.M.E./Music Sales*)
Hans Haug	Prélude, Tiento *and* Toccata (*Bèrben/De Haske*)
Hans Werner Henze	Royal Winter Music: 1st Sonata on Shakespearean Characters: 3rd movt, *Ariel and/or* 6th movt, Oberon (*Schott GA 467/M.D.S.*)
	3 Tentos (from 'Kammermusik 1958'): complete. *Henze 3 Fragments from Hölderlin and 3 Tentos* (*Schott ED 4886/M.D.S.*)
Ibert	Française, arr. Azpiazu (*Leduc/U.M.P.*)
Antonio José	Sonata: 1st *and* 2nd movts (*Bèrben/De Haske*)
Frank Martin	4 Pièces Brèves: complete (*Universal 12711/M.D.S.*)
L. de Narvaez	6 Diferencias sobre el Himno 'O gloriosa Domina' (*Billaudot/U.M.P.*)
Moreno Torroba	Sonatina in A: complete (*Columbia Music 168/M.D.S.* or *Opera Tres/Guitarnotes* or *Opera Tres/Ashley Mark Publishing*)
Ponce *	Concierto del Sur: 1st movt (*Peermusic Classical/William Elkin*)
	Thème varié et Finale (*Schott GA 109/M.D.S.*)
Rawsthorne	Elegy (*O.U.P.*)
Regondi	Rêverie: Notturno, Op.19. *Regondi Collected Guitar Works* (*Chanterelle 441/Guitarnotes*) or *publ. separately* (*Suvini Zerboni/William Elkin*)
Rodrigo *	Concierto de Aranjuez: 1st movt (*Ediciones Joaquín Rodrigo/Guitarnotes* or *Ediciones Joaquín Rodrigo/U.M.P.* or *Schott ED 7242/M.D.S.*)
	Invocación y Danza (Homenaje a Falla) (*Ediciones Joaquín Rodrigo/Guitarnotes* or *Ediciones Joaquín Rodrigo/U.M.P.*)
Roussel	Ségovia, Op.29 (*Durand/U.M.P.*)
Scarlatti	2 Sonatas in D, Kp.480 *and* 491. *Scarlatti 8 Sonatas, trans. Burley* (*Schott ED 12442/M.D.S.*)
Sor	Fantaisie no.7, Op.30 (*Suvini Zerboni/William Elkin*)
	Introduction and Variations on a Theme of Mozart, Op.9 (*Suvini Zerboni/William Elkin*)
Tōru Takemitsu	Any *three* of the 4 pieces from 'All in Twilight' (*Schott SJ 1051/M.D.S.*)
	Folios: complete (*Salabert/U.M.P.*)
Tansman	Variations on a Theme of Scriabin (*Eschig/U.M.P.*)
Tippett	The Blue Guitar Sonata: 2nd movt (*Schott ED 12218/M.D.S.*)
Turina	Fandanguillo, Op.36 (*Schott GA 102/M.D.S.*)
Villa-Lobos *	Concerto: 1st movt (*Eschig/U.M.P.*)
	12 Études: no.7 in E *and* no.8 in C minor *and* no.12 in A minor (*Eschig/U.M.P.*)
S.L. Weiss	Fantasie in C minor *and* Passagaille in D. *Weiss Anthology of Selected Pieces, trans. Burley* (*Schott ED 12320/M.D.S.*)

Guitar: FRSM

* *Works available for guitar and piano reduction to be performed with a keyboard accompaniment.*

Malcolm Arnold *	Concerto, Op.67: complete (*Paterson/Music Sales*)
J.S. Bach	Any *one* of the 4 Suites complete from *Bach Lute Suites for Guitar, ed. Willard* (*Ariel Publications/Music Sales*) or *Bach Solo Lute Works for Guitar, ed. Koonce* (*Neil Kjos Music/Music Sales*)
	Chaconne (from Partita no.2 in D minor for solo violin, BWV 1004) (*trans. Carlevaro: Chanterelle 714/Guitarnotes*) or (*trans. Scheit: Universal 16717/M.D.S.*)
Richard Rodney Bennett	Sonata: complete (*Novello/Music Sales*)
L. Berkeley *	Concerto, Op.88: complete (*Chester/Music Sales*)
	Sonatina, Op.51: complete (*Chester/Music Sales*)
Britten	Nocturnal, Op.70 (*Faber*)
Léo Brouwer *	Concerto no.3 ('Elegiaco'): complete (*Eschig/U.M.P.*)
	Sonata: complete (*Opera Tres/Guitarnotes* or *Opera Tres/Ashley Mark Publishing*)
Elliott Carter	Changes (*Boosey & Hawkes*)

Guitar: FRSM

Castelnuovo-Tedesco * Concerto in D, Op.99: complete (*Schott GA 166/M.D.S.*)
Sonata in D (Omaggio a Boccherini), Op.77: complete (*Schott GA 149/M.D.S.*)

Peter Maxwell Davies Sonata: complete (*Chester/Music Sales*)

Stephen Dodgson * Concerto no.1: complete (*Bèrben/De Haske*)
Partita no.1: complete (*O.U.P.*)
Partita no.2: complete (*O.U.P. archive/Allegro*)
Partita no.3: complete (*Bèrben/De Haske*)

Dowland Any *two* Fantasias from *Dowland 12 Fantasias for Guitar, trans. Ruhe* (*Moeck 7006*)

Françaix * Concerto: complete (*Schott ED 7133/M.D.S.*)

Ginastera Sonata, Op.47: complete (*Boosey & Hawkes*)

M. Giuliani * Concerto no.1 in A, Op.30: complete (*Suvini Zerboni/William Elkin*)
Grande Ouverture, Op.61 (*Schott GA 432/M.D.S.* or *Suvini Zerboni/William Elkin*)
Any *one* of the 6 Rossinianas, Opp.119–124 (*2 vols: P.W.M./M.D.S.*) or *publ. separately* (*Suvini Zerboni/William Elkin*)

Hans Werner Henze Royal Winter Music: 1st Sonata on Shakespearean Characters: complete (*Schott GA 467/M.D.S.*)
Royal Winter Music: 2nd Sonata on Shakespearean Characters: complete (*Schott GA 473/M.D.S.*)

Antonio José Sonata: complete (*Bèrben/De Haske*)

Ohana * Concerto ('Trois Graphiques'): complete (*Amphion/U.M.P.*)

Ponce * Concierto del Sur: complete (*Peermusic Classical/William Elkin*)
Variations on 'Folia de España' *and* Fugue (*Schott GA 135/M.D.S.*)

Rodrigo *Concierto de Aranjuez: complete (*Ediciones Joaquín Rodrigo/Guitarnotes* or *Ediciones Joaquín Rodrigo/U.M.P.* or *Schott ED 7242/M.D.S.*)
3 Piezas Españolas: *Fandango, Passacaglia* and *Zapateado* (*Schott GA 212/M.D.S.*)

Scarlatti Sonata in E minor, Kp.292 *and* Sonata in E, Kp.380 *and* 2 Sonatas in A, Kp.208 *and* 209. *Scarlatti 4 Sonatas, trans. Barrueco* (*Schott GA 521/M.D.S.*)

Sor Fantasia no.2, Op.7 (*Suvini Zerboni/William Elkin*)
Grand Solo, Op.14: complete (*Suvini Zerboni/William Elkin*)
2nd Grand Sonata in C, Op.25: complete (*Suvini Zerboni/William Elkin*)

Tippett The Blue Guitar Sonata: complete (*Schott ED 12218/M.D.S.*)

Tomasi * Concerto: complete (*Leduc/U.M.P.*)

Villa-Lobos * Concerto: complete (*Eschig/U.M.P.*)

Walton 5 Bagatelles: complete (*O.U.P.*)

S.L. Weiss Sonata in A (Dresden no.19), trans. Skiera: complete (*Bärenreiter BA 8003*)
Sonata in A (Dresden), trans. Orbaugh: complete (*Breitkopf & Härtel 8222*)
Sonata in A minor ('L'Infidèle') (Dresden no.15/London no.25), trans. Meunier (*Breitkopf & Härtel 6770*)
Sonata in C (Dresden no.9), trans. Skiera: complete (*Bärenreiter BA 8001*)
Sonata in D minor (Dresden no.5), trans. Scheit: complete (*Universal 14426/M.D.S.*)
Sonata in D minor (Dresden no.6), trans. Skiera: complete (*Bärenreiter BA 8002*)
Suite in D (London no.14), trans. Brojer: complete (*Schott GA 458/M.D.S.*)
Suite in D minor 'from the Moscow Manuscript', trans Duarte: complete (*Universal 29168/M.D.S.*)
Suite in E minor (London no.17): complete ⎫
Suite in F (London no.28): complete ⎭ *Weiss 2 Suites, trans. Biberian* (*Peters EP 7336*)

Harp: DipABRSM

Bernard Andrès Absidioles (*Rideau Rouge/U.M.P.*)

J.S. Bach Études for the Harp, arr. Grandjany: no.6 *or* no.7 (*Carl Fischer/Boosey & Hawkes* or *Carl Fischer – Schott/M.D.S.*)

Derek Bourgeois Fantasy Piece, Op.123 (*Brass Wind*)

Challoner Sonata no.3, Op.11: complete (*Harp Publications/Salvi*)

Chertok Around the Clock Suite: any *three* movts (*Aztec/Salvi*)

J.L. Dussek Sonata in B♭, Op.34 no.2: complete. *Dussek 2 Grandes Sonates* (*Salvi*)

Fauré Impromptu, Op.86 (*Durand/U.M.P.*)

Bàrbara Giuranna Sonatina: complete (*Ricordi/U.M.P.*)

Glinka Variations on a Theme of Mozart (*Salvi*)

Godefroid Étude de Concert, Op.193 (*Salvi*)

Grandjany Children's Hour Suite: any *three* movts (*Boosey & Hawkes*)
Fantasie sur un Thème de Haydn (*Leduc/U.M.P.*)

Alan Hovhaness Nocturne, Op.20 no.1 (*Peters EP 66026*)

Harp: DipABRSM

Howells	Prelude (*Stainer & Bell*)
Hasslemans	Gitana, Op.21 (*Durand/U.M.P.*)
	Guitare, Op.50 (*Leduc/U.M.P.*)
	Nocturne, Op.43 (*Durand/U.M.P.*)
La Presle	Le Jardin Mouillé (*Leduc/U.M.P.*)
Naderman	Sonatina no.6 in D minor, from '7 Sonates Progressives', Op.92: complete (*Leduc/U.M.P.*)
Parish Alvars	Romance in A♭. *An Anthology of English Music for Harp, Book 4, ed. Watkins* (*Stainer & Bell*)
John Parry	Any *one* of the '4 Sonatas' complete (*Salvi*)
Pescetti	Sonata in C minor, trans. Salzedo: complete (*Lyra/Munson & Harbour*)
Pierné	Impromptu-Caprice, Op.9 (*Leduc/U.M.P.*)
Prokofiev	Prelude in C, Op.12 no.7, arr. Forberg (*Salvi*)
Roussel	Impromptu, Op.21 (*Durand/U.M.P.*)
Saint-Saëns	Fantaisie, Op.95 (*Durand/U.M.P.*)
C. Salzedo	Suite of 8 Dances: Seguidilla *and* Tango (*Lyra/Munson & Harbour*)
Samuel-Rousseau	Variations Pastorales sur un vieux Noël (*Leduc/U.M.P.*)
Tournier	Féerie (Prélude et Danse) (*Leduc/U.M.P.*)
	Images, Suite no.1, Op.29: complete (*Lemoine/U.M.P.*)
Gareth Walters	Little Suite: complete (*Ricordi/U.M.P.*)
	Toccata: no.3 from '3 Impromptus' (*Ricordi/U.M.P.*)

Harp: LRSM

J.S. Bach	Études for the Harp, arr. Grandjany: no.10 (*Carl Fischer/Boosey & Hawkes* or *Carl Fischer – Schott/ M.D.S.*)
Britten	Suite, Op.83: any *three* movts (*Faber*)
Caplet	Divertissement no.1: à la française *and* Divertissement no.2: à l'espagnole (*publ. separately: Durand/U.M.P.*)
J.-B. Cardon	Sonata in E♭, Op.7 no.4: complete (*Harp Publications/Salvi*)
Challoner	Sonata no.2, Op.11: complete (*Harp Publications/Salvi*)
Jean-Michel Damase	Sarabande (*Lemoine/U.M.P.*)
Lex van Delden	Impromptu, Op.48 (*Donemus/Boosey & Hawkes*)
J.L. Dussek	Sonata in E♭, Op.34 no.1: complete. *Dussek 2 Grandes Sonates* (*Salvi*)
Gareth Glyn	Triban (*Adlais*)
Grandjany	Rhapsodie (*Leduc/U.M.P.*)
Handel	Concerto in B♭, Op.4 no.6, HWV 294: complete (*unaccompanied*) (*Bärenreiter BA 8347*)
Hindemith	Sonata (1939): complete (*Schott ED 3644*)
J.-B. Krumpholtz	Sonata in B♭, Op.13 no.1: complete (*Harp Publications/Salvi*)
Mathias	Santa Fe Suite: complete (*O.U.P.*)
	Sonata, Op.66: complete (*O.U.P.*)
Nino Rota	Sarabanda *and* Toccata (*Ricordi/U.M.P.*)
C. Salzedo	Suite of 8 Dances: Siciliana, Bolero *and* Rumba (*Lyra/Munson & Harbour*)
Tournier	Jazz-Band (*Lemoine/U.M.P.*)
Zabel	La Source, Op.23 (*Adlais*)
Julien-François Zbinden	3 Esquisses Japonais, Op.72: complete (*Billaudot/U.M.P.*)

Harp: FRSM

C.P.E. Bach	Sonata (Solo) in G, Wq.139: complete (*Breitkopf & Härtel 6593*)
F. Benda	Sonata in B♭: complete (*Salvi*)
Bochsa	Grande Sonate in E♭: complete (*Harp Publications/Salvi*)
Boieldieu	Sonata: complete (*Lyra/Munson & Harbour*)
Britten	Suite, Op.83: complete (*Faber*)
J.-B. Cardon	Sonata in B♭, Op.7 no.2: complete (*Harp Publications/Salvi*)
Casella	Sonata, Op.68: complete (*Suvini Zerboni/William Elkin*)
Cras	2 Impromptus: complete (*Salabert/U.M.P.*)
Heinz Holliger	Sequenzen on John I, 32 (*Schott ED 5472/M.D.S.*)
Pierick Houdy	Sonata no.7: complete (*Leduc/U.M.P.*)

Harp: FRSM

Khatchaturian	Danse Orientale *and* Toccata (*Salvi*)
Krenek	Sonata: complete (*Bärenreiter BA 3230*)
Parish Alvars	Introduction, Cadenza *and* Rondo. *An Anthology of English Music for Harp, Book 4, ed. Watkins* (*Stainer & Bell*)
Paul Patterson	Spiders (*Universal 17668/M.D.S.*)
Ravel	Introduction et Allegro (*to be performed with a piano accomp.*) (*harp & piano trans. by composer: Durand/U.M.P.*)
Renié	Légende d'après 'Les Elfes' de Leconte de Lisle (*Leduc/U.M.P.*)
C. Salzedo	Variations sur un Thème dans le Style ancien (*Leduc/U.M.P.*)
Spohr	Variations in F on an Air by Méhul, Op.36 (*Zimmermann/William Elkin* or *Zimmermann/M.D.S.*)
Tailleferre	Sonata: complete (*Peermusic/William Elkin*)
Tournier	Sonatine, Op.30: complete (*Lemoine/U.M.P.*) Vers la Source dans le Bois (*Leduc/U.M.P.*)
Viotti	Sonata in B♭: complete (*Salvi*)

Recorder: DipABRSM

Candidates may choose to play their programme on any one or any combination of F and C recorders as may be appropriate. All works in the following list are intended for treble (alto) recorder unless otherwise indicated.

J.S. Bach	Sonata in F, BWV 1035: complete (*Schott ED 10272/M.D.S.* or *Universal 18749/M.D.S.*)
Barsanti	Sonata in C, Op.1 no.2: complete (*Bärenreiter HM 183*) Sonata in C minor, Op.1 no.4: complete (*Nova/Spartan Press*)
Christopher Brown	Caprice, Op.68. *Recital Pieces for Treble Recorder, Vol.1* (*Forsyth*)
C. Buterne	Sonata in C minor, Op.2 no.4: complete (*Universal 17124/M.D.S.*)
John Casken	Thymehaze (*Schott TMR 6/M.D.S.*)
Castello	Sonata Prima for descant recorder: complete. *Venetian Music about 1600 for descant or tenor recorder, ed. Linde* (*Schott OFB 122/M.D.S.*)
Alan Davis	Sonata for solo recorder: complete (*Heinrichshofen 2291/Peters*)
Rob Du Bois	Muziek voor Altblokfluit (*Schott TMR 1/M.D.S.*)
van Eyck	Wat zalmen op den Avond doen (2nd version): theme *and* Modo 2–9: no.49 Derde, Doen Daphne d'over: theme *and* Modo 3–4: no.58 from 'Der Fluyten Lust-hof', Vol.2 for solo descant recorder (*Amadeus BP 705 – Schott/M.D.S.*) O slaep, o zoete slaep: complete: no.65
Finger	Sonata in C minor, Op.3 no.2: complete (*Nova NM 105/Spartan Press*)
G.B. Fontana	Sonata Prima in C: complete. *Venetian Music about 1600 for descant or tenor recorder, ed. Linde* (*Schott OFB 122/M.D.S.*)
Norman Fulton	Scottish Suite: complete (*Schott ED 10466/M.D.S.*)
Hans Gal	Any *two* of the '3 Intermezzi', Op.103 (*Schott OFB 134/M.D.S.*)
Handel	Sonata in D minor, HWV 367a: movts 1–5. *Handel Complete Sonatas for Treble Recorder* (*Faber*)
Tony Hewitt-Jones	Suite in F for solo treble recorder: complete. *No.8 from Pieces for Solo Recorder, Vol.1* (*Forsyth*)
J.M. Hotteterre (Le Romain)	Suite in F, Op.2 no.1: any *four* movts (*Nova NM 162/Spartan Press*) Suite in G minor, Op.2 no.3a: any *five* movts (*Nova NM 171/Spartan Press*)
G. Jacob	Sonata: complete (*Musica Rara 1116/Breitkopf & Härtel*)
Hans-Martin Linde	Fantasias and Scherzi for solo treble recorder: complete (*Schott OFB 46/M.D.S.*) Sonata in D minor: complete (*Schott OFB 47/M.D.S.*) 5 Studies for treble recorder and piano: complete (*Schott OFB 160/M.D.S.*)
Nicholas Marshall	4 Haiku: nos.1 *and* 4 for treble, no.2 for descant *and* no.3 for tenor recorder: complete. *No.3 from Pieces for Solo Recorder, Vol.1* (*Forsyth*)
Montalbano	Sinfonia for descant recorder, Op.1 no.4. *Masters of the Early Baroque for descant or tenor recorder* (*Schott OFB 153/M.D.S.*)
Notari	Canzona Passaggiata for descant recorder (*ornamented version*) (*Nova NM 166/Spartan Press*)
Pete Rose	I'd Rather be in Philadelphia – a Jazzy Piece (*Universal 30214/M.D.S.*)
Giuseppe Sammartini	Sonata in G (S.24): complete. *Sammartini 6 Sonatas* (*Faber*)
Hans Ulrich Staeps	Sonata in E♭ (1951): complete (*Universal 12603/M.D.S.*)
Telemann	Concerto in C minor, TWV 42:a2: complete (*Bärenreiter BA 6438*) Fantasia no.7 in F *or* no.8 in G minor: complete, from '12 Fantasias for Treble Recorder without Bass', arr. Harras (*Bärenreiter BA 6440*)

REPERTOIRE LISTS

Recorder: DipABRSM

F.M. Veracini	Sonata no.6 in A minor (1716): complete (*Peters EP 4965b*)
Vivaldi	Concerto in F, Op.10 no.5, RV 434: complete (*Ricordi/U.M.P.* or *Schott FTR 83/M.D.S.*)
Markus Zahnhausen	Herbstmusik (Autumn Music) for solo treble or descant recorder (*Moesler/Peacock Press*)
	Minimal Music: no.4 from '7 Pieces' for solo treble recorder (*Doblinger 04457/M.D.S.*)

Recorder: LRSM

Candidates may choose to play their programme on any one or any combination of F and C recorders as may be appropriate. All works in the following list are intended for treble (alto) recorder unless otherwise indicated.

J.S. Bach	Sonata in G, BWV 1032: complete (*Noetzel 3444/Peters*)
G. Bassano	Ricerata Quinta. *Studies and Solo Pieces for Treble Recorder* (*Ricordi Sy 2612/U.M.P.*)
L. Berkeley	Sonatina, Op.13: complete (*Schott OFB 1040/M.D.S.*)
Boismortier	Suite in D minor, Op.35 no.5: complete. *Boismortier 6 Suites Op.35 for Solo Treble Recorder* (*Schott OFB 147/M.D.S.*)
Donald Bousted	Two Responses to Silence for solo tenor recorder (*Composer Press/Peacock Press*)
Y. Bowen	Sonatina, Op.121: complete (*Emerson*)
Castello	Sonata Seconda for descant recorder: complete (*Amadeus BP 797 – Schott/M.D.S.*)
Dieupart	Suite no.1 in C: complete (*Moeck 1084*)
van Eyck	Psalm 118: complete: no.4 from 'Der Fluyten Lust-hof', Vol.1 for solo descant recorder (*Amadeus BP 704 – Schott/M.D.S.*)
	Variations on Pavane Lachrymae: no.56 from 'Der Fluyten Lust-hof', Vol.2 for solo descant recorder (*Amadeus BP 705 – Schott/M.D.S.*)
G.B. Fontana	Sonata Terza: complete. *Fontana 4 Sonatas for Descant Recorder, Vol.2* (*Doblinger 0014/M.D.S.*)
Handel	Sonata in C, Op.1 no.7, HWV 365: complete (*Schott OFB 39/M.D.S.*) or *Handel Complete Sonatas for Recorder* (*Faber*)
Ryohei Hirose	Meditation for solo treble or tenor recorder (*Zen-On Music/Boosey & Hawkes*)
Maki Ishii	East Green Spring, Op.94, for tenor recorder (*Moeck*)
G. Jacob	Suite for Treble Recorder: complete (*O.U.P. archive/Peacock Press*)
Hans-Martin Linde	Amarilli mia bella (Hommage à Jacob van Eyck) for solo treble or descant recorder (*Schott OFB 133/M.D.S.*)
Pete Rose	Medieval Nights for tenor recorder (*Carus/U.M.P.*)
François Rossé	Renrew (*Billaudot/U.M.P.*)
Rubbra	Sonatina, Op.128: complete (*Lengnick/Faber*)
Makoto Shinohara	Fragmente for tenor recorder (*Schott TMR 3/M.D.S.*)
Hans Ulrich Staeps	Virtuoso Suite (1961) for solo treble recorder (*Schott OFB 95/M.D.S.*)
Telemann	Any *two* Fantasias complete from '12 Fantasias for Treble Recorder without Bass', arr. Harras (*Bärenreiter BA 6440*)
Uccellini	Sonata Sesta, Op.5 no.6: complete (*London Pro Musica CS11*)
Vivaldi	Sonata in G minor, Op.13 no.6, RV 58: complete (*Schott OFB 114/M.D.S.*)
Markus Zahnhausen	Musica Inquieta – Sonata for solo treble recorder: complete (*Doblinger 04461/M.D.S.*)

Recorder: FRSM

Candidates may choose to play their programme on any one or any combination of F and C recorders as may be appropriate. All works in the following list are intended for treble (alto) recorder unless otherwise indicated.

Louis Andriessen	Sweet (*Schott TMR 2/M.D.S.*)
Anon.	Isabella. *Dances of the Jongleurs of Mediaeval Italy, Vol.1, for solo descant recorder* (*Moeck 2510*)
	Lamento di Tristano **and** Rotta. *Dances of the Jongleurs of Mediaeval Italy, Vol.2, for solo descant recorder* (*Moeck 2515*)
Malcolm Arnold	Fantasy for solo descant recorder, Op.127 (*Faber*)
J.S. Bach	Partita in C minor, BWV 1013, for solo treble recorder, arr. Harras: complete (*Bärenreiter BA 6414*)
Berio	Gesti for solo recorder (*Universal 15627/M.D.S.*)
Gerhard Braun	5 Meditations for solo tenor recorder: complete (*Universal 18750/M.D.S.*)
Corelli	Sonata 'La Follia', Op.5 no.12: complete (*Schott OFB 121/M.D.S.*)
van Eyck	Amarilli mia Bella: complete: no.35 from 'Der Fluyten Lust-hof', Vol.1 for solo descant recorder (*Amadeus BP 704 – Schott/M.D.S.*)
G.B. Fontana	Sonata Quarta: complete. *Fontana 4 Sonatas for Descant Recorder, Vol.2* (*Doblinger 0014/M.D.S.*)

Recorder: FRSM

Handel	Sonata in F, HWV 371: complete (*Universal 19929/M.D.S.*)
J.M. Hotteterre (Le Romain)	Suite in E minor, Op.5 no.2: complete (*Bärenreiter HM 198*)
Maki Ishii	Black Intention for solo recorder (*Zen-On Music/Boosey & Hawkes*)
Konrad Lechner	Ludus Juvenalis I for descant recorder: Canzona 2 (*Moeck 2506*)
Nicola LeFanu	Dawn's Dove for solo treble recorder (*Novello/Music Sales*)
Roland Moser	Alrune for solo treble recorder (*Hug 11464/William Elkin*)
Benjamin Thorn	Songs for My Father's Wedding for solo bass recorder (*Carus/U.M.P.*) The Voice of the Crocodile for solo bass recorder (*Moeck 2561*)
Virgiliano	Ricercata per Traversa, Violino, Cornetto et altri Instumenti. *Studies and Solo Pieces for Treble Recorder* (*Ricordi Sy 2612/U.M.P.*)
Vivaldi	Concerto in C, RV 443: complete (*Schott OFB 113/M.D.S.*)
Margaret Lucy Wilkins	Aries, Op.41, for solo descant recorder. *Pieces for Solo Recorder, Vol.1* (*Forsyth*)
Markus Zahnhausen	Harlekins Serenade and Dance: no.2 from '7 Pieces' for solo treble recorder (*Doblinger 04457/M.D.S.*)

Flute: DipABRSM

Malcolm Arnold	Concerto no.2, Op.111: complete (*Faber*)
Arrieu	Sonatine: complete (*Amphion/U.M.P.*)
C.P.E. Bach	Sonata in A minor for solo flute, Wq.132: complete (*Bärenreiter BA 6820*) Sonata in E minor, Wq.124: complete. *C.P.E. Bach Flute Sonatas, Vol.1* (*Bärenreiter HM 71*) Sonata in G, Wq.133 ('Hamburg' Sonata): complete (*Schott FTR 1/M.D.S.*)
J.S. Bach	Sonata no.5 in E minor, BWV 1034: complete } *Bach 4 Flute Sonatas* (*Bärenreiter BA 5198*) or Sonata no.6 in E, BWV 1035: complete } *Bach 6 Sonatas for Flute, Book 2* (*Chester/Music Sales*) Sonata in G minor, BWV 1020: complete. *Bach 3 Flute Sonatas* (*Bärenreiter BA 4418*)
Bartók	Suite Paysanne Hongroise, arr. Arma: complete (*Universal 18666/M.D.S.*)
Richard Rodney Bennett	Sonatina for solo flute: complete (*Universal 12350/M.D.S.*)
L. Berkeley	Sonatina, Op.13: complete (*Schott OFB 1040/M.D.S.*)
attrib. Boccherini	Concerto in D, Op.27: complete (*Bärenreiter BA 6883*)
Anne Boyd	Bali Moods 1 (*Faber*)
Arnold Cooke	Sonatina: complete (*O.U.P.*)
Chaminade	Concertino in D, Op.107: complete (*Enoch/U.M.P.*)
Chopin	Variations on a Theme by Rossini (*International 1952/M.D.S.*)
Debussy	Syrinx for solo flute (*Henle* or *Henle – Schott/M.D.S.*)
Devienne	Sonata in E minor, Op.58 no.1: complete (*International 2734/M.D.S.*) Sonata in E minor, Op.68 no.5: complete (*International 3167/M.D.S.*)
Doppler	Fantaisie Pastorale Hongroise, Op.26 (*Schott FTR 91/M.D.S.*)
Enescu	Cantabile et Presto (*Enoch/U.M.P.*)
Fauré	Fantaisie, Op.79 (*Chester/Music Sales* or *Leduc/U.M.P.*)
Gaubert	Sonata no.3: complete (*Heugel/U.M.P.*)
Hahn	Variations on a Theme of Mozart (*Heugel/U.M.P.*)
Handel	Sonata in G, Op.1 no.5, HWV 363b: complete } *Handel 11 Sonatas for Flute* (*Bärenreiter BA 4225*) or Sonata in C, Op.1 no.7, HWV 365: complete } *Handel Complete Flute Sonatas, Vol.1* (*Emerson*)
Dave Heath	Out of the Cool (*Chester/Music Sales*)
Robert Hinchliffe	The Elements: complete (*O.U.P.*)
Hindemith	Sonata (1936): complete (*Schott ED 2522/M.D.S.*)
Hüe	Fantaisie (*Billaudot/U.M.P.*)
Ibert	Jeux (Sonatine): complete (*Leduc/U.M.P.*)
Maconchy	Colloquy (*Chester/Music Sales*)
Mathias	Sonatina, Op.98: complete (*O.U.P.*)
Milhaud	Sonatine, Op.76: complete (*Durand/U.M.P.*)
Mouquet	Eglogue, Op.29 (*Lemoine/U.M.P.*)
Mozart	Concerto no.1 in G, K.313: 1st *and* 2nd movts (*with cadenzas*), *or* 2nd *and* 3rd movts (*with cadenzas*) (*Bärenreiter BA 6817* or *Novello/Music Sales*) Concerto no.2 in D, K.314: 1st *and* 2nd movts (*with cadenzas*) (*Bärenreiter BA 6818* or *Novello/Music Sales*)
Poulenc	Sonata: complete (*Chester/Music Sales*)

REPERTOIRE LISTS

Flute: DipABRSM

Quantz	Concerto (no.297) in G: complete (*with cadenzas*) (*Editio Musica/Faber*)
	Sonata in D: complete (*Süddeutscher Musikverlag 1985/Bärenreiter*)
John Rutter	Suite Antique: complete (*O.U.P.*)
Taffanel	Andante Pastoral et Scherzettino (*Enoch/U.M.P.*)
Telemann	Concerto in D, TWV Anh.51:D: complete (*International 2407/M.D.S*)
	Any *two* Fantasias complete from '12 Fantasias for Transverse Flute without Bass', TWV 40:2–13 (*Bärenreiter BA 2971*)
	Sonata in F minor, TWV 41:f1: complete (*International 2468/M.D.S.*)
Varèse	Density 21.5 for solo flute (*Ricordi/U.M.P.*)
Vivaldi	Concerto in C minor, RV 441: complete (*Editio Musica/Faber*)
	Concerto in F ('La Tempesta di Mare'), Op.10 no.1, RV 433: complete (*Editio Musica/Faber*)

Flute: LRSM

Malcolm Arnold	Concerto no.1, Op.45: complete (*Paterson/Music Sales*)
J.S. Bach	Partita in A minor for solo flute, BWV 1013: complete (*Bärenreiter BA 4401*)
Boehm	Grande Polonaise in D, Op.16 (*International 3154/M.D.S.*)
Anne Boyd	Cloudy Mountain (*Faber*)
Bozza	Image, Op.38, for solo flute (*Leduc/U.M.P.*)
Briccialdi	Concertino no.2 in G minor: complete (*International 2883/M.D.S.*)
Jean-Michel Damase	Sonate en Concert, Op.17: complete (*Lemoine/U.M.P.*)
Henri Dutilleux	Sonatine: complete (*Leduc/U.M.P*)
Gaubert	Nocturne et Allegro Scherzando (*Enoch/U.M.P.*)
Godard	Suite de Trois Morceaux, Op.116: complete (*Chester/Music Sales*)
Hoffmeister	Concerto no.4 in D: complete (*Billaudot/U.M.P.*)
Honegger	Danse de la chèvre for solo flute (*Salabert/U.M.P.*)
Ibert	Pièce for solo flute (*Leduc/U.M.P.*)
G. Jacob	Concerto: complete (*Stainer & Bell*)
Jolivet	Chant de Linos (*Leduc/U.M.P.*)
Mathias	Concerto: complete (*O.U.P. archive/Allegro*)
Messiaen	Le Merle Noir (*Leduc/U.M.P.*)
Mercadante	Concerto in F: complete (*Lemoine/U.M.P.*)
Mike Mower	Triligence – Jazz Sonatina: complete (*Itchy Fingers Publications/Boosey & Hawkes*)
Mozart	Concerto no.1 in G, K.313: complete (*with cadenzas*) (*Bärenreiter BA 6817* or *Novello/Music Sales*)
	Concerto no.2 in D, K.314: complete (*with cadenzas*) (*Bärenreiter BA 6818* or *Novello/Music Sales*)
Quantz	Concerto in C minor: complete (*International 2693/M.D.S.*)
Reinecke	'Undine' Sonata, Op.167: complete (*Boosey & Hawkes*)
Roussel	All *four* of the pieces from 'Joueurs de Flûte', Op.27 (*Durand/U.M.P.*)
Tulou	Grand Solo no.3, Op.74: complete (*Billaudot/U.M.P.*)
Widor	Suite, Op.34: complete (*Heugel/U.M.P.*)

Flute: FRSM

Alwyn	Divertimento for solo flute: complete (*Boosey & Hawkes*)
J. Andersen	Variations Drolatiques, Op.26, arr. Rampal (*Billaudot/U.M.P.*)
J.S. Bach	Sonata no.1 in B minor, BWV 1030: complete. *Bach 4 Flute Sonatas* (*Bärenreiter BA 5198*) or *Bach 6 Sonatas for Flute, Book 1* (*Chester/Music Sales*)
George Benjamin	Flight for solo flute (*Faber*)
Berio	Sequenza for solo flute (*Suvini Zerboni/William Elkin*)
Boehm	Air Suisse: Variations Brillantes, Op.20 (*Billaudot/U.M.P.*)
Pierre Boulez	Sonatine: complete (*Amphion/U.M.P.*)
Y. Bowen	Sonata, Op.120: complete (*Emerson*)
Robert Dick	Afterlight for solo flute (*MMB Music – Schott/M.D.S.*)
F. Doppler	Airs Valaques (Fantaisie), Op.10 (*Emerson*)
Gaubert	Sonata no.2: complete (*Heugel/U.M.P.*)
Hoffmeister	Concerto in G: complete (*International 3087/M.D.S.*)
Ibert	Concerto: complete (*Leduc/U.M.P.*)
Martinů	Sonata no.1: complete (*Schirmer/Music Sales*)

Mercadante	Concerto in E: complete (*Boccaccini & Spada 1654/M.D.S.*)
Mike Mower	Doodle & Flight – Jazz Suite: complete (*Itchy Fingers Publications/Boosey & Hawkes*)
Nielsen	Concerto: complete (*Chester/Music Sales*)
Prokofiev	Sonata no.2 in D, Op.94: complete (*Boosey & Hawkes*)
Rodrigo	Concierto Pastoral: complete (*Schott ED 11489/M.D.S.*)
Schubert	Introduction and Variations in E minor on 'Trockne Blumen', Op.160, D.802 (*Wiener Urtext/M.D.S.*)
Telemann	Methodical Sonata in A, Op.13 no.2, TWV 41:A3: complete. *Telemann 12 Methodical Sonatas, Vol.1* (*Bärenreiter BA 2241*)

Oboe: DipABRSM

Albinoni	Concerto in B♭, Op.7 no.3: 1st *and* 2nd movts (*Boosey & Hawkes*)
Malcolm Arnold	Concerto, Op.39: 1st *and* 2nd movts (*Paterson/Music Sales*)
C.P.E. Bach	Sonata in G minor, Wq.135: complete (*Amadeus BP 2279 – Schott/M.D.S.*)
Bartók	The Bagpiper, arr. Szeszler (*Editio Musica/Faber*)
Bellini	Concerto in E♭: complete (*Ricordi/U.M.P.*)
L. Berkeley	Sonatina, Op.61: 1st *and* 2nd movts (*Chester/Music Sales*)
Britten	Any *three* of the 6 Metamorphoses after Ovid for solo oboe, Op.49 (*Boosey & Hawkes*) Temporal Variations (*Faber*)
Stephen Dodgson	Suite in D: 1st *and* 4th movts, *Prelude* and *Dance*, *or* 3rd *and* 4th movts, *Canzonet* and *Dance* (*O.U.P. archive/Allegro*)
John Exton	3 Pieces for solo oboe: complete (*Chester/Music Sales*)
Edward Gregson	Sonata: complete (*Emerson*)
Grovlez	Sarabande et Allegro (*Leduc/U.M.P.*)
Handel	Concerto no.3 in G minor, HWV 287: complete (*Boosey & Hawkes*) Sonata in B♭ ('Fitzwilliam'), HWV 357: complete | *Handel 3 Authentic Oboe Sonatas* Sonata in C minor, Op.1 no.8, HWV 366: complete | (*Nova NM 100/Spartan Press*)
Harty	Any *two* of the '3 Miniatures' (*Stainer & Bell*)
Howells	Sonata: 1st movt (*Novello/Music Sales*)
Michael Hurd	Concerto da Camera: 1st movt (*Novello/Music Sales*)
Loeillet	Sonata in D, Op.5 no.4: complete. *Loeillet 6 Sonatas, Op.5, Vol.2* (*European Music Archive EMA 103/ Spartan Press*)
A. Marcello	Concerto in D minor: complete (*Schott OBB 32/M.D.S.*)
Frank Martin	Petite Complainte (*Hug 11129/William Elkin*)
Mozart	Concerto in C, K.314: 1st *and* 2nd movts (*with cadenzas*) (*Bärenreiter BA 4856a*)
Nielsen	2 Fantasiestücke, Op.2: complete (*Chester/Music Sales*)
Poulenc	Sonata: 1st *and* 2nd movts (*Chester/Music Sales*)
György Ránki	Don Quixote and Dulcinea (*Editio Musica/Faber*)
Rubbra	Sonata in C, Op.100: 1st *and* 2nd movts (*Lengnick/Faber*)
Saint-Saëns	Sonata in D, Op.166: 1st *and* 2nd movts (*Peters EP 9196*)
Schumann	Any *two* of the '3 Romances', Op.94 (*Henle* or *Henle – Schott/M.D.S.*)
Seiber	Improvisation (*Schott ED 10648/M.D.S.*)
Telemann	Sonata in A minor (from 'Der getreue Musikmeister'), TWV 41:a3: complete (*Bärenreiter HM 7*) Sonata in E minor (from 'Essercizii musici'), TWV 41:e6: complete (*Schott OBB 23/M.D.S.*)
Vaughan Williams	Concerto in A minor: 1st movt (*O.U.P.*)
Vivaldi	Concerto in A minor, RV 461: complete (*Schott OBB 24/M.D.S.*)

Oboe: LRSM

Albinoni	Concerto in D minor, Op.9 no.2: complete (*International 1025/M.D.S.*)
Malcolm Arnold	Sonatina, Op.28: complete (*Lengnick/Faber*)
Arrieu	Impromptu (*Leduc/U.M.P.*)
C.P.E. Bach	Sonata in G minor, Wq.135: complete (*Amadeus BP 2279 – Schott/M.D.S.*)
J.S. Bach	Sonata (for flute/violin) in G minor, BWV 1020: complete (*Bärenreiter NMA 77*)
Richard Rodney Bennett	Sonata: complete (*Mills Music/I.M.P. express print*)
L. Berkeley	Sonatina, Op.61: complete (*Chester/Music Sales*)
M. Berkeley	3 Moods for solo oboe: complete (*O.U.P. archive/Allegro*)
Boughton	Concerto no.1 in C: complete (*Boosey & Hawkes*)

Oboe: LRSM

Bozza	Fantaisie Pastorale (*Leduc/U.M.P.*)
Britten	6 Metamorphoses after Ovid for solo oboe, Op.49: complete (*Boosey & Hawkes*)
Stephen Dodgson	Suite in D: complete (*O.U.P. archive/Allegro*)
Henri Dutilleux	Sonata: 1st *and* 2nd movts (*Leduc/U.M.P.*)
Handel	Sonata in C minor, Op.1 no.8, HWV 366: complete ⎤ *Handel 3 Authentic Oboe Sonatas* Sonata in F, Op.1 no.5, HWV 363a: complete ⎦ (*Nova NM 100/Spartan Press*)
Hindemith	Sonata (1938): complete (*Schott ED 3676/M.D.S.*)
Howells	Sonata: 1st *and* 2nd movts (*Novello/Music Sales*)
G. Jacob	Concerto no.1: 1st movt (*Stainer & Bell*)
Krommer	Concerto in F, Op.52: 1st *and* 2nd movts (*Bärenreiter*)
Lutosławski	Epitaph (*Chester/Music Sales*)
Maconchy	Any *two* of the '3 Bagatelles' (*O.U.P. archive/Allegro*)
Mozart	Concerto in C, K.314: complete (*with cadenzas*) (*Bärenreiter BA 4856a*)
Poulenc	Sonata: complete (*Chester/Music Sales*)
Rubbra	Sonata in C, Op.100: 1st *and* 2nd movts (*Lengnick/Faber*)
Saint-Saëns	Sonata in D, Op.166: complete (*Peters EP 9196*)
Giuseppe Sammartini	Sonata in G, arr. Rothwell: complete (*Chester/Music Sales*)
Schumann	Any *two* of the '3 Romances', Op.94 (*Henle* or *Henle – Schott/M.D.S.*)
R. Strauss	Concerto: 1st and 2nd movts (*Boosey & Hawkes*)
Telemann	Concerto in C minor, TWV 51:c1: complete (*Schott ANT 109/M.D.S.*) Sonata in B♭ (from 'Essercizii musici'), TWV 41:B6: complete (*Schott OBB 21/M.D.S.*) Sonata in G minor (from 'Tafelmusik, Produktion III') TWV 41:g5: complete (*Schott ED 10195/M.D.S.*)
Vaughan Williams	Concerto in A minor: 1st *and* 2nd movts (*O.U.P.*)
Vivaldi	Concerto in D minor, RV 454: complete (*Ricordi/U.M.P.*) Sonata in C minor, RV 53: complete (*Schott ANT 133/M.D.S.*)

Oboe: FRSM

Arrieu	Impromptu (*Leduc/U.M.P.*)
J.S. Bach	Concerto in F, BWV 1053: complete (*Nova NM 160/Spartan Press*) Sonata in G minor, BWV 1030b: complete (*Peters EP 8118*)
Richard Rodney Bennett	After Syrinx I (*Novello/Music Sales*)
Boughton	Concerto no.1 in C: complete (*Boosey & Hawkes*)
Bozza	Fantaisie Pastorale (*Leduc/U.M.P.*)
Britten	6 Metamorphoses after Ovid for solo oboe, Op.49: complete (*Boosey & Hawkes*)
Henri Dutilleux	Sonata: complete (*Leduc/U.M.P.*)
Goossens	Concerto (in one movement) (*Leduc/U.M.P.*)
Handel	Sonata in F, Op.1 no.5, HWV 363a: complete. *Handel 3 Authentic Oboe Sonatas* (*Nova NM 100/ Spartan Press*) Sonata in G minor, Op.1 no.6, HWV 364a: complete (*Ricordi/U.M.P.*)
Hindemith	Sonata (1938): complete (*Schott ED 3676/M.D.S.*)
Howells	Sonata: complete (*Novello/Music Sales*)
Kalliwoda	Concertino in F, Op.110: complete (*Musica Rara 1656/Breitkopf & Härtel*)
Lutosławski	Epitaph (*Chester/Music Sales*)
Maconchy	3 Bagatelles: complete (*O.U.P. archive/Allegro*)
Martinů	Concerto: complete (*Eschig/U.M.P.*)
Mozart	Concerto in C, K.314: complete (*with cadenzas*) (*Bärenreiter BA 4856a*)
Paul Patterson	Duologue (*Universal 17696/M.D.S.*)
Poulenc	Sonata: complete (*Chester/Music Sales*)
Rainier	Pastoral Triptych for solo oboe: complete (*Schott ED 10636/M.D.S.*)
Rubbra	Sonata in C, Op.100: complete (*Lengnick/Faber*)
Saint-Saëns	Sonata in D, Op.166: complete (*Peters EP 9196*)
Schumann	3 Romances, Op.94: complete (*Henle* or *Henle – Schott/M.D.S.*)
R. Strauss	Concerto: complete (*Boosey & Hawkes*)

Oboe: FRSM

Telemann	Concerto in F minor, TWV 51:f1: complete (*Peters EP 5881*) Sonata in B♭ (from 'Essercizii musici'), TWV 41:B6: complete (*Schott OBB 21/M.D.S.*) Sonata in G minor (from 'Tafelmusik, Produktion III'), TWV 41:g5: complete (*Schott ED 10195/M.D.S.*)
Julia Usher	A Reed in the Wind for solo oboe: complete (*Primavera*)
Vaughan Williams	Concerto in A minor: complete (*O.U.P.*)
Vivaldi	Concerto in F, RV 457: complete (*Ricordi/U.M.P.*)

Clarinet: DipABRSM

Malcolm Arnold	Sonatina, Op.29: complete (*Lengnick/Faber*)
H. Baermann	Introduction and Polonaise, Op.25 (*Musica Rara 2064/Breitkopf & Härtel*)
L. Berkeley	3 Pieces for Solo Clarinet: complete (*Chester/Music Sales*)
L. Bernstein	Sonata: complete (*Boosey & Hawkes*)
Y. Bowen	Sonata, Op.109: 1st *and* 2nd movts (*Emerson*)
Brahms	Sonata in F minor, Op.120 no.1: 1st movt *and* any other movt (*Wiener Urtext/M.D.S.*) Sonata in E♭, Op.120 no.2: 1st movt *and* any other movt (*Wiener Urtext/M.D.S.*)
N. Burgmüller	Duo in E♭, Op.15: complete (*Schott KLB 2/M.D.S.*)
Arnold Cooke	Sonata in B♭: any *two* movts (*Novello/Music Sales*)
Crusell	Concerto no.2 in F minor, Op.5: 1st *and* 2nd movts, *or* 2nd *and* 3rd movts (*Universal 19084/M.D.S.*)
Devienne	Sonata no.1 in C: 1st *and* 2nd movts, *or* 2nd *and* 3rd movts (*Transatlantiques/U.M.P.*)
Donizetti	Studio no.1 for solo clarinet (*Peters EP 8046*)
Dunhill	Phantasy Suite, Op.91: 3rd *and* 6th movts (*Boosey & Hawkes*)
Finzi	5 Bagatelles, Op.23: nos.1, 2 *and* 5, *Prelude*, *Romance* and *Fughetta* (*Boosey & Hawkes*) Concerto, Op.31: 1st *and* 2nd movts, *or* 2nd *and* 3rd movts (*Boosey & Hawkes*)
Gade	4 Fantasiestücke, Op.43: complete (*Hansen/Music Sales*)
Grovlez	Concertino: complete (*Combre/U.M.P.*) Lamento et Tarantelle (*Leduc/U.M.P.*)
Hindemith	Sonata (1939): complete (*Schott ED 3641/M.D.S.*)
Honegger	Sonatine: complete (*Salabert/U.M.P.*)
Joseph Horovitz	2 Majorcan Pieces: complete (*E.M.I./I.M.P.*) Sonatina: any *two* movts (*Novello/Music Sales*)
G. Jacob	Mini Concerto: complete (*Boosey & Hawkes*)
Krommer	Concerto in E♭, Op.36: 1st *and* 2nd movts, *or* 2nd *and* 3rd movts (*Bärenreiter*)
H. Lazarus	Fantasia on Airs from Bellini's 'I Puritani' (*Chester/Music Sales*)
Lutosławski	5 Dance Preludes: complete (*Chester/Music Sales*)
Lutyens	Valediction (in memory of Dylan Thomas), Op.28 (*Mills Music/I.M.P. express print*)
Messager	Solo de Concours (*Leduc/U.M.P.*)
Mozart	Concerto in A, K.622: 1st *and* 2nd movts, *or* 2nd *and* 3rd movts (clarinet in A or B♭ edns: Bärenreiter BA 4773a or c or Boosey & Hawkes)
Poulenc	Sonata: any *two* movts (*Chester/Music Sales*)
Rosetti	Concerto in E♭: 1st *and* 2nd movts, *or* 2nd *and* 3rd movts (*Kunzelmann GM 68/Peters*)
Rossini	Introduction, Theme and Variations, arr. Hermann (*O.U.P.*)
Saint-Saëns	Sonata in E♭, Op.167: 1st *and* 4th movts, *or* 3rd *and* 4th movts (*Peters EP 9290*)
Schumann	3 Fantasiestücke, Op.73: complete (A or B♭ edns: *Peters EP 2366a or c*)
C. Stamitz	Concerto no.3 in B♭: complete (*Peters EP 4859*)
Stanford	3 Intermezzi, Op.13: complete (*Chester/Music Sales*) Sonata, Op.129: complete (*Stainer & Bell*)
Sutermeister	Capriccio for solo clarinet (*Schott ED 10401/M.D.S.*)
Weber	Concertino in E♭, Op.26: complete (*Boosey & Hawkes*) Concerto no.1 in F minor, Op.73: 1st *and* 2nd movts, *or* 2nd *and* 3rd movts (*Boosey & Hawkes*) Concerto no.2 in E♭, Op.74: 1st *and* 2nd movts, *or* 2nd *and* 3rd movts (*Boosey & Hawkes*) Grand Duo Concertant, Op.48: 1st *and* 2nd movts, *or* 2nd *and* 3rd movts (*Boosey & Hawkes*)
Léo Weiner	Peregi Verbunk (Hungarian Dance), Op.40 (*Editio Musica/Faber*)

Clarinet: LRSM

Bax	Sonata (1934): complete (*Studio Music*)
Berg	4 Pieces, Op.5: complete (*Universal 07485/M.D.S.*)
Berio	Lied for solo clarinet (1983) (*Universal 17812/M.D.S.*)
Y. Bowen	Sonata, Op.109: complete (*Emerson*)
Brahms	Sonata in F minor, Op.120 no.1: complete (*Wiener Urtext/M.D.S.*)
	Sonata in E♭, Op.120 no.2: complete (*Wiener Urtext/M.D.S.*)
Gary Carpenter	Sonata: complete (*Camden Music CM 078/Spartan Press*)
Arnold Cooke	Sonata in B♭: complete (*Novello/Music Sales*)
Copland	Concerto: complete (*Boosey & Hawkes*)
Debussy	Première Rapsodie (*Durand/U.M.P.*)
Martin Ellerby	Sonata: complete (*Maecenas Europe*)
Finzi	Concerto, Op.31: complete (*Boosey & Hawkes*)
Gaubert	Fantaisie (*Heugel/U.M.P.*)
Iain Hamilton	3 Nocturnes, Op.6: complete (*Schott ED 10194/M.D.S.*)
Hindemith	Concerto in A (1947): complete (*clarinet in A edn: Schott ED 4025/M.D.S.*)
Alun Hoddinott	Sonata, Op.50: complete (*O.U.P. archive/Allegro*)
Joseph Horovitz	Sonatina: complete (*Novello/Music Sales*)
Howells	Sonata for clarinet in A: complete (*clarinet in A edn: Boosey & Hawkes*)
Ireland	Fantasy-Sonata in E♭ (*Boosey & Hawkes*)
J.X. Lefèvre	Sonata in B♭, Op.12 no.1: complete. *Lefèvre 3 Sonatas, Op.12* (*O.U.P. archive/Allegro*)
Lutosławski	5 Dance Preludes: complete (*Chester/Music Sales*)
John McCabe	3 Pieces, Op.26: complete (*Novello/Music Sales*)
Martinů	Sonatina: complete (*Leduc/U.M.P.*)
Milhaud	Duo Concertant, Op.351: complete (*Heugel/U.M.P.*)
Mozart	Concerto in A, K.622: complete (*clarinet in A or B♭ edns: Bärenreiter BA 4773a or c or Boosey & Hawkes*)
Paul Patterson	Conversations (*Weinberger/William Elkin*)
Poulenc	Sonata: complete (*Chester/Music Sales*)
Reger	Sonata in A♭, Op.49 no.1: complete (*Universal 01231/M.D.S.*)
	Sonata in F♯ minor, Op.49 no.2: complete (*Universal 01232/M.D.S.*)
Rivier	Concerto: complete (*Transatlantiques/U.M.P.*)
Rossini	Introduction, Theme and Variations, arr. Hermann (*O.U.P.*)
Saint-Saëns	Sonata in E♭, Op.167: complete (*Peters EP 9290*)
Schumann	3 Fantasiestücke, Op.73: complete (*A or B♭ edns: Peters EP 2366a or c*)
Seiber	Concertino: complete (*Schott ED 10341/M.D.S.*)
Spohr	Concerto no.1 in C minor, Op.26: complete (*Peters EP 2098a*)
	Concerto no.2 in E♭, Op.57: complete (*Peters EP 2098b*)
	Concerto no.3 in F minor, WoO 19: complete (*International 2257/M.D.S.*)
	Concerto no.4 in E minor for clarinet in A, WoO 20: complete (*clarinet in A edn: International 2258/M.D.S.*)
	Potpourri on Winter's 'Das unterbrochene Operfest', Op.80 (*Musica Rara 2226/Breitkopf & Härtel*)
Stanford	Concerto in A minor, Op.80: complete (*Cramer*)
Stravinsky	3 Pieces for solo clarinet: complete (*Chester/Music Sales*)
Weber	Concerto no.1 in F minor, Op.73: complete (*Boosey & Hawkes*)
	Concerto no.2 in E♭, Op.74: complete (*Boosey & Hawkes*)
	Grand Duo Concertant, Op.48: complete (*Boosey & Hawkes*)

Clarinet: FRSM

A. Benjamin	Le Tombeau de Ravel: complete (*Boosey & Hawkes*)
Brahms	Sonata in F minor, Op.120 no.1: complete (*Wiener Urtext/M.D.S.*)
	Sonata in E♭, Op.120 no.2: complete (*Wiener Urtext/M.D.S.*)
Busoni	Concertino, Op.48: complete (*Breitkopf & Härtel 5140*)
Elliot Carter	Gra for solo clarinet (*Boosey & Hawkes*)
Castelnuovo-Tedesco	Sonata, Op.128: complete (*Ricordi/U.M.P.*)
Copland	Concerto: complete (*Boosey & Hawkes*)
John Corigliano	Concerto: complete (*Schirmer/Music Sales*)

Gordon Crosse	A Year and a Day for solo clarinet (*O.U.P. archive/Allegro*)
Carl Davis	Concerto: complete (*Faber*)
Debussy	Première Rapsodie (*Durand/U.M.P.*)
Denisov	Sonata for solo clarinet: complete (*Breitkopf & Härtel BG 1017*)
Martin Ellerby	Sonata: complete (*Maecenas Europe*)
Finzi	Concerto, Op.31: complete (*Boosey & Hawkes*)
Françaix	Concerto: complete (*Transatlantiques/U.M.P.*)
Alun Hoddinott	Sonata, Op.50: complete (*O.U.P. archive/Allegro*)
Howells	Sonata for clarinet in A: complete (*clarinet in A edn: Boosey & Hawkes*)
Ireland	Fantasy-Sonata in E♭ (*Boosey & Hawkes*)
Martinů	Sonatina: complete (*Leduc/U.M.P.*)
Milhaud	Concerto, Op.230: complete (*Elkan-Vogel/U.M.P.*)
Mozart	Concerto in A, K.622: complete (*clarinet in A or B♭ edns: Bärenreiter BA 4773a or c or Boosey & Hawkes*)
Robert Muczynski	Time Pieces: complete (*Theodore Presser/U.M.P.*)
Nielsen	Concerto, Op.57: complete (*Chester/Music Sales*)
Paul Patterson	Conversations (*Weinberger/William Elkin*)
Poulenc	Sonata: complete (*Chester/Music Sales*)
Anthony Powers	Sea/Air for solo clarinet (*O.U.P.*)
Reger	Sonata in A♭, Op.49 no.1: complete (*Universal 01231/M.D.S.*)
	Sonata in B♭, Op.107: complete (*Bote & Bock/Boosey & Hawkes*)
Humphrey Searle	Cat Variations (*clarinet in A edn: Faber*)
Spohr	Concerto no.1 in C minor, Op.26: complete (*Peters EP 2098a*)
	Concerto no.2 in E♭, Op.57: complete (*Peters EP 2098b*)
	Concerto no.3 in F minor, WoO 19: complete (*International 2257/M.D.S.*)
	Concerto no.4 in E minor for clarinet in A, WoO 20: complete (*clarinet in A edn: International 2258/M.D.S.*)
Karlheinz Stockhausen	In Freundschaft for solo clarinet (*Stockhausen-Verlag, Kettenberg 15, 51515 Kürten, Germany*)
Stravinsky	3 Pieces for solo clarinet: complete (*Chester/Music Sales*)
Tomasi	Sonatine attique for solo clarinet: complete (*Leduc/U.M.P.*)
Weber	Concerto no.2 in E♭, Op.74: complete (*Boosey & Hawkes*)
	Grand Duo Concertant, Op.48: complete (*Boosey & Hawkes*)

Bassoon: DipABRSM

Apostel	Sonatina for solo bassoon, Op.19 no.3: complete (*Universal 12217/M.D.S.*)
J. C. Bach	Concerto in E♭: 1st **and** 2nd movts (*Sikorski/William Elkin*)
J. Bentzon	Study in Variation Form for solo bassoon, Op.34 (*Chester/Music Sales*)
Rainer Bischof	Transfigurazione for solo bassoon, Op.42 (*Doblinger 05576/M.D.S.*)
Bozza	Fantaisie (*Leduc/U.M.P.*)
Elgar	Romance, Op.62 (*Novello/Music Sales*)
Glinka	Sonata, arr. Kostlan: complete (*Sikorski/William Elkin*)
Hurlstone	Sonata in F: 1st, 2nd **and** 4th movts (*Emerson*)
G. Jacob	Concerto: 1st movt (*Stainer & Bell*)
	Partita for solo bassoon: complete (*O.U.P.*)
C. Jacobi	Introduction and Polonaise, Op.9 (*Musica Rara 2208/Breitkopf & Härtel*)
Koechlin	Sonata, Op.71: complete (*Billaudot/U.M.P.*)
C. Kreutzer	Variations for Bassoon (*Universal 18127/M.D.S.*)
Maconchy	Concertino: 1st **and** 2nd movts (*Lengnick/Faber*)
Mozart	Concerto in B♭, K.191: 1st **and** 2nd movts (*Bärenreiter BA 4868a*)
Willson Osborne	Rhapsody for solo bassoon (*Peters EP 6005*)
Ian Parrott	Rondo Giocoso (*Phylloscopus Publications*)
Aleksandër Peçi	Broken Dream for solo bassoon (*Emerson*)
Persichetti	Parable IV for solo bassoon, Op.110 (*Elkan-Vogel/U.M.P.*)
Jeremy Pike	Aria-Commemoration (*Da Capo/Music Exchange*)
Saint-Saëns	Sonata in G, Op.168: 1st **and** 2nd movts, **or** 2nd **and** 3rd movts (*Peters EP 9195*)
Schreck	Sonata, Op.9: complete (*Hofmeister/William Elkin*)

Bassoon: DipABRSM

Zdeněk Šesták	Any *three* of the '5 Virtuosic Inventions' for solo bassoon (*Panton/M.D.S.*)
Øistein Sommerfeldt	Divertimento for solo bassoon, Op.25: complete (*Norsk Musikforlag/De Haske*)
Tansman	Suite for Bassoon: complete (*Eschig/U.M.P.*)
N. Tcherepnin	Esquisse for solo bassoon, Op.45 no.7 (*Forberg/Peters*)
Telemann	Sonata in F minor (from 'Der getreue Musikmeister'), TWV 41:f1: complete (*Amadeus 665 – Schott/M.D.S.*)
Vivaldi	Concerto in A minor, RV 497: complete (*Editio Musica/Faber*) Concerto in G, RV 492: complete (*Accolade Musikverlag/Emerson*)
J.C. Vogel	Concerto in C: 1st *and* 2nd movts, *or* 2nd *and* 3rd movts (*Sikorski/William Elkin*)
Weber	Concerto in F, Op.75: 1st *and* 2nd movts, *or* 2nd *and* 3rd movts (*Universal 18131/M.D.S.*)

Bassoon: LRSM

Malcolm Arnold	Fantasy for solo bassoon, Op.86 (*Faber*)
Richard Rodney Bennett	Sonata: complete (*Novello/Music Sales*)
Berwald	Concert Piece in F, Op.2 (*Bärenreiter BA 8512a*)
Bozza	Concertino, Op.49: complete (*Leduc/U.M.P.*)
Büsser	Concertino, Op.80: complete (*Leduc/U.M.P.*)
Crusell	Airs Suédois (*British Double Reed Society/Emerson*)
Denisov	Sonata for solo bassoon: complete (*Leduc/U.M.P.*)
P.M. Dubois	Sonatine Tango: complete (*Billaudot/U.M.P.*)
Henri Dutilleux	Sarabande et Cortège (*Leduc/U.M.P.*)
Fernström	Concerto: complete (*Forlag Svensk Musik/Emerson*)
Eric Fogg	Concerto in D: complete (*Emerson*)
Françaix	Divertissement: complete (*Schott FAG 17/M.D.S.*)
Hummel	Concerto in F: 2nd *and* 3rd movts (*Boosey & Hawkes*)
G. Jacob	Concerto: complete (*Stainer & Bell*)
C. Jacobi	Concertino, Op.7 (*Musica Rara 2070/Breitkopf & Härtel*)
John Joubert	Concerto, Op.77: complete (*Novello/Music Sales*)
Paul Lewis	Concerto Burlesco: complete (*Goodmusic*)
Mozart	Concerto in B♭, K.191: complete (*Bärenreiter BA 4868a*)
Neruda	Concerto in C: complete (*Bärenreiter*)
Nussio	Variations on an Arietta by Pergolesi (*Universal 12182/M.D.S.*)
Raphael	Sonata for solo bassoon, Op.46 no.9 (*Süddeutscher Musikverlag 1612/Bärenreiter*)
Saint-Saëns	Sonata in G, Op.168: complete (*Peters EP 9195*)
Tansman	Sonatine: complete (*Eschig/U.M.P.*)
Vivaldi	Concerto in E minor, RV 484: complete (*International 2353/M.D.S.*) Concerto in F, RV 485: complete (*Ricordi/U.M.P.*)
Weber	Concerto in F, Op.75: complete (*Universal 18131/M.D.S.*)
Richard Wilson	Profound Utterances for solo bassoon: complete (*Boosey & Hawkes*)
Isang Yun	Monolog for solo bassoon (*Bote & Bock/Boosey & Hawkes*)

Bassoon: FRSM

Maurice Allard	Variations on a Theme from Paganini's Caprice no.24 (*Billaudot/U.M.P.*)
Berio	Sequenza XII for solo bassoon (*Universal 30264/M.D.S.*)
Roger Boutry	Prisme (*Salabert/U.M.P.*) Timbres (*Salabert/U.M.P.*)
Peter Maxwell Davies	Strathclyde Concerto no.8: complete (*Chester/Music Sales*)
Françaix	Concerto: complete (*Schott FAG 18/M.D.S.*)
Peter Hope	Concertino: complete (*Emerson*)
Hummel	Concerto in F: complete (*Boosey & Hawkes*)
Jolivet	Concerto: complete (*Heugel/U.M.P.*)
Maconchy	Concertino: complete (*Lengnick/Faber*)
Mozart	Concerto in B♭, K.191: complete (*Bärenreiter BA 4868a*)
A. Panufnik	Concerto: complete (*Boosey & Hawkes*)
Rimsky-Korsakov	Flight of the Bumble-bee (from 'The Tale of Tsar Saltan'), arr. Waterhouse (*Emerson*)

Graham Sheen	Endsong for solo bassoon (*Emerson*)
Nikos Skalkottas	Sonata Concertante: complete (*A.M.P. – Schirmer/Music Sales*)
Karlheinz Stockhausen	In Freundschaft for solo bassoon (*Stockhausen-Verlag, Kettenberg 15, 51515 Kürten, Germany*)
Yoshihisa Taira	Monodrame II for solo bassoon (*Transatlantiques/U.M.P.*)
Tomasi	Concerto: complete (*Leduc/U.M.P.*)
Vivaldi	Concerto in A minor, RV 498: complete (*Ricordi/U.M.P.*)
	Concerto in B♭, RV 503: complete (*Billaudot/U.M.P.*)
Weber	Andante e Rondo Ungarese, Op.35: complete (*Universal 18134/M.D.S.*)
Adrian Williams	7 Kilvert Sketches: complete (*Eschig/U.M.P.*)
John Williams	Concerto 'The Five Sacred Trees': complete (*Hal Leonard/I.M.P.*)

Saxophone: DipABRSM

Candidates may choose to play their programme on any one or any combination of E♭ and B♭ saxophones as may be appropriate. All works in the following list are published for alto saxophone in E♭ unless otherwise indicated.

J.S. Bach	Sonata in E♭, BWV 1031 (orig. for flute), arr. Leonard: complete (*soprano/tenor sax. edn: Theodore Presser 2237/U.M.P.*)
Ronald Binge	Concerto for alto saxophone: complete (*Weinberger/William Elkin*)
Paul Bonneau	Suite for alto saxophone: complete (*Leduc/U.M.P.*)
Creston	Rapsodie for alto saxophone and piano, Op.108b (*Shawnee Press/Music Sales*)
Fiocco	Concerto for tenor saxophone, arr. Bazelaire and Londeix: complete (*tenor sax. edn: Schott Frères 9260 – Schott/M.D.S.*)
Gál	Suite, Op.102b: complete (*Simrock/Boosey & Hawkes*)
Paul Harvey	Concertino: complete (*soprano/tenor sax. edn: Maurer/U.M.P.*)
Ibert	The following *four* pieces from 'Histoires', arr. Mule: no.2 'Le petit âne blanc', no.6 'Le palais abandonné', no.7 'Bajo la mesa' *and* no.9 'La Marchande d'eau fraîche' (*Leduc/U.M.P.*)
Jolivet	Fantaisie-Impromptu (*Leduc/U.M.P.*)
Koechlin	Études nos.1, 2 *and* 3 from '15 Études pour saxophone alto et piano' (*Billaudot/U.M.P.*)
Lawson Lunde	Sonata (1959): complete (*Southern Music/Emerson*)
Paule Maurice	'Tableaux de Provence' Suite: complete (*Lemoine/U.M.P.*)
Claude Pascal	Impromptu (*Durand/U.M.P.*)
Pierné	Canzonetta, Op.19, arr. Mule (*Leduc/U.M.P.*)
Amy Quate	Light of Sothis (*Leduc/U.M.P.*)
Alan Richardson	3 Pieces, Op.22: complete (*Emerson*)
P. Tate	Concerto for alto saxophone: 1st *and* 2nd movts (*O.U.P. archive/Allegro*)
A. Tcherepnin	Sonatine Sportive, Op.63: complete (*Leduc/U.M.P.*)
Telemann	Sonata in C minor (orig. for oboe, TWV 41:a3), arr. Londeix: complete (*Leduc/U.M.P.*)
	Sonata in D minor (orig. for oboe, TWV 41:a3), arr. Londeix: complete (*soprano sax. edn: Leduc/U.M.P.*)
Mark-Anthony Turnage	Sarabande (*soprano sax. edn: Schott ED 12417/M.D.S.*)
Burnet Tuthill	Sonata for alto saxophone, Op.20: complete (*Southern Music/Emerson*)
	Sonata for tenor saxophone, Op.56: complete (*tenor sax. edn: Southern Music/Emerson*)
Maurice Whitney	Introduction and Samba (*Bourne Music 1006/M.D.S.*)
Phil Woods	Sonata for alto saxophone: 1st *and* 2nd movts (*Kendor Music/William Elkin* or *Advance Music/Music Exchange*)

Saxophone: LRSM

Candidates may choose to play their programme on any one or any combination of E♭ and B♭ saxophones as may be appropriate. All works in the following list are published for alto saxophone in E♭ unless otherwise indicated.

Absil	Sonata, Op.115: complete (*Lemoine/U.M.P.*)
J.S. Bach	Sonata no.4 (orig. for flute), arr. Mule: complete (*Leduc/U.M.P.*)
	Sonata no.6 (orig. for flute), arr. Mule: complete (*Leduc/U.M.P.*)
	Sonata in G minor, BWV 1020, arr. Harle: complete (*soprano/alto/tenor sax. edn: Universal 17774/M.D.S.*)
Warren Benson	Concertino for alto saxophone: 2nd movt (Aeolian Song) (*Theodore Presser 2605/U.M.P.*)
Paul Bonneau	Pièce Concertante dans l'esprit 'Jazz' (*Leduc/U.M.P.*)
Bozza	Fantaisie italienne (*Leduc/U.M.P.*)
Creston	Sonata for alto saxophone, Op.19: complete (*Shawnee Press/Music Sales*)

Saxophone: LRSM

Debussy	Rapsodie (*Durand/U.M.P.*)
Denisov	2 Pièces: complete (*Leduc/U.M.P.*)
P. M. Dubois	Suite Française for solo saxophone: complete (*Leduc/U.M.P.*)
Françaix	5 Danses Exotiques: complete (*Schott ED 4745/M.D.S.*)
Raymond Gallois-Montbrun	6 Pièces Musicales d'Étude: complete (*Leduc/U.M.P.*)
Glazunov	Concerto in E♭, Op.109: complete (*Leduc/U.M.P.*)
Clare Grundman	Concertante (*Boosey & Hawkes*)
Dave Heath	Out of the Cool (*soprano sax. edn: Chester/Music Sales*)
Bernhard Heiden	Sonata for alto saxophone (1937): complete (*Schott ED 11195/M.D.S.*)
Hindemith	Sonata (1943): complete (*Schott ED 4635/M.D.S.*)
G. Jacob	All *seven* of the pieces from 'Miscellanies' (*Emerson*)
Frank Martin	Ballade for alto saxophone (1938) (*Universal 13984/M.D.S.*)
	Ballade for trombone or tenor saxophone (1940) (*tenor sax. edn: Universal 11250/M.D.S.*)
Milhaud	'Scaramouche' Suite, Op.165c: complete (*Salabert/U.M.P.*)
Stephen Morland	Recitatives for solo saxophone (*E♭/B♭ sax.: Broadbent & Dunn*)
Robert Muczynski	Sonata for alto saxophone, Op.29: complete (*Schirmer/Music Sales*)
Dominic Muldowney	… in a hall of mirrors (*Universal 17776/M.D.S.*)
Ryo Noda	Improvisation I for solo alto saxophone (*Leduc/U.M.P.*)
	Improvisation II *or* Improvisation III for solo alto saxophone (*Leduc/U.M.P.*)
Michael Nyman	Miserere Paraphrase for soprano saxophone (*Chester/Music Sales*)
Piazzolla	6 Tango-Etudes: complete (*U.M.P.*)
Robert Planel	Prélude et Saltarelle (*Leduc/U.M.P.*)
Erwin Schulhoff	Hot-Sonate: complete (*Schott ED 7739/M.D.S.*)
Singelée	Adagio et Rondo, Op.63 (*soprano/tenor sax. edn: Roncorp/Emerson*)
	Fantaisie for soprano saxophone, Op.89 (*Roncorp/Emerson*)
Mark-Anthony Turnage	Sarabande (*soprano sax. edn: Schott ED 12417/M.D.S.*)
Villa-Lobos	Fantasia for soprano or tenor saxophone: complete (*soprano/tenor sax. edn: Peer-Southern/William Elkin*)
Phil Woods	Sonata for alto saxophone: complete (*Kendor Music/William Elkin* or *Advance Music/Music Exchange*)

Saxophone: FRSM

Candidates may choose to play their programme on any one or any combination of E♭ and B♭ saxophones as may be appropriate. All works in the following list are published for alto saxophone in E♭ unless otherwise indicated.

Absil	Fantaisie Caprice, Op.152 (*Lemoine/U.M.P.*)
Richard Rodney Bennett	Concerto for Stan Getz: complete (*tenor sax. edn: Novello/Music Sales*)
	Sonata for soprano saxophone: complete (*soprano sax. edn: Novello/Music Sales*)
Berio	Sequenza IXb for solo alto saxophone (*Universal 17447/M.D.S.*)
Michael Berkeley	Keening (*O.U.P.*)
Paul Bonneau	Caprice en forme de Valse for solo saxophone (*E♭/B♭ sax.: Leduc/U.M.P.*)
Roger Boutry	Divertimento: complete (*Leduc/U.M.P.*)
Creston	Concerto for alto saxophone, Op.26: complete (*Schirmer/Music Sales*)
Dahl	Concerto: complete (*European American Music 0442/Emerson*)
Denisov	Sonata for alto saxophone: complete (*Leduc/U.M.P.*)
Désenclos	Prélude, Cadence et Finale: complete (*Leduc/U.M.P.*)
P. M. Dubois	Concerto for alto saxophone: complete (*Leduc/U.M.P.*)
Gaubert	Intermède Champêtre (*Leduc/U.M.P.*)
Ida Gotkovsky	Brilliance (*Billaudot/U.M.P.*)
Karel Husa	Elégie et Rondeau (*Leduc/U.M.P.*)
Ibert	Concertino da Camera: complete (*Leduc/U.M.P.*)
M. William Karlins	Music for Tenor Sax: complete (*tenor sax. edn: Southern Music/Emerson*)
Nicola LeFanu	Ervallagh for solo alto saxophone (*Novello/Music Sales archive*)
Boris Mersson	Fantasia, Op.37 (*Kunzelmann GM 937/Peters*)
Mihalovici	Chant Premier (*alto/tenor sax. edn: Heugel/U.M.P.*)
Ryo Noda	Maï for solo alto saxophone (*Leduc/U.M.P.*)
Michael Nyman	Shaping the Curve (*soprano sax. edn: Chester/Music Sales*)

REPERTOIRE LISTS

Claude Pascal	Sonatine for alto saxophone: complete (*Durand/U.M.P.*)
Lucie Robert	Cadenza (*E.F.M./U.M.P.*)
Ned Rorem	Picnic on the Marne: complete (*Boosey & Hawkes*)
Jeanine Rueff	Sonata for solo alto saxophone: complete (*Leduc/U.M.P.*)
Schmitt	Légende, Op.66 (*Durand/U.M.P.*)
Tomasi	Concerto for alto saxophone: complete (*Leduc/U.M.P.*)
Mark-Anthony Turnage	Two Elegies Framing a Shout: complete (*soprano sax. edn: Schott ED 12492/M.D.S.*)
Nigel Wood	Cries of the Stentor (*soprano/tenor sax. edn: Saxtet Publications*)
Takashi Yoshimatsu	Fuzzy Bird Sonata: complete (*Billaudot/U.M.P.*)

Horn: DipABRSM

All the following works have parts for horn in F, although candidates may choose to offer certain items on horns in other keys where these are indicated as available.

Malcolm Arnold	Fantasy for solo horn, Op.88 (*Faber*)
J.S. Bach	Cello Suite no.1: 7th movt, *Gigue* } *Bach Cello Suites, arr. Hoss* Cello Suite no.3: 5th *and* 6th movts, *Bourrée I* and *II* } (*Southern Music/Emerson*)
Beethoven	Sonata in F, Op.17: complete (*Henle* or *Henle – Schott/M.D.S.*)
Cherubini	Sonata no.2 in F. *Cherubini 2 Sonatas* (*Concert Études*) (*Schirmer/Music Sales*)
Eileen Clews	Partita: complete (*F/E♭ horn edn: Paterson/Music Sales*)
Dukas	Villanelle (*Durand/U.M.P.*)
Fricker	Sonata, Op.24: complete (*Schott ED 10473/M.D.S.*)
Edward Gregson	Concerto: 1st *and* 2nd movts (*Music Sales*)
J. Haydn	Concerto no.1 in D, Hob.VIId/3: complete (*F/D horn edn archive copy: Boosey & Hawkes* or *D horn edn: Henle* or *Henle – Schott/M.D.S.*) Concerto no.2 in D, Hob.VIId/4: complete (*F/D horn edn archive copy: Boosey & Hawkes*)
M. Haydn	Concertino in D: complete (*F/D horn edn: Schirmer/Music Sales*)
Hindemith	Sonata (1939): complete (*Schott ED 3642/M.D.S.*)
Alun Hoddinott	Sonata, Op.78 no.2: complete (*O.U.P. archive/Allegro*)
Larsson	Concertino, Op.45 no.5: complete (*Gehrmans/William Elkin*)
David Lyon	Partita for solo horn: complete (*Studio Music*)
Mozart	Any *one* of the 4 Concertos as follows: Concerto no.1 in D, K.412/514: complete (*F/D horn edn: Bärenreiter BA 5314a*) Concerto no.2 in E♭, K.417: complete (*F/E♭ horn edn: Bärenreiter BA 5311a*) Concerto no.3 in E♭, K.447: complete (*F/E♭ horn edn: Bärenreiter BA 5312a*) Concerto no.4 in E♭, K.495: complete (*F/E♭ horn edn: Bärenreiter BA 5313a*)
Poulenc	Élégie (*Chester/Music Sales*)
Saint-Saëns	Morceau de Concert in F minor, Op.94: complete (*Durand/U.M.P.*) Romance in E, Op.67 (*Durand/U.M.P.*)
F. Strauss	Concerto in C minor, Op.8: complete (*Schirmer/Music Sales*) Introduction, Theme and Variations, Op.13 (*Zimmermann/William Elkin*)
R. Strauss	Concerto no.1 in E♭, Op.11: complete (*Universal 01039/M.D.S.*)
Telemann	Concerto in D, TWV 51:D8: complete (*F horn edn: Peters HG 6119* or *F/D horn edn: Schirmer/Music Sales*) Sonata in F minor (from 'Der getreue Musikmeister'), TWV 41:f1: complete (*International 2403/M.D.S.*)

Horn: LRSM

All the following works have parts for horn in F, although candidates may choose to offer certain items on horns in other keys where these are indicated as available.

Malcolm Arnold	Concerto no.2, Op.58: complete (*F/E♭ horn edn: Paterson/Music Sales*) Fantasy for solo horn, Op.88 (*Faber*)
Derek Bourgeois	Fantasy Pieces for solo horn: no.5, *Allegro or* no.6, *Presto* (*in the written keys*) (*Brass Wind*)
Y. Bowen	Sonata in E♭, Op.101: 1st *and* 2nd movts, *or* 2nd *and* 3rd movts (*Emerson*)
Edward Gregson	Concerto: complete (*Music Sales*)
J. Haydn	Concerto no.1 in D, Hob.VIId/3: complete (*F/D horn edn archive copy: Boosey & Hawkes* or *D horn edn: Henle* or *Henle – Schott/M.D.S.*) Concerto no.2 in D, Hob.VIId/4: complete (*F/D horn edn archive copy: Boosey & Hawkes*)

Horn: LRSM

Hindemith	Concerto (1949): complete (*Schott ED 4024/M.D.S.*) Sonata (1939): complete (*Schott ED 3642/M.D.S.*)
G. Jacob	Concerto: 1st *and* 2nd movts, **or** 2nd *and* 3rd movts (*Stainer & Bell*)
Mozart	Any *one* of the 4 Concertos as follows: Concerto no.1 in D, K.412/514: complete (*F/D horn edn: Bärenreiter BA 5314a*) Concerto no.2 in E♭, K.417: complete (*F/E♭ horn edn: Bärenreiter BA 5311a*) Concerto no.3 in E♭, K.447: complete (*F/E♭ horn edn: Bärenreiter BA 5312a*) Concerto no.4 in E♭, K.495: complete (*F/E♭ horn edn: Bärenreiter BA 5313a*)
Thea Musgrave	Music for Horn and Piano: complete (*Chester/Music Sales*)
Poulenc	Élégie (*Chester/Music Sales*)
Rossini	Prelude, Theme and Variations in F: complete (*Schirmer/Music Sales*)
Saint-Saëns	Romance in E, Op.67 (*Durand/U.M.P.*)
Schumann	Adagio and Allegro in A♭, Op.70 (*Schirmer/Music Sales*)
Seiber	Notturno (*Schott ED 10336/M.D.S.*)
F. Strauss	Introduction, Theme and Variations, Op.13 (*Zimmermann/William Elkin*)
R. Strauss	Concerto no.1 in E♭, Op.11: complete (*Universal 01039/M.D.S.*)
Telemann	Concerto in D, TWV 51:D8: complete (*F horn edn: Peters HG 6119* or *F/D horn edn: Schirmer/* *Music Sales*)

Horn: FRSM

All the following works have parts for horn in F, although candidates may choose to offer certain items on horns in other keys where these are indicated as available.

Malcolm Arnold	Concerto no.2, Op.58: complete (*F/E♭ horn edn: Paterson/Music Sales*)
Derek Bourgeois	Fantasy Pieces for solo horn: no.9, Con fuoco (*in the written key*) (*Brass Wind*)
Y. Bowen	Sonata in E♭, Op.101: complete (*Emerson*)
Peter Maxwell Davies	Sea Eagle for solo horn (*Chester/Music Sales*)
Anthony Halstead	Suite for solo horn: complete (*Emerson*)
Iain Hamilton	Sonata Notturna: complete (*Schott ED 10971/M.D.S.*)
J. Haydn	Concerto no.2 in D, Hob.VIId/4: complete (*F/D horn edn archive copy: Boosey & Hawkes*)
Hindemith	Concerto (1949): complete (*Schott ED 4024/M.D.S.*)
G. Jacob	Concerto: complete (*Stainer & Bell*)
Koechlin	Monodie for solo horn, Op.218 bis (*Billaudot/U.M.P.*)
John McCabe	Any of the 3 pieces from 'The Goddess Trilogy': Castle of Arianrhod, Floraison, Shapeshifter (*published separately: Novello/Music Sales*)
Mozart	Concerto no.2 in E♭, K.417: complete (*F/E♭ horn edn: Bärenreiter BA 5311a*) Concerto no.4 in E♭, K.495: complete (*F/E♭ horn edn: Bärenreiter BA 5313a*)
Thea Musgrave	Music for Horn and Piano: complete (*Chester/Music Sales*)
Schumann	Adagio and Allegro in A♭, Op.70 (*Schirmer/Music Sales*)
Humphrey Searle	Aubade, Op.28 (*Schott ED 10500/M.D.S.*)
Seiber	Notturno (*Schott ED 10336/M.D.S.*)
R. Strauss	Concerto no.2 in E♭: complete (*E♭ horn edn: Boosey & Hawkes*)
Julia Usher	The Old Man of the Sea (*Primavera*)
Weber	Concertino in E minor, Op.45: complete (*F/E horn edn: Schirmer/Music Sales* or *E♭ horn edn:* *International 2337/M.D.S.*)

Trumpet, Cornet in B♭ and Flugelhorn: DipABRSM

All the following works have parts for trumpet in B♭, unless otherwise indicated. Candidates may offer certain items on trumpets in other keys where these are noted as available or, in some cases, are actually specified.

Arban	Carnaval de Venise (Air Varié)(*accompanied*) (*Boosey & Hawkes*)
Malcolm Arnold	Trumpet Concerto, Op.125: complete (*Faber*)
Niels Viggo Bentzon	Sonata for trumpet, Op.73: complete (*Hansen/Music Sales*)
Bloch	Proclamation (*Broude Bros/Emerson*)
O. Böhme	Trumpet Concerto in F minor, Op.18: complete (*Rahter/Schauer*)
Büsser	Andante et Scherzo, Op.44 (*B♭/C trumpet edn: Leduc/U.M.P.*)
Clarke	Suite in D: complete (*D trumpet only*) (*D trumpet part: Musica Rara 1321/Breitkopf & Härtel*)

Trumpet, Cornet in B♭ and Flugelhorn: DipABRSM

Copland	Quiet City, arr. Wastall. *Contemporary Music for Trumpet* (*Boosey & Hawkes*)
Corelli	Sonata in D: complete (*D trumpet only*) (*C trumpet part: Musica Rara 1142/Breitkopf & Härtel*)
Fasch	Trumpet Concerto à 8 in D: complete (*D or A trumpet only*) (*D/A trumpet edn: McNaughtan/MusT*)
Fiala	Divertimento in D: complete (*Faber*)
G. B. Fontana	Sonata no.3 in C: complete (*D trumpet only*). Fontana 2 Sonatas (*C edn: Musica Rara 1959/Breitkopf & Härtel*)
Françaix	Prélude, Sarabande et Gigue: complete (*Eschig/U.M.P.*)
Iain Hamilton	5 Scenes: complete (*Theodore Presser 0102/U.M.P.*)
Handel	Suite in D: complete (*D trumpet only*) (*Musica Rara 1225/Breitkopf & Härtel*)
Haydn	Trumpet Concerto in E♭, Hob.VIIe/1: complete (*with cadenzas*) (*B♭/E♭ trumpet edn: Universal HMP 223/M.D.S.*)
William Himes	Concertino for flugelhorn: complete (*Studio Music*)
Elgar Howarth	Concerto for trumpet: complete (*Chester/Music Sales*)
Ibert	Impromptu (*C trumpet edn: Leduc/U.M.P.*)
Larsson	Concertino in E♭, Op.45 no.6: complete (*Gehrmans/William Elkin*)
J. B. G. Neruda	Concerto in E♭: complete (*with cadenzas*) (*B♭/E♭ trumpet edn: Brass Wind*)
Peeters	Sonata in B♭ for trumpet, Op.51: complete (*Peters EP 6240*)
Ridout	Concertino for trumpet: complete (*Emerson*)
Rivier	Concerto for trumpet: complete (*C trumpet edn: Billaudot/U.M.P.*)
Saint-Saëns	Fantaisie in E♭ (*B♭ or C trumpet edns: Leduc/U.M.P.*)
Scriabin	3 Preludes, arr. Snell: complete (*Emerson*)
Halsey Stevens	Sonata for trumpet: complete (*Peters EP 6030*)
Viviani	Sonata Prima in C for trumpet: complete (*B♭/C trumpet edn: Editions Marc Reift 6006/MusT*) Sonata Seconda in C for trumpet: complete (*B♭/C trumpet edn: Editions Marc Reift 6007/MusT*)
F. D. Weber	Variations in F (*Faber*)
Denis Wright	Concerto for B♭ cornet: complete (*Studio Music*)

Trumpet, Cornet in B♭ and Flugelhorn: LRSM

All the following works have parts for trumpet in B♭, unless otherwise indicated. Candidates may offer certain items on trumpets in other keys where these are noted as available or, in some cases, are actually specified.

John Addison	Concerto for trumpet: complete (*Stainer & Bell*)
Arban	Carnaval de Venise (Air Varié) (*accompanied*) (*Boosey & Hawkes*)
Malcolm Arnold	Trumpet Concerto, Op.125: complete (*Faber*) Fantasy for solo trumpet, Op.100 (*Faber*)
Alexander Arutjunjan	Concerto for trumpet: complete (*Boosey & Hawkes*)
Bozza	Caprice, Op.47 (*B♭/C trumpet edn: Leduc/U.M.P.*) Concertino: complete (*C trumpet edn: Leduc/U.M.P.*)
Edward Gregson	Trumpet Concerto (1983): complete (*Novello/Music Sales*) Prelude and Capriccio for cornet (*or trumpet*) (*Brand Publications/Smith*)
Handel	Overture to the opera 'Atalanta' (*D trumpet only*) (*D trumpet part: Musica Rara 1823a/Breitkopf & Härtel*)
Haydn	Trumpet Concerto in E♭, Hob.VIIe/1: complete (*with cadenzas*) (*B♭/E♭ trumpet edn: Universal HMP 223/M.D.S.*)
Hindemith	Sonata for trumpet (1939): complete (*Schott ED 3643/M.D.S.*)
Honegger	Intrada (*C trumpet edn: Salabert/U.M.P.*)
Joseph Horovitz	Concerto for trumpet: complete (*Novello/Music Sales*)
Hubeau	Sonata for trumpet: complete (*B♭/C trumpet edn: Durand/U.M.P.*)
Hummel	Trumpet Concerto in E: 1st *and* 2nd movts (*B♭/C/E trumpet edn: Universal 25030c/M.D.S.*)
Martinů	Sonatina for trumpet: complete (*B♭/C trumpet edn: Leduc/U.M.P.*)
Paul Patterson	Trumpet Concerto, Op.3: complete (*Weinberger/William Elkin*)
Riisager	Concertino for trumpet, Op.29: complete (*Hansen/Music Sales*)
Philip Sparke	Concerto for trumpet or cornet (1993): complete (*Studio Music*)
Telemann	Concerto in D, TWV 51:D7: complete (*D trumpet only*) (*D trumpet part: Musica Rara 1848a/Breitkopf & Härtel*)

Trumpet, Cornet in Bb and Flugelhorn: LRSM

Torelli	Trumpet Sonata in D, G1: complete (*D trumpet only*) (*D trumpet part: Musica Rara 1646a/Breitkopf & Härtel*)
	Trumpet Sinfonia in D, G8: complete (*D trumpet only*) (*D trumpet part: Musica Rara 1861a/ Breitkopf & Härtel*)
Allen Vizzutti	Sonata no.2 for trumpet: complete (*Bella Musica/Studio Music*)
Denis Wright	Concerto for Bb cornet: complete (*Studio Music*)

Trumpet, Cornet in Bb and Flugelhorn: FRSM

All the following works have parts for trumpet in Bb, unless otherwise indicated. Candidates may offer certain items on trumpets in other keys where these are noted as available or, in some cases, are actually specified.

Peter Maxwell Davies	Sonata for trumpet in D (1955): complete (*D trumpet edn: Schott ED 11067/M.D.S.*)
Enescu	Légende (*C trumpet edn: Enoch/U.M.P.*)
Edward Gregson	Trumpet Concerto (1983): complete (*Novello/Music Sales*)
Anthony Halstead	Suite for solo trumpet: complete (*Emerson*)
Hans Werner Henze	Sonatina for solo trumpet (1974): complete (*Schott TR 19/M.D.S.*)
Gilles Herbillon	Sonatine for trumpet: complete (*Bb/C trumpet edn: Billaudot/U.M.P.*)
J.W. Hertel	Trumpet Concerto no.1 in Eb: complete (*McNaughtan/MusT*)
Hummel	Trumpet Concerto in E: complete (*Bb/C/E trumpet edn: Universal 25030c/M.D.S.*)
Jolivet	Concertino for trumpet: complete (*C trumpet edn: Durand/U.M.P.*)
L. Mozart	Trumpet Concerto in D: complete (*D trumpet only*) (*D trumpet edn: Kunzelmann GM 809/Peters*)
Michael Nyman	Flugelhorn and Piano (*Chester/Music Sales*)
Raymond Premru	Trumpet Concerto (1983): complete (*Tezak 1019/MusT*)
Philip Sparke	Concerto for trumpet or cornet (1993): complete (*Studio Music*)
Eino Tamberg	Trumpet Concerto, Op.42: complete (*Bb/C trumpet edn: Editions Marc Reift 6012/MusT*)
Tartini	Concerto in D: complete (*D trumpet only*) (*D trumpet part: Brass Wind*)
Tomasi	Trumpet Concerto in C: complete (*C trumpet edn: Leduc/U.M.P.*)
	Triptyque: complete (*Bb/C trumpet edn: Leduc/U.M.P.*)
Allen Vizzutti	Andante (*for trumpet*) **and** Capriccio (*for piccolo trumpet*) (*Bella Musica/Studio Music*)

Eb Horn: DipABRSM

Malcolm Arnold	Horn Concerto no.1, Op.11: 1st **and** 2nd, **or** 2nd **and** 3rd movts (*F/Eb horn edn: Lengnick/Faber*)
Eric Ball	September Fantasy for Eb horn (*Wright & Round*)
Bellini	Horn Concerto in Eb, arr. Newsome: complete (*Eb horn edn: Studio Music*)
Arthur Butterworth	Saxhorn Sonata, Op.103: 1st movt (*Eb horn edn: Comus Edition*)
Eileen Clews	Partita for horn: complete (*F/Eb horn edn: Paterson/Music Sales*)
Robert Eaves	Rhapsody for Eb cornet/horn (*Brand Publications/Smith*)
C. Förster	Horn Concerto in Eb: 1st **and** 2nd movts (*F/Eb horn edn: Schirmer/Music Sales*)
John Golland	Rhapsody no.1 for Eb horn, Op.71 (*Studio Music*)
Edward Gregson	Concerto for horn: 1st movt (*Eb horn edn: Chester/Music Sales*)
Hindemith	Sonata for Eb horn (1943): 1st, 2nd **and** 4th movts (*Schott ED 4635/M.D.S.*)
Bryan Kelly	Concert Suite for horn: complete (*F/Eb horn edn: Brand Publications/Smith*)
Peter Kneale	Variations on a Welsh Theme for Eb horn (*Brand Publications/Smith*)
Mozart	Any *one* of the following Horn Concertos:
	Horn Concerto no.2 in Eb, K.417: complete (*F/Eb horn edn: Bärenreiter BA 5311a*)
	Horn Concerto no.3 in Eb, K.447: complete (*F/Eb horn edn: Bärenreiter BA 5312a*)
	Horn Concerto no.4 in Eb, K.495: complete (*F/Eb horn edn: Bärenreiter BA 5313a*)
Rossini	Prelude, Theme and Variations (*F horn edn: Peters EP 7173a*)
Philip Sparke	Masquerade for Eb horn (*Studio Music*)
R. Strauss	Horn Concerto no.1 in Eb, Op.11: 1st **and** 2nd movts (*F horn edn: Universal 01039/M.D.S.*)
Bram Wiggins	Cornucopia for Eb horn (*Kirklees Music*)
Gareth Wood	Concertino for Eb horn (full version): complete (*Brand Publications/Smith*)
	3 Pieces for solo horn: complete (*Eb horn edn: Brand Publications/Smith*)
Ray Woodfield	Concert Suite for horn: complete (*F/Eb horn edn: Hallamshire Music*)

E♭ Horn: LRSM

Malcolm Arnold	Horn Concerto no.1, Op.11: complete (*F/E♭ horn edn: Lengnick/Faber*)
Arthur Butterworth	Saxhorn Sonata, Op.103: 1st **and** 3rd movts (*E♭ horn edn: Comus Edition*)
Eileen Clews	Partita for horn: complete (*F/E♭ horn edn: Paterson/Music Sales*)
Robert Eaves	Rhapsody for E♭ cornet/horn (*Brand Publications/Smith*)
Martin Ellerby	Tenor Horn Concerto: 2nd **and** 3rd movts (*Studio Music*)
C. Förster	Horn Concerto in E♭: complete (*F/E♭ horn edn: Schirmer/Music Sales*)
John Golland	Rhapsody no.1 for E♭ horn, Op.71 (*Studio Music*)
Peter Graham	Episode (*with cadenza*) (*F/E♭ horn edn: Rosehill Music*)
Edward Gregson	Concerto for horn: complete (*E♭ horn edn: Chester/Music Sales*)
Hindemith	Sonata for E♭ horn (1943): complete (*Schott ED 4635/M.D.S.*)
Mozart	Any *one* of the following Horn Concertos: Horn Concerto no.2 in E♭, K.417: complete (*F/E♭ horn edn: Bärenreiter BA 5311a*) Horn Concerto no.3 in E♭, K.447: complete (*F/E♭ horn edn: Bärenreiter BA 5312a*) Horn Concerto no.4 in E♭, K.495: complete (*F/E♭ horn edn: Bärenreiter BA 5313a*)
Rossini	Prelude, Theme and Variations (*F horn edn: Peters EP 7173a*)
Howard Snell	4 Bagatelles for tenor horn: nos.2, 3 **and** 4 (*Kirklees*)
Philip Sparke	Masquerade for E♭ horn (*Studio Music*)
R. Strauss	Horn Concerto no.1 in E♭, Op.11: complete (*F horn edn: Universal 01039/M.D.S.*)
Gareth Wood	Concertino for E♭ horn (full version): complete (*Brand Publications/Smith*)

E♭ Horn: FRSM

Arthur Butterworth	Saxhorn Sonata, Op.103: complete (*E♭ horn edn: Comus Edition*)
Martin Ellerby	Tenor Horn Concerto: complete (*Studio Music*)
John Golland	Sonata for horn, Op.75: complete (*E♭ horn edn: Kirklees*)
Edward Gregson	Concerto for horn: complete (*E♭ horn edn: Chester/Music Sales*)
Hindemith	Sonata for E♭ horn (1943): complete (*Schott ED 4635/M.D.S.*)
Mozart	Horn Concerto no.2 in E♭, K.417: complete (*F/E♭ horn edn: Bärenreiter BA 5311a*) Horn Concerto no.4 in E♭, K.495: complete (*F/E♭ horn edn: Bärenreiter BA 5313a*)
Howard Snell	4 Bagatelles for tenor horn: complete (*Kirklees*)
R. Strauss	Horn Concerto no.2 in E♭: complete (*E♭ horn edn: Boosey & Hawkes*)

Trombone: DipABRSM

Candidates may choose to play their programme on either the tenor or bass trombone as may be appropriate or any combination, which may also include alto trombone. All works in the following list are published for tenor trombone unless otherwise indicated.

J.S. Bach	Cello Suite no.1, BWV 1007: 4th, 5th, 6th **and** 7th movts, *Sarabande, Menuetto I and II* **and** *Gigue* · Cello Suite no.3, BWV 1009: 1st, 5th **and** 6th movts, *Prélude,* **and** *Bourrée I and II* — *Bach Cello Suites, arr. Lafosse (Leduc/U.M.P.) or arr. Barbez for bass trombone (Leduc/U.M.P.)*
Barat	Pièce in E♭ (*Leduc/U.M.P.*)
L. Bernstein	Elegy for Mippy II for solo trombone (*Boosey & Hawkes*)
Derek Bourgeois	Fantasy Pieces for solo trombone: no.7, *Allegro energico* **or** no.9, *Adagio cantabile* (*tenor* or *bass trombone edns: Brass Wind*)
Bozza	Hommage à Bach (*Leduc/U.M.P.*) Allegro et Finale for bass trombone (*Leduc/U.M.P.*) Prélude et Allegro for bass trombone (*Leduc/U.M.P.*)
Ferdinand David	Concertino in E♭ for trombone, Op.4: complete (*International 2008/M.D.S.*)
Jean-Michel Defaye	2 Danses: complete (*tenor* or *bass trombone edns: Leduc/U.M.P.*)
P.M. Dubois	Suite for trombone: complete (*Leduc/U.M.P.*) Piccolo Suite for bass trombone: complete (*Leduc/U.M.P.*) Si trombone m'était conté for bass trombone: complete (*Eschig/U.M.P.*)
Harold East	Sonatina for trombone: complete (*Ricordi/U.M.P.*) Sonatina for bass trombone: complete (*Ricordi/U.M.P.*)
Edward Gregson	Divertimento: complete (*Studio Music*)
Gröndahl	Concerto for trombone: complete (*Dansk Musik/Music Sales*)
Guilmant	Morceau Symphonique, Op.88 (*tenor trombone edn: Schott ED 10484/M.D.S.* or *bass trombone edn: Editions Marc Reift 2007/MusT*)

Trombone: DipABRSM

Handel	Concerto in F minor, arr. Lafosse: any *three* movts (*Leduc/U.M.P.*) *or* arr. Angerer: any *three* movts (*alto/tenor trombone edn: Editions Marc Reift 226/MusT*)
O. Henry	Passacaglia and Fugue for bass trombone (*Robert King/U.M.P.*)
Hindemith	Trombone Sonata (1941): any *three* movts (*Schott ED 3673/M.D.S.*)
G. Jacob	Trombone Sonata: complete (*Emerson*)
Bryan Kelly	Sonatina for trombone: complete (*Weinberger/William Elkin*)
Larsson	Concertino for trombone, Op.45 no.7: 1st *and* 2nd movts, *or* 2nd *and* 3rd movts (*Gehrmans/William Elkin*)
Lebedev	Concerto in One Movement in A minor for bass trombone (*Edition Musicus/MusT*)
B. Marcello	Sonata in A minor, arr. Ostrander: complete (*International 2147/M.D.S.*)
Patrick McCarty	Sonata for bass trombone: complete (*Ensemble Publications/William Elkin*)
Claude Pascal	Sonate en 6 minutes 30 for bass trombone: complete (*Durand/U.M.P.*)
Jiří Pauer	Trombonetta (*Panton – Schott/M.D.S.*)
Pierre Petit	Fantaisie for bass trombone (*Leduc/U.M.P.*)
Pilss	Concerto for bass trombone: 2nd *and* 3rd movts (*Robert King/U.M.P.*)
Raymond Premru	Prelude and Dance for solo bass trombone (*Mohawk/Emerson*)
William Presser	3 Folk Tales for bass trombone: complete (*Theodore Presser 0406/U.M.P.*)
Rimsky-Korsakov	Trombone Concerto in B♭: complete (*with cadenzas*) (*Boosey & Hawkes*)
Ernst Sachse	Concertino for bass trombone: complete (*B♭ edn: Rahter/Schauer or F edn: Editions Marc Reift 221/MusT*)
Saint-Saëns	Cavatine, Op.144 (*Durand/U.M.P.*)
C. Salzedo	Pièce Concertante, Op.27 (*Leduc/U.M.P.*)
Serocki	Sonatina for trombone: complete (*Moeck 5302*)
Telemann	Sonata in A minor, arr. Brown: complete (*International 2486/M.D.S.*)
Alec Wilder	Sonata for bass trombone: 1st *and* 2nd movts, *or* 2nd *and* 5th movts (*Margun/Emerson*)

Trombone: LRSM

Candidates may choose to play their programme on either the tenor or bass trombone as may be appropriate or any combination, which may also include alto trombone. All works in the following list are published for tenor trombone unless otherwise indicated.

Albrechtsberger	Concerto for alto trombone: complete (*alto trombone edn: Editio Musica/Faber*)
Malcolm Arnold	Fantasy for solo trombone, Op.101 (*Faber*)
J.S. Bach	Cello Suite no.2, BWV 1008: 4th, 5th, 6th *and* 7th movts, *Sarabande, Menuetto I and II* and *Gigue*. Bach Cello Suites, arr. Lafosse (*Leduc/U.M.P.*) or arr. Barbez for bass trombone (*Leduc/U.M.P.*)
Barat	Pièce in E♭ (*Leduc/U.M.P.*)
L. Bernstein	Elegy for Mippy II for solo trombone (*Boosey & Hawkes*)
Derek Bourgeois	Trombone Concerto, Op.114: any *two* movts (*Brand Publications/Smith*)
	Fantasy Pieces for solo trombone: no.7, *Allegro energico* *or* no.9, *Adagio cantabile* (*tenor* or *bass trombone edns: Brass Wind*)
Roger Boutry	Capriccio (*Leduc/U.M.P.*)
Bozza	Hommage à Bach (*Leduc/U.M.P.*)
	New Orleans for bass trombone (*Leduc/U.M.P.*)
Jean-Michel Defaye	2 Danses: complete (*tenor* or *bass trombone edns: Leduc/U.M.P.*)
Stephen Dodgson	Concerto for bass trombone: 3rd *and* 4th movts (*Studio Music*)
P.M. Dubois	Piccolo Suite for bass trombone: complete (*Leduc/U.M.P.*)
	Si trombone m'était conté for bass trombone: complete (*Eschig/U.M.P.*)
Harold East	Sonatina for trombone: complete (*Ricordi/U.M.P.*)
	Sonatina for bass trombone: complete (*Ricordi/U.M.P.*)
Edward Gregson	Trombone Concerto: complete (*Novello/Music Sales*)
Gröndahl	Concerto for trombone: complete (*Dansk Musik/Music Sales*)
Guilmant	Morceau Symphonique, Op.88 (*tenor trombone edn: Schott ED 10484/M.D.S. or bass trombone edn: Editions Marc Reift 2007/MusT*)
Handel	Concerto in F minor, arr. Lafosse: complete (*Leduc/U.M.P.*) *or* arr. Angerer: complete (*alto/tenor trombone edn: Editions Marc Reift 226/MusT*)
Hindemith	Trombone Sonata (1941): complete (*Schott ED 3673/M.D.S.*)
Elgar Howarth	Concerto for trombone: complete (*Chester/Music Sales*)

Trombone: LRSM

G. Jacob	Trombone Concerto: any *two* movts (*Stainer & Bell*)
Larsson	Concertino for trombone, Op.45 no.7: complete (*Gehrmans/William Elkin*)
Frank Martin	Ballade (1940) (*Universal 11250/M.D.S.*)
Milhaud	Concertino d'Hiver, Op.327: complete (*A.M.P. – Schirmer/Music Sales*)
Claude Pascal	Sonate en 6 minutes 30 for bass trombone: complete (*Durand/U.M.P.*)
Jiří Pauer	Trombonetta (*Panton – Schott/M.D.S.*)
Pierre Petit	Fantaisie for bass trombone (*Leduc/U.M.P.*)
Pilss	Concerto for bass trombone: complete (*Robert King/U.M.P.*)
Serocki	Sonatina for trombone: complete (*Moeck 5302*)
Robert Spillman	Bass Trombone Concerto: complete (*Edition Musicus/MusT*)
Spisak	Concertino for Trombone: complete (*Leduc/U.M.P.*)
Alec Wilder	Sonata for bass trombone: complete (*Margun/Emerson*)

Trombone: FRSM

Candidates may choose to play their programme on either the tenor or bass trombone as may be appropriate or any combination, which may also include alto trombone. All works in the following list are published for tenor trombone unless otherwise indicated.

Malcolm Arnold	Fantasy for solo trombone, Op.101 (*Faber*)
J.S. Bach	Cello Suite no.2, BWV 1008: 1st *and* 3rd movts, *Prélude and Courante. Bach Cello Suites*, arr. Lafosse (*Leduc/U.M.P.*) or arr. Barbez for bass trombone (*Leduc/U.M.P.*)
Derek Bourgeois	Trombone Concerto, Op.114: complete (*Brand Publications/Smith*) Fantasy Pieces for solo trombone: no.8, *Allegro moderato and* no.9, *Adagio cantabile* (*tenor* or *bass trombone edns: Brass Wind*)
Roger Boutry	Capriccio (*Leduc/U.M.P.*)
Bozza	New Orleans for bass trombone (*Leduc/U.M.P.*) Thème Variée for bass trombone (*Leduc/U.M.P.*)
Büsser	Étude de Concert, Op.79 (*Leduc/U.M.P.*)
Stephen Dodgson	Concerto for bass trombone: 3rd *and* 4th movts (*Studio Music*)
Françaix	Concerto for trombone (1983): complete (*Schott ED 7253/M.D.S.*)
Edward Gregson	Trombone Concerto: complete (*Novello/Music Sales*)
Walter Hartley	Sonata Brève for solo bass trombone: complete (*Theodore Presser 2423/U.M.P.*)
Hindemith	Trombone Sonata (1941): complete (*Schott ED 3673/M.D.S.*)
Elgar Howarth	Concerto for trombone: complete (*Chester/Music Sales*)
G. Jacob	Trombone Concerto: complete (*Stainer & Bell*)
Alain Margoni	Après une Lecture de Goldini for bass trombone (*Leduc/U.M.P.*)
Frank Martin	Ballade (1940) (*Universal 11250/M.D.S.*)
Tomasi	Trombone Concerto: complete (*Leduc/U.M.P.*)
Simon Wills	Concerto for trombone: complete (*Studio Music*)

Baritone and Euphonium: DipABRSM

All works in the following list are published in a bass clef version unless otherwise indicated.

Derek Bourgeois	Euphoria, Op.75 (*Vanderbeek & Imrie*)
Brian Bowen	Euphonium Music: any *two* movts (*bass/treble clef edn: Rosehill Music*)
Arthur Butterworth	Partita, Op.89: complete (*treble clef edn: Comus Edition*)
Jean-Michel Defaye	2 Danses: complete (*bass trombone edn: Leduc/U.M.P.*)
Elgar	Romance, Op.62, arr. Wilson (*bass/treble clef edn: Rosehill Music*)
Fiocco	Arioso and Allegro, arr. Childs and Wilby (*bass/treble clef edn: Rosehill Music*)
Edward Gregson	Prelude and Capriccio (*for cornet*) (*treble clef edn: Brand Publications/Smith*)
Guilmant	Morceau Symphonique, Op.88 (*bass/treble clef edn: Editions Marc Reift 2013/MusT*)
Walter Hartley	Sonata Euphonica (1979): complete (*bass/treble clef edn: Tenuto Publications PR 1624/U.M.P.*)
Joseph Horovitz	Euphonium Concerto: 1st *and* 2nd movts, *or* 2nd *and* 3rd movts (*treble clef edn: Novello/Music Sales*)
Hummel	Fantasy, arr. Childs and Wilby from Op.94 (*bass/treble clef edn: Rosehill Music*)
G. Jacob	Fantasia for euphonium (*bass/treble clef edn: Boosey & Hawkes*)

Baritone and Euphonium: DipABRSM

Philip Sparke	Fantasy for euphonium (*treble clef edn: Brand Publications/Smith*)
	Pantomime for euphonium (*treble clef edn: Studio Music*)
	Party Piece for euphonium (*bass/treble clef edn: Studio Music*)
	Rhapsody for baritone (*treble clef edn: Studio Music*)
Ray Woodfield	Caprice for euphonium (*bass/treble clef edn: Hallamshire Music*)
Ernest Young	Euphonium Sonata (no.1): complete (*bass/treble clef edn: Brand Publications/Smith*)
	Euphonium Sonata no.2: complete (*treble clef edn: Suite Music*)

Baritone and Euphonium: LRSM

All works in the following list are published in a bass clef version unless otherwise indicated.

Jean-Michel Defaye	2 Danses: complete (*bass trombone edn: Leduc/U.M.P.*)
Elgar	Romance, Op.62, arr. Wilson (*bass/treble clef edn: Rosehill Music*)
Martin Ellerby	Euphonium Concerto: 1st *and* 3rd movts, *Fantasy* **and** *Rhapsody* (for Luis) (*bass/treble clef edn: Studio Music*)
John Golland	Rhapsody no.2 for baritone ('Don Quixote'), Op.89 (*treble clef edn: Kirklees Music*)
Guilmant	Morceau Symphonique, Op.88 (*bass/treble clef edn: Editions Marc Reift 2013/MusT*)
Joseph Horovitz	Euphonium Concerto: complete (*treble clef edn: Novello/Music Sales*)
Hummel	Fantasy, arr. Childs and Wilby from Op.94 (*bass/treble clef edn: Rosehill Music*)
G. Jacob	Fantasia for euphonium (*bass/treble clef edn: Boosey & Hawkes*)
Paul Mealor	Baritone Concerto: 2nd *and* 3rd movts (*treble clef edn: Con Moto Publications/Mostyn Music*)
John Reeman	Sonata for euphonium: complete (*bass/treble clef edn: Studio Music*)
Antony Roper	Sonata for euphonium: complete (*bass/treble clef edn: Studio Music*)
Philip Sparke	Euphonium Concerto: 1st movt (*bass/treble clef edn: Studio Music*)
	Fantasy for euphonium (*treble clef edn: Brand Publications/Smith*)
	Pantomime for euphonium (*treble clef edn: Studio Music*)
	Party Piece for euphonium (*bass/treble clef edn: Studio Music*)
Stanford	Caoine (from Sonata, Op.129), arr. Childs and Wilby (*bass/treble clef edn: Rosehill Music*)
Bram Wiggins	Trilogy for euphonium (*treble clef edn: Kirklees Music*)
Christopher Wiggins	Soliloquy IX for solo euphonium, Op.94 no.9 (*treble clef edn: Studio Music*)
Philip Wilby	Concerto for euphonium: Part 2 – 3rd *and* 4th movts (*bass/treble clef edn: Rosehill Music*)

Baritone and Euphonium: FRSM

All works in the following list are published in a bass clef version unless otherwise indicated.

Derek Bourgeois	Euphonium Concerto, Op.120: 1st *and* 2nd movts, *or* 2nd *and* 3rd movts (*treble clef edn: Brass Wind*)
Bozza	Allegro et Finale (*bass trombone/tuba edn: Leduc/U.M.P.*)
Martin Ellerby	Euphonium Concerto: any *three* movts (*bass/treble clef edn: Studio Music*)
John Golland	Euphonium Concerto (no.1), Op.64: complete (*bass/treble clef edn: Chester/Music Sales*)
	Euphonium Concerto no.2, Op.77: complete (*bass/treble clef edn: Studio Music*)
Paul Mealor	Baritone Concerto: complete (*treble clef edn: Con Moto Publications/Mostyn Music*)
Ponchielli	Concerto for euphonium: complete (*bass/treble clef edn: Editions Marc Reift 243/MusT*)
John Reeman	Sonata for euphonium: complete (*bass/treble clef edn: Studio Music*)
Philip Sparke	Euphonium Concerto: complete (*bass/treble clef edn: Studio Music*)
Philip Wilby	Concerto for euphonium: complete (*bass/treble clef edn: Rosehill Music*)

Tuba: DipABRSM

Candidates may choose to play their programme on a tuba in any key, provided that the tuba parts are suitably transposed where necessary. All works in the following list are published in a bass clef version unless otherwise indicated.

Malcolm Arnold	Fantasy for solo tuba, Op.102 (*Faber*)
Derek Bourgeois	Fantasy Pieces for solo tuba: no.8, *Moderato pesante* **or** no.9, *Allegro vivace* (*Brass Wind*)
Harold East	Sonatina for tuba: 1st *and* 2nd movts (*Ricordi/U.M.P.*)
Jennifer Glass	Sonatina for tuba: 1st *and* 2nd movts, *or* 3rd *and* 4th movts (*Emerson*)
Edward Gregson	Tuba Concerto: complete (*Novello/Music Sales*)
Walter Hartley	Suite for solo tuba: complete (*Elkan-Vogel/U.M.P.*)
Bernhard Heiden	Concerto for tuba (1976): 1st *and* 2nd movts, *or* 2nd *and* 3rd movts (*Peer Southern/William Elkin*)
Hindemith	Sonata for tuba (1955): complete (*Schott ED 4636/M.D.S.*)

REPERTOIRE LISTS

Tuba: DipABRSM

Michael Hopkinson	Concerto for tuba ('Concerto Euphonique'): 2nd *and* 3rd movts (*E♭ or B♭ treble clef edns: Kirklees Music*)
Persichetti	Serenade no.12 for solo tuba, Op.88: complete (*Elkan-Vogel/U.M.P.*)
Leonard Salzedo	Sonata for tuba, Op.93: complete (*Chester/Music Sales*)
Roger Steptoe	Concerto for tuba: 1st *and* 3rd movts (*Stainer & Bell*)
Donald Swann	2 Moods for tuba: Elegy *and* Scherzo (*Chamber Music Library/Emerson*)
Tomasi	Danse Sacrée (*B♭/C bass clef edn: Leduc/U.M.P.*)
David Uber	Sonata for tuba: 2nd *and* 3rd movts (*Edition Musicus 964/MusT*)
Julia Usher	Venezia: any *four* movts (*Primavera*)
Vaughan Williams	Tuba Concerto in F minor: 1st *and* 2nd movts (*O.U.P.*)

Tuba: LRSM

Candidates may choose to play their programme on a tuba in any key, provided that the tuba parts are suitably transposed where necessary. All works in the following list are published in a bass clef version unless otherwise indicated.

Malcolm Arnold	Fantasy for solo tuba, Op.102 (*Faber*)
Derek Bourgeois	Fantasy Pieces for solo tuba: no.8, *Moderato pesante and* no.9, *Allegro vivace* (*Brass Wind*)
P.M. Dubois	Piccolo Suite for tuba: complete (*Leduc/U.M.P.*)
Harold East	Sonatina for tuba: complete (*Ricordi/U.M.P.*)
Jennifer Glass	Sonatina for tuba: complete (*Emerson*)
	Prelude, Waltz and Finale for solo tuba: complete (*Griffiths Edition*)
John Golland	Tuba Concerto, Op.46: 1st *and* 2nd movts (*bass/treble clef edn: Con Moto Publications/Mostyn Music*)
Edward Gregson	Tuba Concerto: complete (*Novello/Music Sales*)
Bernhard Heiden	Concerto for tuba (1976): complete (*Peer Southern/William Elkin*)
Hindemith	Sonata for tuba (1955): complete (*Schott ED 4636/M.D.S.*)
Michael Hopkinson	Concerto for tuba ('Concerto Euphonique'): complete (*E♭ or B♭ treble clef edns: Kirklees Music*)
Jan Koetsier	Sonatina for tuba, Op.57: complete (*Editions Marc Reift 239/MusT*)
Claude Pascal	Sonate en 6 minutes 30 for tuba: complete (*Durand/U.M.P.*)
Pierre Petit	Fantaisie for tuba (*Leduc/U.M.P.*)
Leonard Salzedo	Sonata for tuba, Op.93: complete (*Chester/Music Sales*)
Roger Steptoe	Concerto for tuba: complete (*Stainer & Bell*)
David Uber	Sonata for tuba: complete (*Edition Musicus 964/MusT*)
Christopher Wiggins	Soliloquy X for solo tuba, Op.94 no.10 (*Studio Music*)
Vaughan Williams	Tuba Concerto in F minor: complete (*O.U.P.*)

Tuba: FRSM

Candidates may choose to play their programme on a tuba in any key, provided that the tuba parts are suitably transposed where necessary. All works in the following list are published in a bass clef version unless otherwise indicated.

Derek Bourgeois	Tuba Concerto, Op.38: any *three* movts (*Brass Wind*)
Jennifer Glass	Prelude, Waltz and Finale for solo tuba: complete (*Griffiths Edition*)
John Golland	Tuba Concerto, Op.46: complete (*bass/treble clef edn: Con Moto Publications/Mostyn Music*)
Alain Margoni	Après une Lecture de Goldini for tuba (*Leduc/U.M.P.*)
Rodney Newton	Capriccio for tuba (*bass/treble edn: Rosehill Music*)
Philip Sparke	Concertino for tuba: complete (*treble clef edn: Studio Music*)
Christopher Wiggins	Soliloquy X for solo tuba, Op.94 no.10 (*Studio Music*)
Vaughan Williams	Tuba Concerto in F minor: complete (*O.U.P.*)

Percussion: DipABRSM

Candidates must present a programme which includes at least one work from each of three of the following four sections (Tuned Percussion, Timpani, Snare Drum, Multiple Percussion).

Tuned Percussion

Creston	Concertino for marimba and piano: any *two* movts (*Schirmer/Music Sales*)
David Hext	Suite for solo marimba: complete (*Woodsmoor Press/Southern Percussion*)
Toshiro Mayuzumi	Concertino for xylophone and piano: complete (*Peters EP 6856a*)
Mitchell Peters	Yellow after the Rain for marimba (*Southern Percussion*)
Ney Rosauro	Suite Popular Brasileira for marimba solo: complete (*Music for Percussion/Southern Percussion*)

Timpani

John Beck	Sonata for 4 timpani: complete (*Boston Music Co./Southern Percussion*)
David Mancini	Suite (no.1) for 4 timpani: complete (*Kendor/William Elkin* or *Kendor/Southern Percussion*)

Snare Drum

Warren Benson	3 Dances: complete (*Woodsmoor Press/Southern Percussion*)
Siegfried Fink	Trommel-Suite: complete (*Zimmermann/Southern Percussion*)

Multiple Percussion

Tom Gauger	Nomad: Solo Jazz March for multiple percussion (*Southern Percussion*)
Martin Westlake	Percussion Solo no.1 (*Woodsmoor Press/Southern Percussion*)
	Percussion Solo no.2 (*Woodsmoor Press/Southern Percussion*)

Percussion: LRSM

Candidates must present a programme which includes at least one work from each of three of the following four sections (Tuned Percussion, Timpani, Snare Drum, Multiple Percussion), so that at least one item includes a part for a tuned percussion instrument.

Tuned Percussion

Keiko Abe	Michi for marimba (*Meredith Music/Southern Percussion*)
Creston	Concertino for marimba and piano: complete (*Schirmer/Music Sales*)
Mark Glentworth	Blues for Gilbert for vibraphone (*Zimmermann/Southern Percussion*)
David Hext	Plainsong for vibraphone (*Woodsmoor Press/Southern Percussion*)
	Suite for solo marimba: complete (*Woodsmoor Press/Southern Percussion*)
Toshiro Mayuzumi	Concertino for xylophone and piano: complete (*Peters EP 6856a*)
Mitchell Peters	Yellow after the Rain for marimba (*Southern Percussion*)
Ney Rosauro	Suite Popular Brasileira for marimba solo: complete (*Music for Percussion/Southern Percussion*)
Emmanuel Séjourné	5 Pieces for marimba solo: any *two* pieces (*Leduc/U.M.P.*)
Gordon Stout	2 Mexican Dances for marimba: complete (*Studio 4/Southern Percussion*)

Timpani

John Beck	Sonata for 4 timpani: complete (*Boston Music Co./Southern Percussion*)
David Mancini	Suite (no.1) for 4 timpani: complete (*Kendor/William Elkin* or *Kendor/Southern Percussion*)
Nick Woud	Paul's Piece (*Southern Percussion*)

Snare Drum

Warren Benson	3 Dances: complete (*Woodsmoor Press/Southern Percussion*)
Siegfried Fink	Trommel-Suite: complete (*Zimmermann/Southern Percussion*)
Guy Gauthreaux II	American Suite for solo snare drum: complete (*Meredith Music/Southern Percussion*)

Multiple Percussion

Charles Delancey	The Love of l'Histoire (*Southern Percussion*)
Tom Gauger	Nomad: Solo Jazz March for multiple percussion (*Southern Percussion*)
Robert Stern	Adventures for One (*Music for Percussion/Southern Percussion*)
Martin Westlake	Percussion Solo no.1 (*Woodsmoor Press/Southern Percussion*)
	Percussion Solo no.2 (*Woodsmoor Press/Southern Percussion*)

Percussion: FRSM

Candidates must present a programme which includes at least one work from each of three of the following four sections (Tuned Percussion, Timpani, Snare Drum, Multiple Percussion), so that at least one item includes a part for a tuned percussion instrument.

Tuned Percussion

Minoru Miki	Time for marimba (*Ongaku No Tomo Sha Corp./Southern Percussion*)
Ney Rosauro	Bem Vido for vibraphone (*Pro Percussão/Southern Percussion*)
	Marimba Concerto: 1st, 2nd *and* 4th movts (*Southern Percussion*)
Paul Smadbeck	Rhythm Song for one or more marimbas (*Southern Percussion*)
Toshimitsu Tanaka	2 Movements for marimba: complete (*Ongaku No Tomo Sha Corp./Southern Percussion*)

Timpani

John Beck	3 Movements for 5 timpani: complete (*Meredith Music/Southern Percussion*)
Elliot Carter	March: no.8 from '8 Pieces for 4 Timpani' (*Schirmer/Music Sales*)
Graham Whettam	Suite for timpani: any *three* movts (*Meriden Music*)

Snare Drum

Askell Masson	Prime (*Iceland Music/Southern Percussion*)
Geryt Mortensen	March-Cadenza (*Southern Percussion*)

Multiple Percussion

Morton Feldman	King of Denmark (*Peters EP 6963*)
Dave Hollinden	Cold Pressed (*Southern Percussion*)
Poul Rugers	Cha cha cha (*Southern Percussion*)

Singing: DipABRSM

The repertoire lists below are presented according to standard voice categories. As well as choosing items from the list appropriate to their voice, candidates may perform suitable items from other of the DipABRSM Singing lists. Candidates should include in their programme at least one song or aria which is in a different language from the other chosen items. All opera and oratorio items should be sung in the keys in which they were written, respecting original pitch if appropriate; otherwise, all songs may be sung in any key suited to the candidate's voice. See p. 7 for performing from memory.

Soprano

Arne	Recit. and Air 'O ravishing delight!' (*Novello/Music Sales*)
J.S. Bach	Aria: Blute nur: from 'St Matthew Passion', Part 1, BWV 244 (*vocal score Ger/Eng: Bärenreiter BA 5038a*)
	Aria: Quia respexit humilitatem: no.3 from Magnificat in D, BWV 243 (*vocal score: Bärenreiter BA 5103a*) *or* no.3 from Magnificat in E♭, BWV 243a (*vocal score: Bärenreiter BA 5208a*)
	Aria: Seufzer, Tränen, Kummer, Not: no.3 from Cantata no.21 'Ich hatte viel Bekümmernis', BWV 21 (*vocal score Ger/Eng: Breitkopf & Härtel 7021*)
Barber	The Monk and his Cat: no.8 from 'Hermit Songs', Op.29 (*high*) (*Schirmer/Music Sales*)
Bax	Shieling Song. *Bax Album of 7 Songs* (*Chester/Music Sales*)
Beethoven	Wonne der Wehmut, Op.83 no.1. *Beethoven Songs Complete, Vol.2* (*Henle* or *Henle – Schott/M.D.S.*)
Berg	Die Nachtigall: no.2 from '7 Early Songs' (*Ger/Eng edn: Universal 08853/M.D.S.*)
Berlioz	Villanelle: no.1 from 'Les Nuits d'Été', Op.7 (*high*) (*Bärenreiter BA 5784a* or *Fr/Eng edn: International 1355/M.D.S.*)
Brahms	Junge Lieder I 'Meine Liebe ist grün', Op.63 no.5. *Brahms 70 Songs* (*high*) (*Ger/Eng edn: International 1270/M.D.S.*) or *Brahms Complete Songs, Vol.1* (*high*) (*Peters EP 3201a*)
Britten	Corpus Christi Carol (arr. as solo song from 'A Boy was Born', Op.3) (*high*) (*O.U.P.*)
Chausson	Le Colibri, Op.2 no.7 (*Leduc/U.M.P.*)
Fauré	Après un Rêve, Op.7 no.1 ⎤
	Nell, Op.18 no.1 ⎦ *Fauré 25 Selected Songs* (*high*) (*Fr/Eng edn: Schirmer/Music Sales*)
	Pie Jesu: no.4 from 'Requiem', Op.48 (*vocal score: Novello/Music Sales*)
Grieg	Solveig's Song, Op.23 no.11 (*high*) (*Ger/Eng/Fr edn: Peters EP 2453a*)
Gurney	Sleep: no.4 from '5 Elizabethan Songs' (*Boosey & Hawkes* or *separately: Boosey & Hawkes*)
Handel	Recit.: Oh! didst thou know the pains of absent love *and* Air: As when the dove laments her love: from 'Acis and Galatea', Part 1, HWV 49a (*vocal score: Novello/Music Sales*)
	Recit.: Ye sacred priests *and* Air: Farewell, ye limpid springs and floods: from 'Jephtha', Part 3, HWV 70 (*vocal score: Novello/Music Sales*)
	Aria: Oh! had I Jubal's lyre (from 'Joshua', HWV 64) (*aria separately: Schirmer/Music Sales*)
	Recit.: Ah me! what refuge now *and* Air: Oh Jove! in pity teach me: from 'Semele', Act 1, HWV 58 (*vocal score: Novello/Music Sales*)

Singing: DipABRSM

Soprano

Haydn Recit.: And God said, let the waters *and* Aria: On mighty pens uplifted: from 'The Creation', Part 2 (*vocal score Eng: Novello/Music Sales* or *vocal score Ger/Eng: Peters EP 66*)

Head Make a joyful noise unto the Lord (Psalm 100) (*high*) (*Roberton/Goodmusic*)

Mahler Wer hat dies Liedlein erdacht? (Up there on the Hill) (from 'Des Knaben Wunderhorn') (*high*) (*Ger/Eng edn: Universal 03642A/M.D.S.*)

Mozart Alleluia (from motet 'Exsultate, jubilate', K.165) (*Novello/Music Sales*)
Aria: Batti, batti, o bel Masetto: from 'Don Giovanni', Act 1, K.527 (*vocal score Ital/Ger: Bärenreiter BA 4550a* or *vocal score Ital/Eng: Boosey & Hawkes*)
Aria: In uomini, in soldati: from 'Così fan tutte', Act 1, K.588 (*vocal score Ital/Ger: Bärenreiter BA 4606a* or *vocal score Ital/Eng: Schirmer/Music Sales*)

Thea Musgrave The Man-in-the-Mune *and* Daffins: nos.1 *and* 2 from 'A Suite O Bairnsangs' (*Chester/Music Sales*)

Perti Aria: Scioglie omai le nevi. *A Selection of Italian Arias 1600–1800, Vol.1* (*high*) (*Ital/Eng edn: Associated Board*)

Poulenc Air vif: no.4 from 'Airs chantés' (*Salabert/U.M.P.*)

Puccini Aria: O mio babbino caro: from 'Gianni Schicchi' (*aria separately Ital/Eng edn: Ricordi/U.M.P.* or *vocal score Ital/Eng: Ricordi/U.M.P.*)

Purcell Bonvica's Song 'O lead me to some peaceful gloom' (from 'Bonduca', Z.574). *Purcell Songs, Vol.2* (*high*) (*Schott ED 12411/M.D.S.*)
Hark! the echoing air: from 'The Fairy Queen', Act 5, Z.629 (*vocal score: Faber* or *Novello/Music Sales*)

Rossini Crucifixus: no.9 from 'Petite Messe Solenelle' (*vocal score: Ricordi/U.M.P.*)

A. Scarlatti Aria: Ergiti, amor (from 'Scipione nelle Spagne'). *Scarlatti 10 Arias for High Voice* (*Schirmer/Music Sales*)

Schubert Liebesbotschaft: no.1 from 'Schwanengesang', D.957. *Schubert Lieder, Vol.9* (*high*) (*Bärenreiter BA 7016*) or *Schubert Songs, Vol.1* (*high*) (*Peters EP 8303a*)
Lied der Mignon 'Nur wer die Sehnsucht kennt', Op.62 no.4, D.877/4. *Schubert Lieder, Vol.4* (*high*) (*Bärenreiter BA 7006*) or *Schubert Songs, Vol.3* (*high*) (*Peters EP 8305a*)

Schumann Du bist wie eine Blume: no.24 from 'Myrthen', Op.25. *Schumann 85 Selected Songs* (*high*) (*Ger/Eng edn: International 1487/M.D.S.*) or *Schumann Complete Songs, Vol.1* (*high*) (*Peters EP 2383a*)
Röselein, Röselein!, Op.89 no.6. *Schumann 85 Selected Songs* (*high*) (*Ger/Eng edn: International 1487/ M.D.S.*) or *Schumann Complete Songs, Vol.3* (*high*) (*Peters EP 2385a*)

R. Strauss Du meines Herzens Krönlein, Op.21 no.2. *Strauss Lieder, Vol.1* (*high*) (*Universal 05463A/M.D.S.*)

Tippett Solo: The Mother 'What have I done to you, my son?': no.23 from 'A Child of Our Time', Part 2 (*vocal score: Schott ED 10065/M.D.S.*)

Vivaldi Domine Deus: no.6 from Gloria in D, RV 589 (*vocal score: Ricordi/U.M.P.*)

Wolf Frühling übers Jahr: no.28 from 'Goethe Lieder', Vol.3 (*high-medium*) (*Peters EP 3158*)

Mezzo-soprano, Contralto and Countertenor

C.P.E. Bach Aria: Suscepit Israel: no.7 from Magnificat in D minor, Wq.215 (*vocal score Lat/Eng: Schirmer/ Music Sales*)

J.S. Bach Aria: Et exultavit spiritus meus: no.2 from Magnificat in D, BWV 243 (*vocal score: Bärenreiter BA 5103a*) *or* no.2 from Magnificat in E♭, BWV 243a (*vocal score: Bärenreiter BA 5208a*)
Aria: Esurientes implevit bonis: no.9 from Magnificat in D, BWV 243 (*vocal score: Bärenreiter BA 5103a*) *or* no.9 from Magnificat in E♭, BWV 243a (*vocal score: Bärenreiter BA 5208a*)

Bantock Song to the Seals (*medium*) (*Cramer*)

Barber The Crucifixion *or* The Monk and his Cat: no.5 *or* no.8 from 'Hermit Songs', Op.29 (*low*) (*Schirmer/ Music Sales*)

Brahms Die Mainacht, Op.43 no.2. *Brahms 70 Songs* (*low*) (*Ger/Eng edn: International 1271/M.D.S.*) or *Brahms Complete Songs, Vol.2* (*medium-low*) (*Peters EP 3202b*)
Sapphische Ode, Op.94 no.4. *Brahms 70 Songs* (*low*) (*Ger/Eng edn: International 1271/M.D.S.*) or *Brahms Complete Songs, Vol.1* (*medium or low*) (*Peters EP 3201b or c*)
Wie Melodien zieht es mir, Op.105 no.1. *Brahms 70 Songs* (*low*) (*Ger/Eng edn: International 1271/ M.D.S.*) or *Brahms Complete Songs, Vol.1* (*medium or low*) (*Peters EP 3201b or c*)

Britten The Nurse's Song: no.5 from 'A Charm of Lullabies', Op.41 (*Boosey & Hawkes*)

Geoffrey Bush Carol: no.7
It was a lover and his lass: no.1 from ⎱ '8 Songs for Medium Voice' (*Novello/Music Sales*)

T. Campion Come you pretty false-eyed wanton
Follow your saint ⎱ *English Lute Songs, Book 1* (*Stainer & Bell*)

Canteloube Berceuse (Brezairola): no.4 from 'Chants d'Auvergne', Vol.3 (*Heugel/U.M.P.*)

Debussy Les Cloches (*medium*) (*Fr/Eng edn: Durand/U.M.P.*)

Elgar In Haven (Capri): no.2 from 'Sea Pictures', Op.37 (*Boosey & Hawkes*)
Queen Mary's Song (*medium*) (*Banks Music BSS 2019*)
The Shepherd's Song, Op.16 no.1 (*medium*) (*Banks Music BSS 2029*)

Fauré Les Berceaux, Op.23 no.1. *Fauré 25 Selected Songs* (*low*) (*Fr/Eng edn: Schirmer/Music Sales*)

Gurney Sleep: no.4 from '5 Elizabethan Songs' (*Boosey & Hawkes* or *separately* (*low*): *Boosey & Hawkes archive copy*)

Handel Air: Hymen, haste, thy torch prepare: from 'Semele', Act 1, HWV 58 (*vocal score: Novello/Music Sales*)
Air: Your tuneful voice: from 'Semele', Act 1, HWV 58 (*vocal score: Novello/Music Sales*)
Recit.: Awake, Saturnia *and* Air: Hence, Iris, hence away: from 'Semele', Act 2, HWV 58 (*vocal score: Novello/Music Sales*)
Solo: Virgam virtutis: no.2 from 'Dixit Dominus', HWV 232 (*vocal score: Novello/Music Sales*)

Mahler Hans und Grethe. *Mahler 24 Songs, Vol.1* (*low*) (*Ger/Eng edn: International 1237/M.D.S.*)

B. Marcello Recit.: Misero! io vengo meno *and* Aria: Non m'è grave morir per amore. *Anthology of Italian Songs of the 17th and 18th Centuries, Book 2* (*low*) (*Ital/Eng edn: Schirmer/Music Sales*)

Massenet Recit: Va! Laisse couler mes larmes *and* Aria: Les larmes qu'on ne pleure pas (The Tears): from 'Werther', Act 3 (*separately Fr/Eng edn: International 0490/M.D.S.*)

Menotti Aria: I shall find for you shells and stars: from 'The Consul' (*vocal score: Schirmer/Music Sales*)

Monteverdi E pur io torno: from 'L'Incoronazione di Poppea', Act 1 scene 1 (*vocal score: Novello/Music Sales*)
Recit.: Adagiati, Poppea *and* Aria: Oblivion soave: from 'L'Incoronazione di Poppea', Act 3. *A Selection of Italian Arias 1600–1800, Vol.1* (*low*) (*Ital/Eng edn: Associated Board*)

Mozart Aria: È amore un ladroncello: from 'Così fan tutte', Act 2, K.588 (*vocal score Ital/Ger: Bärenreiter BA 4606a* or *vocal score Ital/Eng: Schirmer/Music Sales*)

Pergolesi Fac ut portem Christi mortem: no.10 from 'Stabat Mater' (*vocal score Lat/Eng: O.U.P.* or *vocal score Lat: Ricordi/U.M.P.*)

Purcell An Evening Hymn 'Now that the sun hath veiled his light', Z.193. *Purcell Songs, Vol.5* (*low*) (*Schott ED 12494/M.D.S.*)
Here the deities approve: from 'Welcome to all the pleasures' (St Cecilia's Day Ode), Z.339 (*Novello/Music Sales*)
Sweeter than Roses (from 'Pausanias', Z.585). *Purcell Songs, Vol.4* (*low*) (*Schott ED 12493/M.D.S.*)

Saint-Saëns La Cloche (*medium*) (*Fr/Eng edn: Durand/U.M.P.*)

Schoenberg Waldesnacht. *Schoenberg 7 Early Songs* (*Faber*)

Schubert Bei dir allein!, Op.95 no.2, D.866/2. *Schubert Songs, Vol.4* (*medium* or *low*) (*Peters EP 8306b* or *c*)
Lied der Mignon 'So lasst mich scheinen', Op.62 no.3, D.877/3. *Schubert Songs, Vol.3* (*medium* or *low*) (*Peters EP 8305b* or *c*)

Schumann Abschied von der Welt, Op.135 no.4. *Schumann Complete Songs, Vol.3* (*medium-low*) (*Peters EP 2385b*)
Die Soldatenbraut, Op.64 no.1. *Schumann 90 Selected Songs* (*low*) (*Ger/Eng edn: International 1402/M.D.S.*) or *Schumann Complete Songs, Vol.1* (*medium* or *low*) (*Peters EP 2383b* or *c*)
Frauenliebe und Leben, Op.42: any of the 8 songs (*low*) (*Ger/Eng edn: International 2131/M.D.S.*) or *Schumann Complete Songs, Vol.1* (*medium* or *low*) (*Peters EP 2383b* or *c*)

Sibelius Black Roses, Op.36 no.1 (*low*) (*Eng/Ger/Swe edn: Breitkopf & Härtel 5906*)

R. Strauss Schlagende Herzen, Op.29 no.2. *Strauss Lieder, Vol.3* (*medium* or *low*) (*Universal 05465b* or *c/M.D.S.*)
Traum durch die Dämmerung, Op.29 no.1 (*medium* or *low*) (*Universal 05445b* or *c/M.D.S.*)

Vaughan Williams The Water Mill. *Vaughan Williams Collected Songs for medium voice, Vol.2* (*O.U.P.*)

Walton Beatriz's Song (Romanza from 'Christopher Columbus'). *Walton Song Album* (*O.U.P.*)

Warlock Fair and True (*O.U.P.*)
Late Summer. *Warlock Collected Solo Songs, Vol.3* (*medium*) (*Thames Publishing/William Elkin*)

Wolf Mausfallen-Sprüchlein. *Wolf Lieder by Various Poets, Vol.1* (*high-medium*) (*Ger/Eng edn: Peters EP 3153*) or *Wolf 51 Selected Songs* (*medium-low*) (*Ger/Eng edn: Peters EP 4290b*)

Tenor

Arne Now Phoebus sinketh in the West (from 'Comus'). *Arne Selected Songs* (*Cramer*)

J.S. Bach Aria: Benedictus qui venit: no.25 from Mass in B minor, Part 5, BWV 232 (*vocal score: Bärenreiter BA 5102a*)
Aria: Deposuit potentes: no.8 from Magnificat in D, BWV 243 (*vocal score: Bärenreiter BA 5103a*) *or* no.8 from Magnificat in E♭, BWV 243a (*vocal score: Bärenreiter BA 5208a*)

L. Berkeley The Horseman: no.1 from '5 Songs (of de la Mare)', Op.26 (*Chester/Music Sales*)

Singing: DipABRSM

Tenor

Brahms   Minnelied, Op.71 no.5. *Brahms 70 Songs* (*high*) (*Ger/Eng edn: International 1270/M.D.S.*) or *Brahms Complete Songs, Vol.1* (*high*) (*Peters EP 3201a*)

Sehnsucht 'Hinter jenen dichten Wäldern', Op.49 no.3. *Brahms 70 Songs* (*high*) (*Ger/Eng edn: International 1270/M.D.S.*) or *Brahms Complete Songs, Vol.3* (*high*) (*Peters EP 3691a*)

Wir wandelten, Op.96 no.2. *Brahms 70 Songs* (*high*) (*Ger/Eng edn: International 1270/M.D.S.*) or *Brahms Complete Songs, Vol.1* (*high*) (*Peters EP 3201a*)

Britten   Corpus Christi Carol (arr. as solo song from 'A Boy was Born', Op.3) (*high*) (*O.U.P.*)

The Choirmaster's Burial: no.5 from 'Winter Words', Op.52 (*high*) (*Boosey & Hawkes*)

Delius   Twilight Fancies (Evening Voices) | *Delius 19 Songs* (*O.U.P.*)
Young Venevil (Sweet Venevil) |

Duparc   Soupir: no.11 from 'Mélodies' (*high*) (*Salabert/U.M.P.*)

Fauré   Après un Rêve, Op.7 no.1 | *Fauré 25 Selected Songs* (*high*) (*Fr/Eng edn: Schirmer/Music Sales*)
Toujours, Op.21 no.2 |

Grieg   Ein Traum (A Dream), Op.48 no.6 (*high*) (*Ger/Eng/Fr edn: Peters EP 2622a*)

Gurney   Desire in Spring. *Gurney 20 Favourite Songs* (*O.U.P.*)

Sleep: no.4 from '5 Elizabethan Songs' (*Boosey & Hawkes* or *separately: Boosey & Hawkes*)

Handel   Recit.: Horror! confusion! harsh this music grates *and* Air: Open thy marble jaws, O tomb: from 'Jephtha', Part 2, HWV 70 (*vocal score: Novello/Music Sales*)

Recit.: Lo! Here my love! *and* Air: Love in her eyes sits playing: from 'Acis and Galatea', Part 1, HWV 49a (*vocal score: Novello/Music Sales*)

Recit.: His hideous love provokes my rage *and* Air: Love sounds the alarm: from 'Acis and Galatea', Part 2, HWV 49a (*vocal score: Novello/Music Sales*)

Haydn   Recit.: And God created man *and* Aria: In native worth: from 'The Creation', Part 2 (*vocal score Eng: Novello/Music Sales* or *vocal score Ger/Eng: Peters EP 66*)

Ireland   The Lent Lily *and* Goal and Wicket: nos.1 *and* 3 from 'The Land of Lost Content' (*Stainer & Bell*) or *Ireland Complete Works for Voice, Vol.1* (*high*) (*Stainer & Bell*)

Mozart   Aria: Il mio tesoro intanto: from 'Don Giovanni', Act 2, K.527 (*vocal score Ital/Ger: Bärenreiter BA 4550a* or *vocal score Ital/Eng: Boosey & Hawkes*)

Aria: Un'aura amorosa: from 'Così fan tutte', Act 1, K.588 (*vocal score Ital/Ger: Bärenreiter BA 4606a* or *vocal score Ital/Eng: Schirmer/Music Sales*)

O. Nicolai   Aria: Hark, the Lark (Horch, die Lerche singt im Hain!): from 'The Merry Wives of Windsor', Act 2 (*vocal score Eng: Schirmer/Music Sales*)

Rachmaninov   In the silent night, Op.4 no.3. *Rachmaninov Songs, Vol.1* (*Boosey & Hawkes*)

Rossini   La Danza (no.8 from 'Soirées Musicales') (*high*) (*Ital/Eng edn: Ricordi/U.M.P.*)

Aria: Se il mio nome: from 'Il Barbiere di Siviglia', Act 1 (*vocal score Ital/Eng: Ricordi/U.M.P.* or *Schirmer/Music Sales*)

A. Scarlatti   Già il sole dal Gange (from 'L'Honestà negli amore'). *Italian Songs of the 17th and 18th Centuries, Vol.1* (*high*) (*Ital/Eng edn: International 2231/M.D.S.*)

Schubert   Liebesbotschaft: no.1 from 'Schwanengesang', D.957 | *Schubert Lieder, Vol.9* (*high*)
Ihr Bild: no.9 from 'Schwanengesang', D.957 | (*Bärenreiter BA 7016*) or *Schubert Songs,*
Das Fischermädchen: no.10 from 'Schwanengesang', D.957 | *Vol.1* (*high*) (*Peters EP 8303a*)

Schumann   Dichterliebe, Op.48: any of the 16 songs (*high*) (*Ger/Eng edn: International 1823/M.D.S.*) or *Schumann Complete Songs, Vol.1* (*high*) (*Peters EP 2383a*)

Ich wandelte unter den Bäumen, Op.24 no.3. *Schumann Complete Songs, Vol.2* (*high*) (*Peters EP 2384a*)

Warlock   Yarmouth Fair (*medium*) (*O.U.P.*)

Wolf   Der Tambour: no.5 from 'Mörike Lieder', Vol.1 (*high-medium*) (*Ger/Eng edn: Peters EP 3140a*)

Schlafendes Jesukind: no.25 from 'Mörike Lieder', Vol.3 (*high-medium*) (*Ger/Eng edn: Peters EP 3142a*)

Baritone and Bass

J. S. Bach   Aria: Gebt mir meinen Jesum wieder: from 'St Matthew Passion', Part 2, BWV 244 (*vocal score Ger/Eng: Bärenreiter BA 5038a*)

Recit.: Mein Gott! wann kommt das schone Nun! *and* Aria: Ich freue mich auf meinen Tod: nos.4 *and* 5 from Cantata no.82 'Ich habe genug', BWV 82 (*vocal score Ger/Eng: Breitkopf & Härtel 7082*)

Aria: Quia fecit mihi magna: no.5 from Magnificat in D, BWV 243 (*vocal score: Bärenreiter BA 5103a*) *or* no.5 from Magnificat in E♭, BWV 243a (*vocal score: Bärenreiter BA 5208a*)

L. Berkeley   The Song of the Soldiers: no.4 from '5 Songs (of de la Mare)', Op.26 (*Chester/Music Sales*)

Brahms   Auf dem Kirchhofe, Op.105 no.4. *Brahms 70 Songs* (*low*) (*Ger/Eng edn: International 1271/M.D.S.*) or *Brahms Complete Songs, Vol.1* (*medium* or *low*) (*Peters EP 3201b* or *c*)

Nicht mehr zu dir zu gehen, Op.32 no.2. *Brahms 70 Songs* (*low*) (*Ger/Eng edn: International 1271/M.D.S.*) or *Brahms Complete Songs, Vol.2* (*medium-low*) (*Peters EP 3202b*)

Britten She's like the swallow: no.2 from '8 Folk Song Arrangements' (*medium*) (*Faber*)

Geoffrey Bush The Impatient Lover: no.3 from '8 Songs for Medium Voice' (*Novello/Music Sales*)

Duparc Testament: no.8 from 'Mélodies' (*medium*) (*Salabert/U.M.P.*)

Elgar Through the Long Days, Op.16 no.2. (*I.M.P. archive copy*)

Fauré Adieu, Op.21 no.3
Rencontre, Op.21 no.1 } *Fauré 25 Selected Songs (low) (Fr/Eng edn: Schirmer/Music Sales)*

Finzi It was a lover and his lass: no.5 from 'Let us Garlands Bring', Op.18 (*Boosey & Hawkes*)
Proud Songsters: no.10 from 'Earth and Air and Rain', Op.15 (*Boosey & Hawkes*)

Galuppi Aria: La mia ragion è questa (from 'Il Filosofo di Campagna'). *A Selection of Italian Arias 1600–1800, Vol.1 (low) (Ital/Eng edn: Associated Board)*

C.A. Gibbs The Ballad of Semmerwater (*Curwen/Music Sales*)

Gurney Hawk and Buckle. *Gurney A Second Volume of 10 Songs (O.U.P. archive copy)*
Severn Meadows. *Gurney 20 Favourite Songs (O.U.P.)*
Sleep: no.4 from '5 Elizabethan Songs' (*Boosey & Hawkes* or *separately (low): Boosey & Hawkes archive copy*)

Handel Air: Honour and arms scorn such a foe: from 'Samson', Part 2, HWV 57 (*vocal score: Novello/Music Sales*)
Recit.: I feel the Deity within **and** Air: Arm, arm ye brave!: from 'Judas Maccabaeus', Part 1, HWV 63 (*vocal score: Novello/Music Sales*)
Air: That God is great: no.4 from Chandos Anthem no.9 'O praise the Lord with one consent', HWV 254 (*vocal score: Novello/Music Sales*)

Haydn Recit.: At last the bounteous sun **and** Aria: With joy the impatient husbandman: from 'The Seasons', Spring (*vocal score Eng: Novello/Music Sales* or *vocal score Ger/Eng: Peters EP 67*)

Ireland Hope the Hornblower. *Ireland 11 Songs (Stainer & Bell)*

Mendelssohn Intro.: Draw near, all ye people **and** Aria: Lord God of Abraham: from 'Elijah', Part 1, Op.70 (*vocal score Eng: Novello/Music Sales* or *vocal score Ger: Peters EP 1749*)

Mozart Aria: In diesen heil'gen Hallen: from 'Die Zauberflöte', Act 2, K.620 (*vocal score Ger: Bärenreiter BA 4553a* or *vocal score Ger/Eng: Boosey & Hawkes*)
Aria: La Vendetta: from 'Le Nozze di Figaro', Act 1, K.492 (*vocal score Ital/Ger: Bärenreiter BA 4565a* or *vocal score Ital/Eng: Boosey & Hawkes*)

C.W. Orr When as I wake: no.2 from '2 Seventeenth-Century Poems' (*Roberton/Goodmusic*)

Puccini Aria: Vecchia zimarra: from 'La Bohème', Act 4 (*aria separately: Ricordi/U.M.P.* or *vocal score Ital/Eng: Ricordi/U.M.P.*)

Purcell Wond'rous machine: from 'Ode on St Cecilia's Day' (Hail, bright Cecilia), Z.328 (*vocal score: Novello/Music Sales*)

Quilter Blow, blow thou winter wind: no.3
Come away, death: no.1 from } '3 Shakespeare Songs', Op.6 (*low*) (*Boosey & Hawkes*)

Ravel Chanson Romanesque (from 'Don Quichotte à Dulcinée') (*Fr/Eng edn: Durand/U.M.P.*)

Schubert Auf der Donau, Op.21 no.1, D.553 } *Schubert Lieder, Vol.17 for Bass Voice (Bärenreiter BA 7032)* or
Der Schiffer 'Im Winde', Op.21 no.2, D.536 } *Schubert Songs, Vol.2 (medium or low) (Peters EP 8304b or c)*
Ihr Bild: no.9 from 'Schwanengesang', D.957. *Schubert Lieder, Vol.9 (medium) (Bärenreiter BA 7017)* or *Schubert Songs, Vol.1 (medium or low) (Peters EP 8303b or c)*

Schumann Auf das Trinkglas eines verstorbenen Freundes, Op.35 no.6. *Schumann Complete Songs, Vol.2 (medium) (Peters EP 2384b)*
Die beiden Grenadiere, Op.49 no.1. *Schumann 90 Selected Songs (low) (Ger/Eng edn: International 1402/M.D.S.)* or *Schumann Complete Songs, Vol.1 (medium or low) (Peters EP 2383b or c)*
Wehmut: no.9 from 'Liederkreis', Op.39. *Schumann 90 Selected Songs (low) (Ger/Eng edn: International 1402/M.D.S.)* or *Schumann Complete Songs, Vol.1 (medium or low) (Peters EP 2383b or c)*

Vaughan Williams Any of the following from 'Songs of Travel' (*low*): no.2 Let Beauty Awake, no.3 The Roadside Fire, no.6 The Infinite Shining Heavens (*Boosey & Hawkes*)

Warlock Jillian of Berry. *Warlock A First Book of Songs (O.U.P. archive/Banks)*
Whenas the rye reach to the chin. *Warlock Song Album (Boosey & Hawkes)*

Wolf Der Tambour: no.5 from 'Mörike Lieder', Vol.1 } (*high-medium or low*)
Fussreise: no.10 from 'Mörike Lieder', Vol.1 } (*Ger/Eng edn: Peters EP 3140a or b*)
Der Mond hat eine schwere Klag erhoben: no.7 from 'Italienisches Liederbuch', Vol.1 (*high-medium*) (*Ger/Eng edn: Peters EP 3144*) or *Wolf 15 Selected Songs from Italian Lyrics (low) (Ger/Eng edn: Peters EP 3184b)*

Singing: LRSM

The repertoire lists below are presented according to standard voice categories. As well as choosing items from the list appropriate to their voice, candidates may perform suitable items from other of the LRSM Singing lists. Candidates should include in their programme at least one song or aria which is in a different language from the other chosen items. All opera and oratorio items should be sung in the keys in which they were written, respecting original pitch if appropriate; otherwise, all songs may be sung in any key suited to the candidate's voice. See p. 11 for performing from memory.

Soprano

J.S. Bach	Recit.: Wiewohl mein Herz in Tränen schwimmt *and* Aria: Ich will dir mein Herze schenken: from 'St Matthew Passion', Part 1, BWV 244 (*vocal score Ger/Eng: Bärenreiter BA 5038a*)
Barber	Lord Jesus Christ (from 'Prayers of Kierkegaard', Op.30) (*Schirmer/Music Sales*)
L. Berkeley	Silver: no.5 from '5 Songs (of de la Mare)', Op.26 (*Chester/Music Sales*)
Berlioz	Le Spectre de la Rose: no.2 from 'Les Nuits d'Été', Op.7 (*high*) (*Bärenreiter BA 5784a* or *Fr/Eng edn: International 1355/M.D.S.*)
Brahms	Botschaft, Op.47 no.1. *Brahms 70 Songs* (*high*) (*Ger/Eng edn: International 1270/M.D.S.*) or *Brahms Complete Songs, Vol.1* (*high*) (*Peters EP 3201a*)
Britten	Nocturne 'Now through night's caressing grip': no.4 from 'On this Island', Op.11 (*Boosey & Hawkes*)
Chausson	Sérénade, Op.13 no.2. *Chausson 20 Songs* (*high*) (*Fr/Eng edn: International 1130/M.D.S.*)
Debussy	Green (Aquarelles I): no.5 from 'Ariettes Oubliées' (*high*) (*Fr/Eng edn.: International 1224/M.D.S.*)
Delius	The Nightingale. *Delius 19 Songs* (*O.U.P.*)
J. Eccles	Ah, whither shall I fly? *Eccles 8 Songs* (*Stainer & Bell*)
Fauré	Mandoline, Op.58 no.1. *Fauré 25 Selected Songs* (*high*) (*Fr/Eng edn: Schirmer/Music Sales*)
C.A. Gibbs	Why do I love? *New Imperial Edition of Soprano Songs* (*Boosey & Hawkes*)
Gurney	I shall be ever maiden. *Gurney A Third Volume of 10 Songs* (*O.U.P. archive copy*)
Gluck	Aria: Divinités du Styx: from 'Alceste', Act 1 (*aria separately: Choudens/U.M.P.* or *vocal score Fr/Ger: Bärenreiter BA 2291*)
Handel	Recit.: E pur così in un giorno *and* Aria: Piangerò la sorte mia: from 'Julius Caesar' (Giulio Cesare in Egitto), Act 3, HWV 17 (*vocal score Ital/Ger: Bärenreiter BA 4019a* or *vocal score Ital/Ger: Peters EP 3783*)
	Solo: Tecum principium: no.3 from 'Dixit Dominus', HWV 232 (*vocal score: Novello/Music Sales*)
Harty	A Lullaby. *New Imperial Edition of Soprano Songs* (*Boosey & Hawkes*)
Head	On the Wings of the Wind. *Head Song Album, Vol.1 – Songs of the Countryside* (*Boosey & Hawkes*)
Holst	Envoi: no.7 from '12 Humbert Wolfe Songs', Op.48 (*Stainer & Bell*)
Ireland	All in a garden green: no.2 from 'Five 16th-Century Poems'. *Ireland Complete Works for Voice, Vol.3* (*medium*) (*Stainer & Bell*)
	Love is a sickness full of woes. *Ireland Complete Works for Voice, Vol.1* (*high*) (*Stainer & Bell*)
Mozart	Aria: Ach, ich fühl's: from 'Die Zauberflöte', Act 2, K.620 (*vocal score Ger: Bärenreiter BA 4553a* or *vocal score Ger/Eng: Boosey & Hawkes*)
	Recit.: Giunse alfin il momento *and* Aria: Deh vieni non tardar: from 'Le Nozze di Figaro', Act 4, K.492 (*vocal score Ital/Ger: Bärenreiter BA 4565a* or *vocal score Ital/Eng: Boosey & Hawkes*)
	Exsultate, jubilate: from motet 'Exsultate, Jubilate' K.165 (*vocal score: Bärenreiter BA 4897a* or *Peters EP 8697*)
	Cavatina: Porgi amor qualche ristoro: from 'Le Nozze di Figaro', Act 2, K.492 (*vocal score Ital/Ger: Bärenreiter BA 4565a* or *vocal score Ital/Eng: Boosey & Hawkes*)
	Recit.: Solitudini amiche *and* Aria: Zeffiretti lusinghieri: from 'Idomeneo', Act 3, K.366 (*vocal score Ital/Ger: Bärenreiter BA 4562a* or *vocal score Ital/Eng: International 1315/M.D.S.*)
Parry	My heart is like a singing bird (*Novello/Music Sales*)
Poulenc	Air Champêtre: no.2 from 'Airs Chantés' (*Salabert/U.M.P.*)
Puccini	Aria: Quando me'n vo' soletta per la via (Musetta's Waltz Song): from 'La Bohème', Act 2 (*aria separately Ital/Eng: Ricordi/U.M.P.* or *vocal score Ital/Eng: Ricordi/U.M.P.*)
Purcell	From rosy bow'rs (from 'Don Quixote', Part 3, Z.578). *Purcell Songs, Vol.2* (*high*) (*Schott ED 12411/M.D.S.*)
Schubert	Auf dem Wasser zu singen, Op.72, D.774. *Schubert Lieder, Vol.8* (*high*) (*Bärenreiter BA 7014*) or *Schubert Songs, Vol.3* (*high*) (*Peters EP 8305a*)
Schumann	Nur wer die Sehnsucht kennt, Op.98a no.3. *Schumann Complete Songs, Vol.3* (*high*) (*Peters EP 2385a*)
M. Shaw	When daisies pied. *Shaw 7 Songs* (*Stainer & Bell*)
R. Strauss	Meinem Kinde, Op.37 no.3. *Strauss Lieder, Vol.1* (*high*) (*Universal 05463A/M.D.S.*)
A. Sullivan	Orpheus with his Lute. *Sullivan Songs, Book 1* (*Stainer & Bell*)
Tippett	Solo: The Mother 'What have I done to you, my son?': no.23 from 'A Child of Our Time', Part 2 (*vocal score: Schott ED 10065/M.D.S.*)

REPERTOIRE LISTS

Singing: LRSM

Soprano

Verdi Recit.: Gualtier Maldè *and* Aria: Caro nome che il mio cor: from 'Rigoletto', Act 1 (*separately: Ricordi/ U.M.P. or vocal score Ital/Eng: Ricordi/U.M.P. or Schirmer/Music Sales*)

Warlock Robin Goodfellow. *Warlock A First Book of Songs* (*O.U.P. archive/Banks*)
Lillygay: any of the 5 songs (*Chester/Music Sales*)
To the memory of a great singer. *Warlock 13 Songs for High Voice* (*Stainer & Bell*)

Wolf Elfenlied: no.16 from 'Mörike Lieder', Vol.2 (*high-medium*) (*Ger/Eng edn: Peters EP 3141a*)
In dem Schatten meiner Locken: no.2 from 'Spanisches Liederbuch', Vol.2 (*high*) (*Ger/Eng edn: Peters EP 3150*)
Zur Ruh', zur Ruh', ihr müden Glieder. *Wolf Lieder by Various Poets, Vol.2* (*high-medium*) (*Ger/Eng edn: Peters EP 3154*)

Mezzo-soprano, Contralto and Countertenor

J.S. Bach Aria: Ach bleibe doch: no.4 from Cantata no.11 'Lobet Gott in seinen Reichen', BWV 11 (*vocal score Ger/Eng: Breitkopf & Härtel 7011*)
Aria: Agnus Dei qui tollis: no.26 from Mass in B minor, BWV 232 (*vocal score: Bärenreiter BA 5102a*)
Recit.: Du lieber Heiland du *and* Aria: Buss und Reu: from 'St Matthew Passion', Part 1, BWV 244 (*vocal score Ger/Eng: Bärenreiter BA 5038a*)
Aria: Schlafe, mein Liebster: from 'Christmas Oratorio', Part 2, BWV 248 (*vocal score Ger/Eng: Bärenreiter BA 5014a*)

Barber Rain has fallen, Op.10 no.1. *Barber Collected Songs* (*low*) (*Schirmer/Music Sales*)

Bax I heard a piper piping (from '5 Irish Songs') (*Warner Chappell/I.M.P.*)

Bizet Habanera: 'L'amour est un oiseau rebelle' (from 'Carmen', Act 1) (*Choudens/U.M.P.*)

Brahms Auf dem See 'Blauer Himmel, blaue Wogen', Op.59 no.2. *Brahms Complete Songs, Vol.2* (*medium-low*) (*Peters EP 3202b*)
Immer leiser wird mein Schlummer, Op.105 no.2. *Brahms 70 Songs* (*low*) (*Ger/Eng edn: International 1271/M.D.S.*) or *Brahms Complete Songs, Vol.1* (*medium or low*) (*Peters EP 3201b or c*)

Britten A Charm: no.4 from 'A Charm of Lullabies', Op.41 (*Boosey & Hawkes*)
O Waly, Waly: no.6 from 'Folksong Arrangements', Vol.3 British Isles (*medium*) (*Boosey & Hawkes*)

Caldara Come raggio di sol. *Anthology of Italian Song of the 17th and 18th Centuries, Book 1* (*low*) (*Ital/Eng edn: Schirmer/Music Sales*)

T. Campion There is a garden in her face. *English Lute Songs, Book 1* (*Stainer & Bell*)

Cavalli Aria: Lucedissima face: from 'La Calisto', Act 2 (*vocal score: Faber archive copy*)

Chausson Le Temps des Lilas, Op.19 no.3b (*medium*) (*Salabert/U.M.P.*) or (*low*) (*Fr/Eng edn: International 2401/M.D.S.*)

Copland Going to Heaven: no.11 from '12 Poems of Emily Dickinson' (*Boosey & Hawkes*)

Debussy Mandoline (*Fr/Eng edn: Durand/U.M.P.*) or *Debussy 43 Songs* (*low*) (*International 1136/M.D.S.*)

Donizetti Recit.: È sgombro il loco *and* Cavatina: Ah! parea che per incanto: from 'Anna Bolena', Act 1 (*vocal score: Ricordi/U.M.P.*)

Dowland Flow my tears. *Dowland 50 Songs, Book 1* (*low*) (*Stainer & Bell*)

Duparc Chanson triste (no.9 from 'Mélodies') (*Salabert/U.M.P.*)

Elgar A Song of Autumn (*I.M.P. archive copy*)
Sea Slumber Song: no.1 from | 'Sea Pictures', Op.37 (*Boosey & Hawkes*)
Where Corals Lie: no.4

Fauré En Sourdine, Op.58 no.2. *Fauré 25 Selected Songs* (*low*) (*Fr/Eng edn: Schirmer/Music Sales*)

Finzi Song of Ver 'When daisies pied': from Music for 'Love's Labour's Lost', Op.28 (*Boosey & Hawkes*)

T. Ford Fair sweet cruel. *English Lute Songs, Book 1* (*Stainer & Bell*)

Gluck Recit.: Che disse! *and* Aria: Addio, addio, o miei sospiri: from 'Orfeo ed Euridice', Act 1 (*vocal score Ital/Ger: Bärenreiter BA 2294a*)
Recit. from: Caro sposa! Euridice *and* Aria: Che farò senza Euridice?: from 'Orfeo ed Euridice', Act 3 (*separately: Ricordi/U.M.P.*) or *vocal score Ital/Ger: Bärenreiter BA 2294a*)

Gurney The Singer. *Gurney 20 Favourite Songs* (*O.U.P.*)

Handel Air: Father of Heav'n!: from 'Judas Maccabaeus', Part 3, HWV 63 (*vocal score: Novello/Music Sales*)
Aria: Ombra cara: from 'Radamisto', Act 2, HWV 12b (*vocal score: Bärenreiter BA 4066a*)
Recit. from: This grief, O Josabeth *and* Air: Gloomy tyrants! we disdain: from 'Athalia', Act 1, HWV 52 (*vocal score: O.U.P. archive copy*)

Harty Sea Wrack. *New Imperial Edition of Contralto Songs* (*Boosey & Hawkes*)

Howells A Madrigal, Op.22 no.2. *Howells Songs with Piano* (*Boosey & Hawkes*)

Humfrey A Hymne to God the Father (*low*) (*Schott ED 11909/M.D.S.*)

Ireland Weathers (*medium or low*) (*Boosey & Hawkes*)

REPERTOIRE LISTS

Singing: LRSM

Mezzo-soprano, Contralto and Countertenor

Mahler	Ich atmet' einen linden Duft (*low*) (*Ger/Eng edn: International 1956/M.D.S.*)
Meyerbeer	Aria: Ah! mon fils, sois béni! (from 'Le Prophète', Act 2). *Meyerbeer Opera Arias for Alto/Mezzo-Soprano* (*Bärenreiter BA 7543*) or *Operatic Album, Vol.2* (*Ricordi/U.M.P.*)
Monteverdi	Recit.: I miei subiti sdegni **and** Ritornello: Sprezza mi quanto sai: from 'L'Incoronazione di Poppea', Act 2 (*vocal score: Novello/Music Sales*)
Mozart	Recit.: Ah! scostati **and** Aria: Smanie implacabili : from 'Così fan tutte', Act 1, K.588 (*vocal score Ital/Ger: Bärenreiter BA 4606a* or *vocal score Ital/Eng: Schirmer/Music Sales*)
Ponchielli	Recit.: Ho il cor **and** Aria: Stella del marinar!: from 'La Gioconda', Act 2 (*separately: Ricordi/U.M.P.* or *vocal score It/Eng: Ricordi/U.M.P.*)
	Aria: Voce di donna o d'angelo: from 'La Gioconda', Act 1 (*aria separately: Ricordi/U.M.P.* or *vocal score It/Eng: Ricordi/U.M.P.*)
Purcell	Mad Bess 'From silent shades and the Elysian groves', Z.370. *Purcell Songs, Vol.5* (*low*) (*Schott ED 12494/M.D.S.*)
Quilter	Hey, ho, the Wind and the Rain: no.5 from '5 Shakespeare Songs', Op.23 (*Boosey & Hawkes*)
Rosseter	When Laura smiles. *Elizabethan Love Songs, Set 1* (*low*) (*Boosey & Hawkes*)
A. Scarlatti	Spesso vibra per suo gioco. *Anthology of Italian Song of the 17th and 18th Centuries, Book 1* (*low*) (*Ital/Eng edn: Schirmer/Music Sales*)
Schubert	Der Einsame, Op.41, D.800. *Schubert Songs, Vol.3* (*medium* or *low*) (*Peters EP 8305b* or *c*)
	Ganymed, Op.19 no.3, D.544. *Schubert Lieder, Vol.3* (*medium*) (*Bärenreiter BA 7005*) or *Schubert Songs, Vol.2* (*medium* or *low*) (*Peters EP 8304b* or *c*)
Schumann	Liebeslied, Op.51 no.5. *Schumann Complete Songs, Vol.2* (*medium*) (*Peters EP 2384b*)
	Meine Rose, Op.90 no.2. *Schumann 90 Selected Songs* (*low*) (*Ger/Eng edn: International 1402/M.D.S.*) or *Schumann Complete Songs, Vol.3* (*medium-low*) (*Peters EP 2385b*)
	Zwielicht: no.10 from 'Liederkreis', Op.39 (*low*) (*Ger/Eng edn: International 3072/M.D.S.*) or *Schumann Complete Songs, Vol.1* (*medium* or *low*) (*Peters EP 2383b* or *c*)
R. Strauss	Allerseelen, Op.10 no.8 (*medium* or *low*) (*Ger/Eng edn: Universal 05464b* or *c/M.D.S.*)
	Ruhe, meine Seele, Op.27 no.1. *Strauss Lieder, Vol.2* (*medium* or *low*) (*Universal 05464b* or *c/M.D.S.*)
Tchaikovsky	Recit.: Oui, Dieu le veut! **and** Joan's Aria: Adieu, fôrets: from 'Jeanne d'Arc', Act 1. *Schirmer's Singer's Library, Arias for Mezzo-Soprano and Alto, Vol.1* (*Fr/Eng vers: Schirmer/Music Sales*)
	Recit. from: Tanya, Tanya, you dream the whole day long! **and** Olga's Aria: I'm not the sort to sit in silence: from 'Eugene Onegin', Act 1, Op.24 (*Rus/Eng vocal score, revised version: Boosey & Hawkes*)
Tippett	Songs for Ariel: any of the 3 songs (*Schott ED 10871/M.D.S.*)
	Solo: The soul of man: no.27 from 'A Child of Our Time', Part 3 (*vocal score: Schott ED 10065/ M.D.S.*)
Vaughan Williams	The New Ghost. *Vaughan Williams Collected Songs, Vol.2* (*O.U.P.*)
Warlock	Pretty ring time. *Warlock A First Book of Songs* (*O.U.P. archive/Banks*)
	Sleep (*O.U.P.*)
Wolf	Die ihr schwebet um diese Palmen: no.4 from 'Spanisches Liederbuch', Vol.1 (*high*) (*Ger/Eng edn: Peters EP 3149*) or *Wolf 4 Sacred Songs from 'Spanisches Liederbuch'* (*low*) (*Peters EP 3185a*)
	Um Mitternacht: no.19 from 'Mörike Lieder', Vol.2 (*high-medium* or *low*) (*Ger/Eng edn: Peters EP 3141a* or *b*)

Tenor

J.S. Bach	Recit.: Ach heile mich, du Artz der Seelen **and** Aria: Tröste mir, Jesu: nos.2 **and** 3 from Cantata no.135 'Ach Herr, mich armen Sünder', BWV 135 (*vocal score: Breitkopf & Härtel 7135*)
	Recit.: So geht! genug, mein Schatz **and** Aria: Nun mögt ihr stolzen Feinde schrecken: from 'Christmas Oratorio', Part 6, BWV 248 (*Ger/Eng vocal score: Bärenreiter BA 5014a*)
Beethoven	Adelaide, Op.46 (*high/medium*) (*Schott ED 01115/M.D.S.*)
L. Berkeley	Autumn's Legacy, Op.58: any of the 7 songs (*Chester/Music Sales*)
Bizet	Flower Song: 'La fleur que tu m'avais jetée': from 'Carmen', Act 2 (*vocal score Fr/Ger: Bärenreiter AE 129a* or *vocal score Fr/Eng: Schirmer/Music Sales*)
Brahms	In Waldeseinsamkeit, Op.85 no.6. *Brahms 70 Songs* (*high*) (*Ger/Eng edn: International 1270/M.D.S.*) or *Brahms Complete Songs, Vol.1* (*high*) (*Peters EP 3201a*)
Bridge	Thy hand in mine. *Bridge Song Album* (*Boosey & Hawkes*)
Britten	The little old table: no.4 from 'Winter Words', Op.52 (*Boosey & Hawkes*)
	The plough boy: no.1 from 'Folksong Arrangements', Vol.3 British Isles (*high*) (*U.M.P.*)
Delius	Love's Philosophy. *Delius 19 Songs* (*O.U.P.*)
Donizetti	Aria: Una furtiva lagrima: from 'L'Elisir d'Amore', Act 2 (*aria separately: Ricordi/U.M.P.*)
Duparc	L'Invitation au Voyage (no.1 from 'Mélodies') (*high*) (*Salabert/U.M.P.*)
Fauré	Lydia, Op.4 no.2. *Fauré 25 Selected Songs* (*high*) (*Fr/Eng edn: Schirmer/Music Sales*)

Tenor

Finzi	Since we loved: no.7 from 'Oh Fair to See', Op.13 (*Boosey & Hawkes*)
Gurney	All night under the moon. *Gurney 20 Favourite Songs* (*O.U.P.*)
Handel	Recit.: Thanks to my bretheren *and* Air: How vain is man who boasts in fight: from 'Judas Maccabaeus', Part 2, HWV 63 (*vocal score: Novello/Music Sales*)
	Recit.: He that dwelleth in heaven shall laugh them to scorn *and* Air: Thou shalt break them: from 'Messiah', Part 2, HWV 56 (*vocal score: Bärenreiter BA 4012b*)
Head	Oh, for a March wind. *Head Song Album, Vol.1 – Songs of the Countryside* (*Boosey & Hawkes*)
Holst	A Little Music: no.4 from '12 Humbert Wolfe Songs', Op.48 (*Stainer & Bell*)
Ireland	The Heart's Desire. *Ireland Complete Works for Voice, Vol.1* (*high*) (*Stainer & Bell*)
Mozart	Aria: Dies Bildnis ist bezaubernd schön: from 'Die Zauberflöte', Act 1, K.620 (*vocal score Ger: Bärenreiter BA 4553a or vocal score Ger/Eng: Boosey & Hawkes*)
	Recit.: In qual fiero contrasto *and* Cavatina: Tradito, schernito dal perfido cor: from 'Così fan tutte', Act 1, K.588 (*vocal score Ital/Ger: Bärenreiter BA 4606a or vocal score Ital/Eng: Schirmer/Music Sales*)
Puccini	Aria: Recondita armonia: from 'Tosca', Act 1 (*aria separately: Ricordi/U.M.P. or vocal score Ital/Eng: Ricordi/U.M.P.*)
Purcell	Celia has a thousand charms (from 'The Rival Sisters', Z.609) (*Bayley & Ferguson/Kerr Music*)
Quilter	Weep you no more: no.1 from '7 Elizabethan Lyrics', Op.12 (*high*) (*Boosey & Hawkes*)
Rossini	Domine Deus: no.4 from 'Petite Messe Solenelle' (*vocal score: Novello/Music Sales*)
Schubert	Am Meer: no.12 from 'Schwanengesang', D.957. *Schubert Lieder, Vol.9* (*high*) (*Bärenreiter BA 7016*) or *Schubert Songs, Vol.1* (*high*) (*Peters EP 8303a*)
	Der Müller und der Bach: no.19 from 'Die schöne Müllerin', Op.25, D.795. *Schubert Lieder, Vol.1* (*high*) (*Bärenreiter BA 7000*) or *Schubert Songs, Vol.1* (*high*) (*Peters EP 8303a*)
Schumann	Geständnis: no.7 from 'Spanisches Liederspiel', Op.74. *Schumann Complete Songs, Vol.2* (*high*) (*Peters EP 2384a*)
	Stille Tränen, Op.35 no.10. *Schumann 85 Selected Songs* (*high*) (*Ger/Eng edn: International 1487/M.D.S.*) or *Schumann Complete Songs, Vol.2* (*high*) (*Peters EP 2384a*)
R. Strauss	Heimliche Aufforderung, Op.27 no.3. *Strauss Lieder, Vol.3* (*high*) (*Universal 05465a/M.D.S.*)
Verdi	Recit.: Lunge da lei *and* Aria: De' miei bollenti spiriti: from 'La Traviata', Act 2 (*separately: Ricordi/U.M.P. or vocal score Ital/Eng: Ricordi/U.M.P. or Schirmer/Music Sales*)
Warlock	And wilt thou leave me thus. *Warlock A First Book of Songs* (*O.U.P. archive/Banks*)
Wolf	Ganymed: no.50 from 'Goethe Lieder', Vol.2 (*high-medium*) (*Peters EP 3157*)
	Verschwiegene Liebe: no.3 from 'Eichendorff Lieder', Vol.1 (*high-medium*) (*Ger/Eng edn: Peters EP 3147a*)

Baritone and Bass

J.S. Bach	Recit.: Ich habe genug *and* Aria: Schlummert ein, ihr matten Augen: nos.2 and 3 from Cantata no.82 'Ich habe genug', BWV 82 (*vocal score Ger/Eng: Breitkopf & Härtel 7082*)
	Aria: Grosser Herr und starker König: from 'Christmas Oratorio', Part 1, BWV 248 (*vocal score Ger/Eng: Bärenreiter BA 5014a*)
	Aria: Quoniam tu solus sanctus: no.11 from Mass in B minor, BWV 232 (*vocal score: Bärenreiter BA 5102a*)
Beethoven	Aus Goethes Faust, Op.75 no.3. *Beethoven Songs Complete, Vol.1* (*Henle or Henle/M.D.S.*)
L. Berkeley	5 Poems of Auden, Op.53: any song(s) (*Chester/Music Sales*)
Brahms	Verrat, Op.105 no.5. *Brahms 70 Songs* (*low*) (*Ger/Eng edn: International 1271/M.D.S.*) or *Brahms Complete Songs, Vol.4* (*medium-low*) (*Peters EP 3692b*)
	Wie bist du, meine Königin, Op.32 no.9. *Brahms 70 Songs* (*low*) (*Ger/Eng edn: International/M.D.S.*) or *Brahms Complete Songs, Vol.2* (*medium-low*) (*Peters EP 3202b*)
Britten	Now you may save your scornful looks: from 'Owen Wingrave', Act 2 (fig. 243–257), Op.85 (*vocal score Eng/Ger: Faber*)
	The Salley Gardens: no.1 from 'Folksong Arrangements', Vol.1 British Isles (*low*) (*Boosey & Hawkes*)
	You've got your maps there?: from 'Owen Wingrave', Act 1 (fig. 12–15), Op.85 (*vocal score Eng/Ger: Faber*)
G. Butterworth	Is my team ploughing?: no.6 / Loveliest of trees: no.1 — from | 'A Shropshire Lad' (*Stainer & Bell*)
Debussy	Le Temps a laissé son Manteau (Rondel I): no.1 from '3 Chansons de France' (*medium*) (*Peters EP 9241*) or *Debussy 43 Songs* (*low*) (*International 1136/M.D.S.*)
Donizetti	Aria: Bella siccome un angelo: from 'Don Pasquale', Act 1 (*aria separately: Ricordi/U.M.P. or vocal score Ital/Eng: Ricordi/U.M.P.*)
Duparc	Le Manoir de Rosemonde: no.6 from 'Mélodies' (*medium*) (*Salabert/U.M.P.*)

Singing: LRSM
Baritone and Bass

J. Eccles	I gently touched her hand. *Eccles 8 Songs* (*Stainer & Bell*)
Fauré	Le Voyageur, Op.18 no.2 ⎤ *Fauré 60 Mélodies, Vol.2* (*medium*) (*Hamelle/U.M.P.*) Nocturne, Op.43 no.2 ⎦ Prison, Op.83 no.1. *Fauré 25 Selected Songs* (*low*) (*Fr/Eng edn: Schirmer/Music Sales*)
Finzi	Chilhood among the Ferns: no.1 from 'Before and after Summer', Op.16 (*Boosey & Hawkes*) Fear no more the heat o' the sun: no.3 from 'Let us Garlands Bring', Op.18 (*Boosey & Hawkes*) The Phantom: no.4 from 'Earth and Air and Rain', Op.15 (*Boosey & Hawkes*) Song of Hiems 'When icicles hang by the wall': from Music for 'Love's Labour's Lost', Op.28 (*Boosey & Hawkes*)
C.A. Gibbs	The Ship of Rio. *A Heritage of 20th-Century British Song, Vol.3* (*Boosey & Hawkes*)
Gurney	The Scribe. *Gurney 20 Favourite Songs* (*O.U.P.*)
Handel	Recit.: I rage, I melt, I burn! *and* Aria: O ruddier than the cherry: from 'Acis and Galatea', Part 2, HWV 49a (*vocal score: Novello/Music Sales*) Recit.: Be comforted *and* Air: The Lord worketh wonders: from 'Judas Maccabaeus', Part 2, HWV 63 (*vocal score: Novello/Music Sales*) Recit.: The good we wish for *and* Air: Thy glorious deeds inspir'd my tongue: from 'Samson', Part 1, HWV 57 (*vocal score: Novello/Music Sales*)
Haydn	Recit.: Lo! where the plenteous harvest wav'd *and* Aria: Behold, along the dewy grass: from 'The Seasons', Autumn (*vocal score Eng: Novello/Music Sales* or *vocal score Ger/Eng: Peters EP 67*)
Head	Limehouse Reach: no.2 from 'Sea Songs' (*Boosey & Hawkes archive copy*) Lavender Pond (no.5 from 'Sea Songs'). *A Heritage of 20th-Century British Song, Vol.3* (*Boosey & Hawkes*)
Holst	Betelgeuse: no.12 from '12 Humbert Wolfe Songs', Op.48 (*Stainer & Bell*) The Sergeant's Song, Op.15 no.3 (*Ashdown/Music Sales*)
Ireland	In Boyhood. *Ireland Complete Works for Voice, Vol.3* (*medium*) (*Stainer & Bell*) Tryst. *Ireland Complete Works for Voice, Vol.2* (*medium*) (*Stainer & Bell*)
Mozart	Recit.: Tutto è disposto *and* Aria: Aprite un po' quegli occhi: from 'Le Nozze di Figaro', Act 4, K.492 (*vocal score Ital/Ger: Bärenreiter BA 4565a* or *vocal score Ital/Eng: Boosey & Hawkes*) Recit. from: Eh, consolatevi *and* Aria: Madamina! Il catalogo è questo: from 'Don Giovanni', Act 1, K.527 (*vocal score Ital/Ger: Bärenreiter BA 4550a* or *vocal score Ital/Eng: Boosey & Hawkes*)
Purcell	Anacreon's Defeat: 'This poet sings the Trojan wars', Z.423. *Purcell 6 Songs for Bass* (*International 1657/M.D.S.*)
Ravel	Chanson Épique (no.2 from 'Don Quichotte à Dulcinée') (*Fr/Eng edn: Durand/U.M.P.*)
Rossini	Quoniam tu solus sanctus: no.6 from 'Petite Messe Solennelle' (*vocal score: Novello/Music Sales*) Aria: Resta immobile: from 'Guglielmo Tell', Act 3 (*aria separately: Ricordi/U.M.P.* or *vocal score: Ricordi/U.M.P.*)
Schubert	Aufenthalt: no.5 from 'Schwanengesang', D.957. *Schubert Lieder, Vol.9* (*medium*) (*Bärenreiter BA 7017*) or *Schubert Songs, Vol.1* (*medium* or *low*) (*Peters EP 8303b* or *c*) Gesänge des Harfners, Op.12, D.478–80: any of the 3 songs in any version. *Schubert Lieder, Vol.3* (*medium*) (*Bärenreiter BA 7005*) or *Schubert Songs, Vol.2* (*medium* or *low*) (*Peters EP 8304b* or *c*)
Schumann	Dein Angesicht, Op.127 no.2. *Schumann 90 Selected Songs* (*low*) (*Ger/Eng edn: International 1402/M.D.S.*) or *Schumann Complete Songs, Vol.1* (*medium* or *low*) (*Peters EP 2383b* or *c*) Wer nie sein Brot mit Tränen ass, Op.98a no.4. *Schumann 90 Selected Songs* (*low*) (*Ger/Eng edn: International 1402/M.D.S.*) or *Schumann Complete Songs, Vol.3* (*medium-low*) (*Peters EP 2385b*)
M. Shaw	Song of the Palanquin Bearers. *Shaw 7 Songs* (*Stainer & Bell*)
Somervell	The lads in their hundreds: no.10 from 'A Shropshire Lad' (*Boosey & Hawkes*)
Stanford	The Fairy Lough (no.2 from 'An Irish Idyll in 6 Miniatures', Op.77). *A Heritage of 20th-Century British Song, Vol.2* (*Boosey & Hawkes*) The rain it raineth every day (no.1 from 'Clown's Songs from Twelfth Night', Op.65). *A Heritage of 20th-Century British Song, Vol.1* (*Boosey & Hawkes*)
R. Strauss	Der Einsame, Op.51 no.2. *Strauss Lieder, Vol.2* (*Boosey & Hawkes*) Mein Herz ist stumm, Op.19 no.6. *Strauss Lieder, Vol.3* (*medium* or *low*) (*Universal 05465b* or *c/M.D.S.*)
Vaughan Williams	Bright is the Ring of Words: no.8 ⎤ In Dreams: no.5 from ⎨ 'Songs of Travel' (*medium* or *low*) (*Boosey & Hawkes*) Youth and Love: no.4 ⎦
Verdi	Recit.: Studia il passo *and* Aria: Come dal ciel precipita: from 'Macbeth', Act 2 (*separately: Ricordi/U.M.P.* or *vocal score: Ricordi/U.M.P.* or *vocal score Ital/Eng: Schirmer/Music Sales*) Aria: Di Provenza il mar: from 'La Traviata', Act 2 (*aria separately: Ricordi/U.M.P.* or *vocal score Ital/Eng: Ricordi/U.M.P.* or *Schirmer/Music Sales*)

Baritone and Bass

Wagner Recit.: Wie Todesahnung *and* O du mein holder Abendstern: from 'Tannhäuser', Act 3 (*vocal score: Peters EP 8217*)

Wolf Auf dem grünen Balkon: no.5 from 'Spanisches Liederbuch', Vol.2 (*high*) (*Ger/Eng edn: Peters EP 3150*) or *Wolf 9 Secular Songs from 'Spanisches Liederbuch'* (*low*) (*Ger/Eng edn: Peters EP 3185b*)
Der Rattenfänger: no.11 from 'Goethe Lieder', Vol.1 (*high-medium*) (*Peters EP 3156*) or *Wolf 35 Baritone-Bass Songs* (*Ger/Eng edn: Peters EP 4291*)
Harfenspieler I 'Wer sich der Einsamkeit ergibt': no.1 from 'Goethe Lieder', Vol.1 (*high-medium*) (*Peters EP 3156*) or *Wolf 35 Baritone-Bass Songs* (*Ger/Eng edn: Peters EP 4291*)
Über Nacht. *Wolf 51 Selected Songs* (*medium-low*) (*Ger/Eng edn: Peters EP 4290b*)

Singing: FRSM

Candidates may choose items from the list appropriate to their voice and/or the list marked 'All voices' on pp. 94–97. They should include in their programme at least one song or aria which is in a different language from the other chosen items. All opera and oratorio items should be sung in the keys in which they were written, respecting original pitch if appropriate; otherwise, all songs may be sung in any key suited to the candidate's voice. See p. 14 for performing from memory.

Soprano

C.P.E. Bach Aria: Quia respexit humilitatem: no.2 from Magnificat in D minor, Wq.215 (*vocal score Lat/Eng: Schirmer/Music Sales*)

J.S. Bach Recit.: Er hat uns allen wohlgetan *and* Aria: Aus Liebe will mein Heiland sterben: from 'St Matthew Passion', Part 1, BWV 244 (*vocal score Ger/Eng: Bärenreiter BA 5038a*)
Aria: Zerfliesse, mein Herze: from 'St John Passion', Part 2, BWV 245 (*vocal score Ger/Eng: Bärenreiter BA 5037a*)

Brahms Ihr habt nun Traurigkeit: no.5 from 'Ein deutsches Requiem' (German Requiem), Op.45 (*vocal score Ger: Peters EP 3672* or *vocal score Eng: Peters EP 3672a*)

Britten Come, now a roundel: from 'A Midsummer Night's Dream', Act 1, Op.64 (*vocal score Eng/Ger: Boosey & Hawkes*) or *Britten Opera Arias, Vol.2* (*Eng/Ger edn: Boosey & Hawkes*)
Embroidery Aria 'Embroidery in childhood': from 'Peter Grimes', Act 3, Op.33 (*vocal score: Boosey & Hawkes*) or *Britten Opera Arias, Vol.1* (*Eng/Ger edn: Boosey & Hawkes*)
Beautiful it is: from 'The Turn of the Screw', Act 1 (The Tower), Op.54 (*vocal score Eng/Ger: Boosey & Hawkes*) or *Britten Opera Arias, Vol.2* (*Eng/Ger edn: Boosey & Hawkes*)

G. Charpentier Aria: Depuis le jour où je me suis donnée: from 'Louise', Act 3 (*aria separately: Heugel/U.M.P.*)

Delibes Aria: Où va la jeune indou (Bell Song): from 'Lakmé', Act 2 (*aria separately: Fr/Eng edn: U.M.P.*)

Elgar Solo: The sun goeth down: from 'The Kingdom', Part 4, Op.51 (*vocal score: Novello/Music Sales*)

Gounod Recit.: O Dieu! que de bijoux! *and* Air des Bijoux (Jewel Song): Ah! je ris: from 'Faust', Act 3 (*separately: Choudens/U.M.P.* or *vocal score Fr/Eng: Schirmer/Music Sales*)

Handel Air: Let the bright Seraphim in burning row: from 'Samson', Part 3, HWV 57 (*vocal score: Novello/Music Sales*)
Air: Through the land, so lovely blooming: from 'Athalia', Act 2, HWV 52 (*vocal score: O.U.P. archive copy*)

Haydn Recit.: And God said, Let the earth *and* Aria: With verdure clad: from 'The Creation', Part 1 (*vocal score Eng: Novello/Music Sales* or *vocal score Ger/Eng: Peters EP 66*)

Massenet Aria: Pleurez! Pleurez, mes yeux: from 'Le Cid', Act 3 (*aria separately: Heugel/U.M.P.*)

Mendelssohn Aria: Hear ye, Israel: from 'Elijah', Part 2, Op.70 (*vocal score Eng: Novello/Music Sales* or *vocal score Ger: Peters EP 1749*)

Mozart Recit. from: Temerari! sortite fuori di questo loco *and* Aria: Come scoglio: from 'Così fan tutte', Act 1, K.588 (*vocal score Ital/Ger: Bärenreiter BA 4606a* or *vocal score Ital/Eng: Schirmer/Music Sales*)
Recit.: E Susanna non vieni *and* Aria: Dove sono i bei momenti: from 'Le Nozze di Figaro', Act 3, K.492 (*vocal score Ital/Ger: Bärenreiter BA 4565a* or *vocal score Ital/Eng: Boosey & Hawkes*)
Solo: Et incarnatus est: from Mass no.18 in C minor, K.427 (*vocal score: Bärenreiter BA 4846a*)

Ponchielli Aria: Suicido!: from 'La Gioconda', Act 4 (*aria separately: Ricordi/U.M.P.* or *vocal score Ital/Eng: Ricordi/U.M.P.*)

Puccini Aria: Si. Mi chiamano Mimì: from 'La Bohème', Act 1 (*aria separately: Ricordi/U.M.P.* or *vocal score Ital/Eng: Ricordi/U.M.P.*)
Aria: Sola, perduta, abbandonata: from 'Manon Lescaut', Act 4 (*aria separately: Ricordi/U.M.P.* or *vocal score Ital/Eng: Ricordi/U.M.P.*)

Purcell The Blessed Virgin's Expostulation ('Tell me, some pitying angel'), Z.196: complete. *Purcell Songs, Vol.1* (*high*) (*Schott ED 12409/M.D.S.*)

Singing: FRSM

Soprano

J. Strauss II Csárdás 'Klänge der Heimat': from 'Die Fledermaus', Act 2 (*aria separately Ger/Eng edn: Cranz/ U.M.P. or vocal score Ger/Eng: Cranz/U.M.P.*)

Aria: Spiel' ich die Unschuld vom Lande (Audition Song): from 'Die Fledermaus', Act 3 (*aria separately Ger/Eng edn: Cranz/U.M.P. or vocal score Ger/Eng: Cranz/U.M.P.*)

Tippett Solo: How can I cherish my man in such days *and the first 8 bars of the solo soprano part of* A Spiritual: no.7 *and* the first 8 bars of no.8 from 'A Child of Our Time', Part 1 (*vocal score: Schott ED 10065/M.D.S.*)

Verdi Aria: Pace, pace, mio Dio: from 'La Forza del Destino', Act 4 (*aria separately: Ricordi/U.M.P. or vocal score Ital/Eng: Schirmer/Music Sales*)

Recit.: Sorta è la notte *and* Aria: Ernani! Ernani, involami *and* Cabaletta: Tutto sprezzo che d'Ernani: from 'Ernani', Act 1 (*separately: Ricordi/U.M.P. or vocal score: Ricordi/U.M.P.*)

Mezzo-soprano, Contralto and Countertenor

J.S. Bach Aria: Erbarme dich, mein Gott: from 'St Matthew Passion', Part 2, BWV 244 (*vocal score Ger/Eng: Bärenreiter BA 5038a*)

Aria: Es ist vollbracht: from 'St John Passion', Part 2, BWV 245 (*vocal score Ger/Eng: Bärenreiter BA 5037a*)

Aria: Vergnügte Ruh, beliebte Seelenlust: no.1 from Cantata no.170 'Vergnügte Ruh', BWV 170 (*vocal score Ger/Eng: Breitkopf & Härtel 7170*)

Bizet Séguidilla: 'Près des ramparts de Séville': from 'Carmen', Act 1 (*separately: Choudens/U.M.P.*)

Brahms Aber abseits, wer ist's?: no.1 from 'Alto Rhapsody', Op.53 (*Novello/Music Sales*)

Britten Recit.: Give him this orchid *and* Flowers bring to ev'ry year the same perfection: from 'The Rape of Lucretia', Act 2, Op.37 (*vocal score Eng/Ger: Boosey & Hawkes*) or *Britten Opera Arias, Vol.3* (*Eng/Ger edn: Boosey & Hawkes*)

I know a bank where the wild thyme blows: from 'A Midsummer Night's Dream', Act 1, Op.64 (*vocal score Eng/Ger: Boosey & Hawkes*) or *Britten Opera Arias, Vol.3* (*Eng/Ger edn: Boosey & Hawkes*)

Donizetti Recit.: Fia dunque vero? *and* Aria: O mio Fernando: from 'La Favorita', Act 3 (*separately: Ricordi/ U.M.P. or vocal score: Ricordi/U.M.P.*)

Dvořák Inflammatus et accensus: no.9 from 'Stabat Mater', Op.58 (*vocal score: Novello/Music Sales*)

Elgar Solo: Softly and gently, dearly ransomed soul (Angel's Farewell): from 'The Dream of Gerontius', Part 2 (fig. 126), Op.38 (*vocal score: Novello/Music Sales*)

Handel Air: But who may abide the day of His coming?: from 'Messiah', Part 1, HWV 56 (*vocal score: Bärenreiter BA 4012b*)

Aria: A dispetto: from 'Tamerlano', Act 3, HWV 18 (*vocal score: Bärenreiter BA 4052a*)

Recit.: Pompe vane di morte *and* Aria: Dove sei?: from 'Rodelinda', Act 1, HWV 19 (*vocal score: Bärenreiter BA 4064a*)

Massenet Recit: Werther! Qui m'aurait dit la place *and* Aria starting with: Je vous écris de ma petite chambre (The Letters): from 'Werther', Act 3 (*separately: Fr/Eng edn: International 3014/M.D.S.*)

Mozart Solo: Laudamus te: from Mass no.18 in C minor, K.427 (*vocal score: Bärenreiter BA 4846a*)

Aria: Parto, parto, ma tu ben mio: from 'La Clemenza di Tito', Act 1, K.621 (*vocal score Ital/Ger: Bärenreiter BA 4554a or vocal score Ital/Eng: International 1109/M.D.S.*)

Purcell Lord, what is Man? (*Stainer & Bell*)

The fife and all the harmony: from 'Ode on St Cecilia's Day' (Hail, bright Cecilia), Z.328
'Tis Nature's voice: (*vocal score: Novello/Music Sales*)

Rossini Solo: Fac, ut portem Christi mortem: no.7 from 'Stabat Mater' (*vocal score: Novello/Music Sales*)

Aria: Una voce poco fa *and* Io son docile: from 'Il Barbiere di Siviglia', Act 1 (*aria separately: Ricordi/ U.M.P. or vocal score Ital/Eng: Ricordi/U.M.P. or Schirmer/Music Sales*)

Recit.: O Patria! *and* Cavatina: Tu che accendi *and* Cabaletta: Di tanti palpiti: from 'Tancredi', Act 1 (*vocal score: Ricordi/U.M.P.*)

Saint-Saëns Recit.: Samson, recherchant ma présence *and* Air: Amour! viens aider ma faiblesse!: from 'Samson et Dalila', Act 2 (*separately: Durand/U.M.P.*)

Verdi Solo: Liber scriptus (*finishing at bar 68*): no.4 from 'Messa da Requiem' (*vocal score Lat/Eng: Ricordi/ U.M.P.*)

Aria: Stride la vampa!: from 'Il Trovatore', Act 2 (*vocal score Ital/Eng: Ricordi/U.M.P. or Schirmer/ Music Sales*)

Vivaldi Solo: from Nisi Dominus in G minor, RV 608 (*vocal score Lat/Eng: Ricordi/U.M.P.*)

Singing: FRSM

Tenor

C.P.E. Bach Aria: Quia fecit mihi magna: no.3 from Magnificat in D minor, Wq.215 (*vocal score Lat/Eng: Schirmer/Music Sales*)

J.S. Bach Aria: Ach, mein Sinn: from 'St John Passion', Part 1, BWV 245 (*vocal score Ger/Eng: Bärenreiter BA 5037a*)

Aria: Frohe Hirten, eilt: from 'Christmas Oratorio', Part 1, BWV 248 (*vocal score Ger/Eng: Bärenreiter BA 5014a*)

Recit.: Mein Jesus schweigt *and* Aria: Geduld, Geduld: from 'St Matthew Passion', Part 2, BWV 244 (*vocal score Ger/Eng: Bärenreiter BA 5038a*)

Britten Heaven helps those who help themselves: from 'Albert Herring', Act 2 (fig. 85), Op.39 (*vocal score: Boosey & Hawkes*)

Tarquinius does not wait for his servant to wake: from 'The Rape of Lucretia', Act 1 (Interlude), Op.37 (*vocal score Eng/Ger: Boosey & Hawkes*)

Coleridge-Taylor Solo: Onaway!, Awake, beloved!: from 'Hiawatha's Wedding Feast', Op.30 no.1 (*vocal score: Novello/Music Sales*)

Elgar Solo: Sanctus fortis, Sanctus Deus: from 'The Dream of Gerontius', Part 1 (fig. 40), Op.38 (*vocal score: Novello/Music Sales*)

Handel Recit.: My arms! against this Gorgias I will go *and* Air: Sound an alarm! your silver trumpets sound: from 'Judas Maccabaeus', Part 2, HWV 63 (*vocal score: Novello/Music Sales*)

Massenet Aria: Pourquoi me réveiller?: from 'Werther', Act 3 (*aria separately: Fr/Eng edn: International 1358/ M.D.S.*)

Meyerbeer Recit.: Pays merveilleux *and* Cavatina: O Paradis sorti de l'onde: from 'L'Africaine', Act 4. *Schirmer's Singer's Library, Arias for Tenor, Vol.1* (*Fr/Eng edn: Schirmer/Music Sales*)

Mozart Aria: Se all'impero, amici Dei: from 'La Clemenza di Tito', Act 2, K.621 (*vocal score Ital/Ger: Bärenreiter BA 4554a or vocal score Ital/Eng: International 1109/M.D.S.*)

Puccini Aria: E lucevan le stelle: from 'Tosca', Act 3 (*aria separately: Ricordi/U.M.P. or vocal score Ital/Eng: Ricordi/U.M.P.*)

Tchaikovsky Lensky's Aria: How far away you seem now, O happy days when I was young: from 'Eugene Onegin', Act 2, Op.24 (*aria separately Rus/Eng edn: Boosey & Hawkes EE 3378a or Rus/Eng vocal score, revised version: Boosey & Hawkes*)

Verdi Solo: Ingemisco tam quam reus: no.8 from 'Messa da Requiem' (*vocal score Lat/Eng: Ricordi/U.M.P.*)

Recit.: Oh! fede negar potessi *and* Aria: Quando le sere al placido: from 'Luisa Miller', Act 2 (*separately: Ricordi/U.M.P. or vocal score: Ricordi/U.M.P.*)

Baritone and Bass

C.P.E. Bach Aria: Fecit potentiam: no.5 from Magnificat in D minor, Wq.215 (*vocal score Lat/Eng: Schirmer/ Music Sales*)

J.S. Bach Aria: Et in spiritum sanctum: no.19 from Mass in B minor, Part 3, BWV 232 (*vocal score: Bärenreiter BA 5102a*)

Recit.: Mein Wandel auf der Welt *and* Aria: Endlich, endlich wird mein Joch: nos.2 *and* 3 from Cantata no.56 'Ich will den Kreuzstab gerne tragen', BWV 56 (*vocal score Ger/Eng: Breitkopf & Härtel 7056*)

Bizet Recit.: L'orage s'est calmé *and* Aria: O Nadir, tendre ami de mon jeune âge: from 'Les Pêcheurs de Perles', Act 3 (*vocal score Fr/Eng: Choudens/U.M.P.*)

Britten Bottom's Dream: 'When my cue comes, call me, and I will answer': from 'A Midsummer Night's Dream', Act 3 (fig.25), Op.64 (*separately or vocal score Eng/Ger: Boosey & Hawkes*)

Look! Through the port comes the moonshine astray!: from 'Billy Budd', Act 1 (fig.105), Op.50 (*vocal score: Boosey & Hawkes*)

O beauty, o handsomeness, goodness: from 'Billy Budd', Act 2, Op.50 (*vocal score: Boosey & Hawkes*)

Donizetti Cavatina: Come Paride vezzoso: from 'L'Elisir d'Amore', Act 1 (*vocal score: Ricordi/U.M.P.*)

Elgar Solo: Angel of Agony 'Jesu! by that shudd'ring dread': from 'The Dream of Gerontius', Part 2 (fig. 106), Op.38 (*vocal score: Novello/Music Sales*)

Handel Recit.: Behold, I tell you a mystery *and* Air: The trumpet shall sound: from 'Messiah', Part 3, HWV 56 (*vocal score: Bärenreiter BA 4012b*)

Air: Revenge, revenge, Timotheus cries: from 'Alexander's Feast', Part 2, HWV 75 (*vocal score: Novello/Music Sales*)

Haydn Recit.: And God said, Let the waters *and* Aria: Rolling in foaming billows: from 'The Creation', Part 1 (*vocal score Eng: Novello/Music Sales or vocal score Ger/Eng: Peters EP 66*)

Massenet Recit.: Ce breauvage pourrait me donner un tel rêvel *and* Aria: Vision fugitive: from 'Hérodiade', Act 2 (*separately: Heugel/U.M.P. or vocal score Fr/Eng: Heugel/U.M.P.*)

Mendelssohn Recit.: Tarry here, my servant *and* Aria: It is enough: from 'Elijah', Part 2, Op.70 (*vocal score Eng: Novello/Music Sales or vocal score Ger: Peters EP 1749*)

Singing: FRSM
Baritone and Bass

Mozart Recit.: Ehi, capitano *and* Aria: Non più andrai: from 'Le Nozze di Figaro', Act 1, K.492 (*vocal score Ital/Ger: Bärenreiter BA 4565a or vocal score Ital/Eng: Boosey & Hawkes*)
Recit.: Hai già vinta la causa! *and* Aria: Vedrò, mentr'io sospiro: from 'Le Nozze di Figaro', Act 3, K.492 (*vocal score Ital/Ger: Bärenreiter BA 4565a or vocal score Ital/Eng: Boosey & Hawkes*)

Offenbach Recit.: Allez! Pour te livrer combat *and* Aria: Scintille, diamant: from 'Les Contes d'Hoffmann', Act 2 (*vocal score Fr/Eng: Bärenreiter AE 333c or Schirmer/Music Sales*)

Purcell Let the dreadful engines of eternal will (from 'Don Quixote', Z.578). *Purcell Songs, Vol.5 (low) (Schott ED 12494/M.D.S.)*
These are the sacred charms: from Birthday Ode 'Come ye sons of art away', Z.323 (*vocal score: Novello/Music Sales*)

Rossini Solo: Pro peccatis suae gentis: no.4 from 'Stabat Mater' (*vocal score: Novello/Music Sales*)

Tchaikovsky Prince Gremin's Aria: A wasted, melancholy life is what I led: from 'Eugene Onegin', Act 3, Op.24 (*aria separately Rus/Eng edn: Boosey & Hawkes EE 3379c or Rus/Eng vocal score, revised version: Boosey & Hawkes*)

Vaughan Williams Easter (*small notes to be sung in place of chorus part*): no.1 from '5 Mystical Songs' (*vocal score: Stainer & Bell*)

Verdi Solo: Confutatis maledictis: no.9 from 'Messa da Requiem' (*vocal score Lat/Eng: Ricordi/U.M.P.*)
Aria: Ella giammai m'amò: from 'Don Carlo', Act 4 (*aria separately: Ricordi/U.M.P. or vocal score: Ricordi/U.M.P. or vocal score Ital/Eng: Schirmer/Music Sales*)
Recit.: Alzati! Là tuo figlio *and* Aria: Eri tu che macchiavi quell'anima: from 'Un Ballo in Maschera', Act 3 (*separately: Ricordi/U.M.P. or vocal score: Ricordi/U.M.P. or vocal score Ital/Eng: Schirmer/Music Sales*)

All voices

Bax Across the door (no.4 from '5 Irish Songs') (*Warner Chappell/I.M.P.*)
The Enchanted Fiddle. *Bax Album of 7 Songs (Chester/Music Sales)*

Beethoven Abendlied unterm gestirnten Himmel, WoO 150. *Beethoven Songs Complete, Vol.2 (Henle or Henle – Schott/M.D.S.)*
Neue Liebe, neues Leben (version 2), Op.75 no.2. *Beethoven Songs Complete, Vol.1 (Henle or Henle – Schott/M.D.S.)*

Blow Self Banished. *Blow 10 Songs for High Voice (Stainer & Bell)*

Brahms An die Äolsharfe, Op.19 no.5. *Brahms 70 Songs (high or low) (Ger/Eng edn: International 1270 or 1271/M.D.S.) or Brahms Complete Songs, Vol.1 (high, medium or low) (Peters EP 3201a, b or c)*
An ein Bild, Op.63 no.3. *Brahms Complete Songs, Vol.3 (high or medium-low) (Peters EP 3691a or b)*
Das Mädchen, Op.95 no.1. *Brahms 70 Songs (high or low) (Ger/Eng edn: International 1270 or 1271/M.D.S.) or Brahms Complete Songs, Vol.4 (high or medium-low) (Peters EP 3692a or b)*
Erinnerung, Op.63 no.2. *Brahms 70 Songs (high or low) (Ger/Eng edn: International 1270 or 1271/M.D.S.) or Brahms Complete Songs, Vol.3 (high or medium-low) (Peters EP 3691a or b)*
4 Ernste Gesänge (4 Serious Songs), Op.121: any song(s). *Brahms 70 Songs (low) (Ger/Eng edn: International 1271/M.D.S.) or Brahms Complete Songs, Vol.4 (high or medium-low) (Peters EP 3692a or b)*
Treue Liebe dauert lange, Op.33 no.15. *Brahms Complete Songs, Vol.2 (high or medium-low) (Peters EP 3202a or b)*
Unbewegte, laue Luft, tiefe Ruhe der Natur, Op.57 no.8. *Brahms Complete Songs, Vol.2 (high or medium-low) (Peters EP 3202a or b)*
Willst du, dass ich geh?, Op.71 no.4. *Brahms 70 Songs (high or low) (Ger/Eng edn: International 1270 or 1271/M.D.S.) or Brahms Complete Songs, Vol.4 (high or medium-low) (Peters EP 3692a or b)*

Britten Fish in the unruffled lakes (*Boosey & Hawkes*)
Funeral Blues: no.2 from '4 Cabaret Songs' (*high*) (*Faber*)
Johnny: no.3 from '4 Cabaret Songs' (*high*) (*Faber*)
Let the florid music praise!: no.1 from 'On this Island', Op.11 (*high*) (*Boosey & Hawkes*)
London: no.1 from 'Songs and Proverbs of William Blake', Op.74 (*baritone*) (*Faber*)
Now the leaves are falling fast: no.2 from 'On this Island', Op.11 (*high*) (*Boosey & Hawkes*)
The Tyger: no.4 from 'Songs and Proverbs of William Blake', Op.74 (*baritone*) (*Faber*)
Wild with passion (Song, on the water): no.5 from 'The Red Cockatoo and other songs' (*high or medium-low*) (*Faber*)

Carissimi Vittoria, mio cuore! *Italian Songs of the 17th and 18th Centuries, Vol.1 (high, medium or low) (Ital/Eng edn: International 2231, 2232 or 2233/M.D.S.)*

Cesti Tu mancavi a tormentarmi. *Anthology of Italian Song of the 17th and 18th Centuries, Book 2 (high or low) (Ital/Eng edn: Schirmer/Music Sales)*

REPERTOIRE LISTS

Singing: FRSM
All voices

Chausson Cantique à l'Épouse, Op.36 no.1
Chanson Perpétuelle, Op.37   *Chausson 20 Songs (high or low) (Fr/Eng edn:*
La Caravane, Op.14   *International 1130 or 1131/M.D.S.)*

Danyel Like as the lute delights. *English Lute Songs, Book 1 (Stainer & Bell)*

Debussy Colloque Sentimental: no.3 from 'Fêtes Galantes', Set 2 (*high* or *low*) (*Fr/Eng edn: International 1230*
or *1231/M.D.S.)*

Fantoches: no.2 from 'Fêtes Galantes', Set 1 (*high* or *low*) (*Fr/Eng edn: International 1713* or *1714/*
M.D.S.)

5 Poèmes de Baudelaire: any song(s)   *Debussy 43 Songs (high or low)*
4 Proses Lyriques: any song(s)   *(International 1135 or 1136/M.D.S.)*

Delibes Chanson Espagnole 'Les Filles de Cadiz' (*Consortium/U.M.P.*)

Delius Indian Love Song
The Bird's Story   *Delius 19 Songs (O.U.P.)*
To the Queen of my Heart

Duparc Au pays où se fait la guerre: no.13   from   *'Mélodies' (high* or *medium) (Salabert/U.M.P.)*
La Vague et la Cloche: no.3

Elgar A Sabbath Morning at Sea: no.3 from 'Sea Pictures', Op.37 (*Boosey & Hawkes*)

Falla 7 Canciones Populares Españolas: any *two* songs (*high* or *medium*) (*Sp/Fr edn: Chester/Music Sales*)

Fauré Au Cimetière, Op.51 no.2
C'est l'extase, Op.58 no.5
Fleur Jetée, Op.39 no.2   *Fauré 25 Selected Songs (high or low) (Fr/Eng edn: Schirmer/Music Sales)*
Green, Op.58 no.3

Finzi Budmouth Dears: no.3
Former Beauties: no.9   from   *'A Young Man's Exhortation', Op.14 (Boosey & Hawkes)*
The dance continued: no.10
Summer Schemes: no.1 from 'Earth and Air and Rain', Op.15 (*Boosey & Hawkes*)

T. Ford Unto the temple of thy beauty. *English Lute Songs, Book 1 (Stainer & Bell)*

R. Greaves Ye bubbling springs. *English Lute Songs, Book 1 (Stainer & Bell)*

Grieg Dein Rat ist wohl gut (Thanks for your advice), Op.21 no.4   *Grieg 60 Selected Songs*
Herbststurm (Autumn Storms), Op.18 no.4   *(high* or *medium-low)*
Mein Ziel (The Goal), Op.33 no.12   *(Ger edn: Peters EP 3208a* or *b)*

Gurney Is my team ploughing?: no.6 from 'The Western Playland' (*baritone*) (*Stainer & Bell*)
Ludlow Fair: no.4 from 'Ludlow and Teme' (*tenor*) (*Stainer & Bell*)
March: no.8 from 'The Western Playland' (*baritone*) (*Stainer & Bell*)
The Folly of being comforted. *Gurney A Second Volume of 10 Songs (O.U.P. archive copy)*
The Lent Lily: no.7 from 'Ludlow and Teme' (*tenor*) (*Stainer & Bell*)

Head 3 Songs of Venice: any song(s) (*Boosey & Hawkes archive copy*)
The Estuary. *A Heritage of 20th-Century British Song, Vol.3 (Boosey & Hawkes)*

Holst The Floral Bandit: no.6 from '12 Humbert Wolfe Songs', Op.48 (*Stainer & Bell*)

Ireland Friendship in misfortune   *Ireland 11 Songs (Stainer & Bell)*
My true love hath my heart
5 Poems by Thomas Hardy: any song(s) (*O.U.P.*)
The One Hope   *Ireland 11 Songs (Stainer & Bell)*
The Trellis

Mahler Die zwei blauen Augen: no.4 from 'Lieder eines fahrenden Gesellen' (*high* or *medium*) (*Ger/Eng edn:
International 2146* or *1020/M.D.S.)*
Ich hab' ein glühend' Messer: no.3 from 'Lieder eines fahrenden Gesellen' (*high* or *medium*) (*Ger/Eng
edn: International 2146* or *1020/M.D.S.)*
Oft denk' ich, sie sind nur ausgegangen: no.4 from 'Kindertotenlieder' (*high* or *medium*) (*Ger/Eng
edn: International 2144* or *1040/M.D.S.)*
Um Mitternacht (from '5 Rückert-Lieder'). *Mahler 24 Songs, Vol.4 (high* or *low) (Ger/Eng edn:
International 1216* or *1234/M.D.S.)*
Wenn dein Mütterlein: no.3 from 'Kindertotenlieder' (*high* or *medium*) (*Ger/Eng edn: International
2144* or *1040/M.D.S.)*
Wo die schönen Trompeten blasen (from 'Lieder aus Des Knaben Wunderhorn'). *Mahler 24 Songs,
Vol.2 (high* or *low) (Ger/Eng edn: International 1214* or *1232/M.D.S.)*

J.P. E Martini Plaisir d'Amour (Piacer d'Amor) (*high* or *medium*) (*Fr edn: Durand/U.M.P.* or *Fr/Ital edn: Ricordi/
U.M.P.)*

Singing: FRSM

All voices

Poulenc
Il vole: no.3 from 'Fiançailles pour Rire' (*Salabert/U.M.P.*)
Le Mendiant: no.4
Les gars qui vont à la fête: no.2 ⎤ from ⎤ 'Chansons Villageoises' (*Fr/Eng edn: Eschig/U.M.P.*)
Sanglots: no.5 from 'Banalités' (*Eschig/U.M.P.*)

Ravel
Chanson à boire (no.3 from 'Don Quichotte à Dulcinée') (*Fr/Eng edn: Durand/U.M.P.*)
La Flûte enchantée (no.2 from 'Shéhérazade') (*Fr/Eng edn: Durand/U.M.P.*)

D. Scarlatti
Consolati e spera! *Anthology of Italian Song of the 17th and 18th Centuries, Book 1* (*high* or *low*)
(*Ital/Eng edn: Schirmer/Music Sales*)

Schubert
Auf der Bruck, Op.93 no.2, D.853. *Schubert Lieder, Vol.5* (*high*) (*Bärenreiter BA 7008*) or *Schubert Songs, Vol.4* (*high, medium* or *low*) (*Peters EP 8306a, b* or *c*)
Die Almacht, Op.79 no.2, D.852. *Schubert Lieder, Vol.7* (*high*) (*Bärenreiter BA 7012*) or *Schubert Songs, Vol.3* (*high, medium* or *low*) (*Peters EP 8305a, b* or *c*)
Erlkönig, Op.1, D.328. *Schubert Lieder, Vol.3* (*high* or *medium*) (*Bärenreiter BA 7004* or *7005*) or *Schubert Songs, Vol.2* (*high, medium* or *low*) (*Peters EP 8304a, b* or *c*)
Gretchen am Spinnrade, Op.2, D.118. *Schubert Lieder, Vol.3* (*high* or *medium*) (*Bärenreiter BA 7004* or *7005*) or *Schubert Songs, Vol.2* (*high, medium* or *low*) (*Peters EP 8304a, b* or *c*)
Grenzen der Menschheit, D.716. *Schubert Lieder, Vol.17 for Bass Voice* (*Bärenreiter BA 7032*) or *Schubert Complete Songs, Vol.3* (*high, medium* or *low*) (*Peters EP 790a, b* or *c*)
Im Frühling, D.882. *Schubert Complete Songs, Vol.2* (*high, medium* or *low*) (*Peters EP 178a, b* or *c*)
Prometheus, D.674. *Schubert Lieder, Vol.17 for Bass Voice* (*Bärenreiter BA 7032*) or *Schubert Complete Songs, Vol.3* (*high, medium* or *low*) (*Peters EP 790a, b* or *c*)
Rastlose Liebe, Op.5 no.1, D.138. *Schubert Lieder, Vol.3* (*high* or *medium*) (*Bärenreiter BA 7004* or *7005*) or *Schubert Songs, Vol.2* (*high, medium* or *low*) (*Peters EP 8304a, b* or *c*)
Suleika II 'Ach um deine feuchten Schwingen', Op.31, D.717. *Schubert Lieder, Vol.4* (*high*) (*Bärenreiter BA 7006*) or *Schubert Songs, Vol.2* (*high, medium* or *low*) (*Peters EP 8304a, b* or *c*)

Schumann
Belsazar, Op.57. *Schumann 85 Selected Songs* (*high*) or *Schumann 90 Selected Songs* (*low*) (*Ger/Eng edn: International 1487* or *1402/M.D.S.*) or *Schumann Complete Songs, Vol.2* (*high* or *medium*) (*Peters EP 2384a* or *b*)
Der Hidalgo, Op.30 no.3. *Schumann Complete Songs, Vol.2* (*high* or *medium*) (*Peters EP 2384a* or *b*)
Der Kontrabandiste, Op.74 no.10. *Schumann 85 Selected Songs* (*high*) or *Schumann 90 Selected Songs* (*low*) (*Ger/Eng edn: International 1487* or *1402/M.D.S.*) or *Schumann Complete Songs, Vol.2* (*high* or *medium*) (*Peters EP 2384a* or *b*)
Provenzalisches Lied, Op.139 no.4. *Schumann Complete Songs, Vol.3* (*high* or *medium-low*) (*Peters EP 2385a* or *b*)
Waldesgespräch: no.3 from 'Liederkreis', Op.39 (*high* or *low*) (*Ger/Eng edn: International 3071* or *3072/M.D.S.*) or *Schumann Complete Songs, Vol.1* (*high, medium* or *low*) (*Peters EP 2383a, b* or *c*)

Stradella
Pièta, Signore! *24 Italian Songs and Arias of the 17th and 18th Centuries* (*medium high* or *medium low*) (*Ital/Eng edn: Schirmer/Music Sales*)
Se amor m'annoda il piede. *Anthology of Italian Song of the 17th and 18th Centuries, Book 2* (*high* or *low*) (*Ital/Eng edn: Schirmer/Music Sales*)

R. Strauss
Cäcilie, Op.27 no.2 (*high, medium* or *low*) (*Ger/Eng edn: Universal 05442a, b* or *c/M.D.S.*)
Für funfzehn Pfennige, Op.36 no.2. *Strauss Lieder, Vol.1* (*high, medium* or *low*) (*Universal 05463a, b* or *c/M.D.S.*)
Geduld, Op.10 no.5. *Strauss Lieder, Vol.2* (*high, medium* or *low*) (*Universal 05464a, b* or *c/M.D.S.*)
Hat gesagt – bleibt's nicht dabei, Op.36 no.3. *Strauss Lieder, Vol.4* (*high, medium* or *low*) (*Universal 05466a, b* or *c/M.D.S.*)
Hochzeitlich Lied, Op.37 no.6. *Strauss Lieder, Vol.2* (*high, medium* or *low*) (*Universal 05464a, b* or *c/M.D.S.*)
Kling!, Op.48 no.3. *Strauss Lieder, Vol.2* (*Boosey & Hawkes*)
Nachtgang, Op.29 no.3. *Strauss Lieder, Vol.2* (*high, medium* or *low*) (*Universal 05464a, b* or *c/M.D.S.*)
Das Rosenband, Op.36 no.1. *Strauss Lieder, Vol.3* (*high, medium* or *low*) (*Universal 05465a, b* or *c/M.D.S.*)
Sehnsucht, Op.32 no.2. *Strauss Lieder, Vol.3* (*high, medium* or *low*) (*Universal 05465a, b* or *c/M.D.S.*)
Wie sollten wir geheim sie halten, Op.19 no.4. *Strauss Lieder, Vol.2* (*high, medium* or *low*) (*Universal 05464a, b* or *c/M.D.S.*)

Vivaldi
Un certo non so che. *Anthology of Italian Song of the 17th and 18th Centuries, Book 1* (*high* or *low*) (*Ital/Eng edn: Schirmer/Music Sales*)

Wagner
5 Wesendonck Lieder: any song(s) (*high* or *low*) (*Ger/Eng edn: Peters EP 3445a* or *b*)

Walton
Anon. in Love: any of the 6 songs
Holy Thursday: no.4 from 'A Song for the Lord Mayor's Table' ⎤ *Walton Song Album (O.U.P.)*
3 Songs by Edith Sitwell: any song(s)
The Lord Mayor's Table: no.1 from 'A Song for the Lord Mayor's Table' ⎦

Singing, FRSM

All voices

Warlock   Sweet Content. *Warlock Song Album* (*Boosey & Hawkes*)

Wolf   An die Geliebte: no.32 from 'Mörike Lieder', Vol.3 (*high-medium*) (*Ger/Eng edn: Peters EP 3142a*) or
Wolf 35 Baritone-Bass Songs (*Ger/Eng edn: Peters EP 4291*)

An eine Äolsharfe: no.11 from 'Mörike Lieder', Vol.1 (*high-medium* or *low*) (*Ger/Eng edn: Peters EP 3140a or b*)

Im Frühling: no.13 from 'Mörike Lieder', Vol.2 (*high-medium* or *low*) (*Ger/Eng edn: Peters EP 3141a or b*)

3 Michelangelo Lieder for bass: any song(s) (*Ger/Eng edn: Peters EP 3155*)

Mignon 'Kennst du das Land': no.9 from 'Goethe Lieder', Vol.1 (*high-medium*) (*Peters EP 3156*) or
Wolf 51 Selected Songs (*medium-low*) (*Ger/Eng edn: Peters EP 4290b*)

Nachtzauber: no.8 from 'Eichendorff Lieder', Vol.1 (*high-medium* or *low*) (*Ger/Eng edn: Peters EP 3147a or b*)

Prometheus: no.49 from 'Goethe Lieder', Vol.2 (*high-medium*) (*Peters EP 3157*) or *Wolf 35 Baritone-Bass Songs* (*Ger/Eng edn: Peters EP 4291*)

Orchestral excerpts for FRSM

Violin

Brahms   Symphony no.4 in E minor, Op.98: 1st movt (letter O to the end)

Elgar   Enigma Variations, Op.36: 2nd variation ('H.D.S.-P.') (fig. 5 –8)

R. Strauss   Don Juan, Op.20 (opening to letter B)

Viola

Mendelssohn   A Midsummer Night's Dream, Op.61: Scherzo (bars 187–208 *and* 296–323)

Shostakovich   Symphony no.5 in D minor, Op.47: 1st movt (fig. 15–17)

R. Strauss   Don Juan, Op.20 (opening to letter B)

Cello

Beethoven   Symphony no.5 in C minor, Op.67: 2nd movt (opening to bar 10 *and* bars 49–59, 98–106 *and* 114–123)

Mendelssohn   A Midsummer Night's Dream, Op.61: Scherzo (bars 70–93 *and* 296–323)

R. Strauss   Don Juan, Op.20 (opening to letter B)

Double Bass

Beethoven   Symphony no.5 in C minor, Op.67: 3rd movt (opening to bar 18 *and* bars 44–61 *and* 140–160)

Mozart   Symphony no.39 in E♭, K.543: 1st movt (bars 40–54) *and* 4th movt (bars 115–137)

R. Strauss   Ein Heldenleben, Op.40 (fig. 9–11 *and* 77–78)

Harp

R. Strauss   Don Juan, Op.20 (bars 104–149)

Stravinsky   Symphony in Three Movements: 2nd movt (fig. 118–134)

Tchaikovsky   'Swan Lake' Suite, Op.20: no.4 – Scène (Second Dance of the Queen) (opening to fig. 1)

Flute

Beethoven   Leonore Overture no.3, Op.72b (29 bars after letter E for 33 bars)

Mendelssohn   A Midsummer Night's Dream, Op.61: Scherzo (bar 338 to the end)

Ravel   Suite no.2 from 'Daphnis et Chloé' (fig. 176–179)

Oboe

Brahms   Violin Concerto in D, Op.77: 2nd movt (opening to bar 30)

Ravel   Le Tombeau de Couperin: Prélude (opening to fig. 2) *and* Menuet (opening to fig. 4 *and* fig. 9–10)

Rossini   Overture to 'La Scala di Seta' (The Silken Ladder) (Introduction *and* bars 37–53)

Clarinet

Beethoven   Symphony no.6 in F ('Pastoral'), Op.68: 1st movt (bars 474–492)

Kodály   Dances of Galánta (bars 31–65)

Shostakovich   Symphony no.9 in E♭, Op.70: 2nd movt (fig. 28–32)

Bassoon

Beethoven   Symphony no.4 in B♭, Op.60: 4th movt (bars 184–189)

Shostakovich   Symphony no.7 in C ('Leningrad'), Op.60: 1st movt (fig. 60–66)

Stravinsky   The Rite of Spring (Le Sacre du Printemps): Part 1 – Introduction (opening to fig. 3)

Orchestral excerpts for FRSM

Horn

Brahms	Symphony no.2 in D, Op.73: 1st movt (bars 454–477) *and* 2nd movt (bars 17–31 – letters A to B)
R. Strauss	Ein Heldenleben, Op.40 (opening to fig. 1 *and* fig. 109 to the end)
Tchaikovsky	Symphony no.4 in F minor, Op.36: 1st movt (opening to moderato *and* bars 300–306)

Trumpet

Bizet	'Carmen' Suite no.1: Prélude (Andante moderato to the end)
Mahler	Symphony no.5 in C♯ minor: 1st movt (opening to fig. 1)
Stravinsky	Petrushka: Scene 3 – Waltz (Ballerina and Moor) (fig. 140–143 *and* 149–153)

Trombone

Mozart	Requiem (Mass no.19) in D minor, K.626: no.3 – Tuba mirum (opening to bar 18)
Ravel	Boléro (fig. 10 to two bars after fig. 11)
Rossini	Overture to 'Guillaume Tell' (William Tell) (bars 92–131)

Tuba

Dvořák	'Carnival' Concert Overture, Op.92 (bars 387–404)
Stravinsky	The Rite of Spring (Le Sacre du Printemps): Part 1 – Dance of the Earth (from five bars after fig. 78 for two bars)
Wagner	Prelude (Overture) to 'Die Meistersinger von Nürnberg' (bars 158–188)

Tuned Percussion

Dukas	L'Apprenti Sorcier (The Sorcerer's Apprentice) (fig. 17–20 *and* 22–24)
Gershwin	'Porgy and Bess' Concert Suite (fig. 13–17)
Kabalevsky	'Colas Breugnon' Suite, Op.24: 1st movt (fig. 9–12) *and* 4th movt (fig. 12–13)

Timpani

Beethoven	Violin Concerto in D, Op.61: 1st movt (opening to bar 9)
Hindemith	Symphonic Metamorphosis on Themes of Carl Maria von Weber: 2nd movt 'Turandot' (Scherzo) (five bars after letter V to eight bars after letter W *and* two bars before letter Z to the end)
Stravinsky	The Rite of Spring (Le Sacre du Printemps): Part 2 – Sacrificial Dance (fig. 189 to the end)

Snare Drum

Rimsky-Korsakov	Capriccio Espagnol, Op.34: 4th movt 'Scena e canto gitano' (opening to five bars after letter L)
Shostakovich	Symphony no.7 in C ('Leningrad'), Op.60: 1st movt (fig. 19 to three bars before fig. 52)
Suppé	Overture to 'Pique Dame' (Queen of Spades) (from four bars before letter C to ten bars before letter D)

Cymbals

Mussorgsky	A Night on the Bare Mountain, arr. Rimsky-Korsakov (from letter S for seven bars)
Rachmaninov	Piano Concerto no.2 in C minor, Op.18: 3rd movt (opening to meno mosso after bars 37/38)
Tchaikovsky	Symphony no.4 in F minor, Op.36: 4th movt (bar 272 to the end)

REPERTOIRE LISTS

Accepted related instruments

(see pp. 8, 12 and 15)

Main Instrument	Related Instrument(s)
Harpsichord	Spinet, Virginal
Violin	Viola
Viola	Violin
Cello	Viola da Gamba
Recorder	Sopranino, Descant, Treble, Tenor
Flute	Piccolo
Oboe	Cor Anglais
Clarinet	E♭ Clarinet, Bass Clarinet
Bassoon	Contrabassoon
Saxophone	Soprano, Alto, Tenor, Baritone
Trumpet	Cornet in B♭, Flugelhorn
Cornet in B♭	Trumpet, Flugelhorn
Flugelhorn	Cornet in B♭, Trumpet
Trombone	Bass Trombone
Baritone	Euphonium
Euphonium	Baritone
Tuba	Sousaphone, Euphonium

NB Candidates wishing to perform part of their Recital on an instrument not listed among the accepted related instruments above should apply in writing to the Director of Examinations.

REPERTOIRE LISTS

APPENDICES

Specimen questions and indicative responses

The **specimen questions** on pp. 102–104 are intended to provide a clear sense of how the examiners might address the various areas of the Viva Voce. The selected **indicative responses** on pp. 105–111 provide an indication of the sorts of response that would be expected from candidates within the main marking bands (Distinction, Pass, Fail). It is important to note that these are specimen questions only, and that none of them may actually be asked in the exam. Additionally, not all areas specified below will necessarily be covered by examiners in their questioning.

SPECIMEN QUESTIONS

DipABRSM

Musical and instrumental outlook
- What attracted you to your own-choice item?
- What were your considerations in selecting the repertoire for your Recital programme?

Repertoire and Programme Notes
- Where does this particular work stand in the creative output of the composer? What features characterize his works of this time?
- In your Programme Notes you state that Haydn was 'a Romantic before his time'. How do you account for that opinion?
- Tell us about *The Well-Tempered Clavier* – why did Bach write it?
- ** In your Programme Notes you describe Fauré as 'one of the leading figures in the history of French music'. What important contributions did he make to the field of vocal music in particular?
- Are there any nationalistic influences in this piece or features that might indicate the nationality of the composer?

Musical language and form
- What form is this piece in? What features of the structure affect the way you play its various sections?
- ** Can you outline the structure of the sonata's first movement with reference to the score? How do you make this structure clear to the listener?
- Please could you map out the exposition of the fugue for us? What happens to the subject at this point?

Style and interpretation
- Your own-choice item was a contemporary song – tell us about your interpretation of this piece.
- What are the differences in your approaches to the Beethoven and the Brahms?
- What mood are you trying to create in the Poulenc? How do you achieve it?
- How did you decide to characterize each of the variations?
- ** Is playing from memory helpful to a harpist?
- What stylistic issues did you consider throughout your programme?
- As this Mozart concerto was originally written for natural horn, could you explain which notes would have sounded different when played at the first performance?
- How has the cello changed since Bach's time?
- ** Are there any specific aspects of the piano part that have influenced your performance?

*   *indicative responses to these specimen questions are to be found on pp. 105–106.*

APPENDICES

LRSM

Musical and instrumental outlook
- How did you prepare the detail needed to play Berg's *Four Pieces*, Op. 5?
- How do you set about preparing a song in a language other than your own? How do you ensure that the meaning of the text is conveyed to your audience?

Repertoire and Programme Notes
- Is this piece typical of the composer's style?
- Who were the main influences on this composer?
- * For whom did Copland write his Clarinet Concerto? Do you think the dedicatee influenced the music in any way?
- Tell us about the contribution made by Hindemith to the brass repertoire.
- What were the main influences on Debussy's compositional style?
- * In your Programme Notes you write that the D minor Sonata belongs to Beethoven's 'middle period'. Describe some of the features of his works of this time.

Musical language and form
- Explain the compositional techniques used in this piece, particularly in relation to its harmony.
- How did you show in your performance the ways in which Stravinsky's *Three Pieces* link together?
- How does Handel achieve variety in this Chaconne?
- How does this movement's structure differ from a textbook sonata-form plan? How does this influence your performance?

Style and interpretation
- You write in your Programme Notes that, 'unlike Debussy, Ravel was not an Impressionist'. Is the piece you performed an Impressionist work?
- How do you judge how much *rubato* is appropriate in this piece?
- When playing an arrangement, to what extent do you try to simulate the sound of the original instrument? Or do you try to make the music sound appropriate to your instrument?
- How would you research ornamentation for Baroque pieces?
- For many years, scholars and performers have tried to define authentic performance practice. How has this impinged on your work?
- Who were the great violinists in Elgar's time? Some wrote books of studies that are still in use today. Can you name any of them?
- What are the main differences between the pianos of Mozart's era and Rachmaninov's? How do these differences affect the sound and colour that performers aim to produce on a modern instrument, in order for their playing to be regarded as stylish?
- * Other than technical security and musical sensitivity, what factors contribute to a successful recital?
- How has the development of material used for making strings affected the sound?
- What were the differences in the seventeenth century between English organs and their counterparts in Germany? How did this affect the development of organ composition in England?
- * Which performers do you particularly admire? Do you find that listening to their live performances or recordings helps you in matters of interpretation and style? Explain how, or why not?

* *indicative responses to these specimen questions are to be found on pp. 107–109.*

FRSM

Musical and instrumental outlook

- How did you address the issue of stamina in preparing this piece?
- Ravel's *Gaspard de la Nuit* is widely regarded as one of the most challenging pieces in the piano repertoire. What particular difficulties did it present for you and how did you overcome them?

Repertoire and Written Submission

- How do you see the function and techniques of your instrument changing in the twenty-first century? What contemporary music do you know which presents new challenges?
- What is the origin of the word 'Partita'? Do Bach's Partitas differ from his other Suites in any way?
- It could be said that in the first half of the twentieth century the French organ composers were the only 'school' of composers for the organ. What happened in the latter half of the century?
- Describe the development of the Toccata as a genre.
- To what extent is this work 'of its time'?
- * ● In the chamber music repertoire, the voice has been used by a number of composers. Tell us about some examples and any that you consider to be important in the historical context of the voice.
- What other works are there in the French repertoire for saxophone?
- Paul Patterson's *Conversations* is a very popular work. What other British clarinet music from the late twentieth century has become accepted as standard repertoire?
- The Concerto you played today was written for Dennis Brain. Tell us about other works written for him and how they suited his particular style of playing.

Musical language and form

- How does Bach's keyboard writing differ from that of his contemporary, Scarlatti?
- How important is French influence in this composer's works?
- To what extent could this piece be regarded as 'late Romantic'?
- * ● How does the composer achieve unity within this series of varied pieces?
- Are there any particular aspects of the work's structure that have helped you in developing your interpretation?

Style and interpretation

- You ornamented the repeat of the Sarabande – is there any evidence that Bach would have done this?
- Can you describe the various styles that influenced this piece? How does this knowledge affect your interpretation?
- Is there a Russian style of playing this music? If so, does this influence you in any way?
- Are there any features of the piano part that have helped you to develop your performance?
- What part have commissions played in promoting the instrument?
- How have performing conventions changed from the nineteenth century? How have these changes influenced your performance?
- How did this composer's works affect the development of the instrument?
- Why did the virtuoso trumpet style of the Baroque period not continue into the Classical era?
- * ● What do you know of the composer's own performances? To what extent should a performer be influenced by them?
- Tell us about how the leading harp makers of the twentieth century contributed to the development of the instrument.
- Where do you think the organ is going as an instrument in the twenty-first century? Do you think it is becoming more of a secular than liturgical instrument?
- In the Maxwell Davies piece, you had to produce many varied tone colours. How did you decide to highlight these and how did you achieve the range of tone?
- * ● What criteria did you use when selecting your edition? How do the main editions of this piece differ?

* *indicative responses to these specimen questions are to be found on pp. 109–111.*

INDICATIVE RESPONSES

DipABRSM

Repertoire and Programme Notes

In your Programme Notes you describe Fauré as 'one of the leading figures in the history of French music'. What important contributions did he make to the field of vocal music in particular?

Distinction

The candidate demonstrated an understanding of Fauré's place in the development of the *mélodie* and an awareness of the three periods of compositional activity in Fauré's creative output. Comparisons were made with contemporary *Lied* composers, most notably Schumann, to demonstrate nationalistic differences of style. The candidate considered Fauré's setting of poetry to be evocative rather than using words as mere vehicles of sonority – a novel approach which also influenced the songs of Debussy, Ravel and Poulenc. The candidate acknowledged that Fauré's intimate style was not always best suited to works on a grander scale, citing the rarely performed opera *Pénélope*, but named the *Requiem* as a lasting choral monument to rank alongside Fauré's prolific output of songs.

Pass

The candidate clearly understood the historical context of Fauré's works and enthused about some songs which had previously been studied. Several other composers in this genre who preceded Fauré were named, but the candidate did not elaborate on the influences (musical or poetic) to which Fauré was subjected, and references to his influence on later *mélodie* composers were sound but lacked depth. The candidate was more comfortable when referring to Fauré's chamber music, commenting on his subtle harmonic innovations and classical elegance. It was suggested that the *Requiem* carries a resonance that reoccurs in later French compositions, such as Duruflé's *Requiem*.

Fail

The candidate appreciated the period and style to which Fauré belonged, but had difficulty in expressing the place of the composer as a catalyst in the development of the *mélodie*. The candidate's knowledge of Fauré's vocal output was very limited, and suggestions of any other French composers of this genre who might have been influenced by his style were not forthcoming. A knowledge of Fauré's instrumental composition also lacked depth, but the candidate suggested that the *Requiem* (from which the *Pie Jesu* comes) would be a lasting favourite of the concert-going public.

Musical language and form

Can you outline the structure of the sonata's first movement with reference to the score? How do you make this structure clear to the listener?

Distinction

The candidate showed clearly and confidently where the main structural features of the movement were in the score, and pointed out how they conformed to conventional sonata form. A commanding understanding of the importance of key to the form was also shown. The candidate then demonstrated how the various stages in the formal argument could be highlighted by the performer, using subtle nuances of balance and tempo, in order to make the listener fully aware of the principal motifs and the structure overall. Particular success was achieved in showing the tension raised by the dominant preparation. An understanding of the need not to overstress these points in performance was also shown.

Pass

The candidate showed a good awareness of the importance of key to the form, with a little hesitation and misreading of the dominant preparation in the development section. However, the structural features were clearly grasped. There was some illustration of the main turning-points, with a little overemphasis at the second subject area in particular. The candidate was less successful, however, in explaining how his/her playing could highlight these elements. The structural importance of the recapitulation was understood and demonstrated with some success.

Fail

The candidate was unsure in response and showed little awareness of the main structural points, confusing the recapitulation with the coda. The significance of the development section was not clearly shown or explained and the end of the exposition was not identified, despite some prompting. The importance of key to the form was not successfully articulated or demonstrated. While showing some theoretical knowledge of the workings of sonata form, the candidate was unable to explain how a performance could clarify the shape of the structure and aid the listener's understanding – and therefore enjoyment – of the music.

Style and interpretation

Is playing from memory helpful to a harpist?

Distinction

The candidate showed exactly why memorization is vital for a harpist. The visual aspects of playing the harp were fully explained and why having to look at, and turn the pages of, a score would greatly detract from the stage performance, technically and visually. Stage presentation from the audience's point of view was also mentioned, as the music stand could block both the sound and sightlines for the audience. The expressive freedom gained, the focus on tone quality and the overall flow of the performance were also stressed. The candidate explained the best way to manage a score in cases where playing from memory was not possible (i.e. the height of the stand and practical ways to minimize page-turning).

Pass

The candidate explained the different aspects of playing from memory from a harpist's point of view. The expressive and visual freedom that this permitted was outlined, as were the practical details of managing a score, if required. The visual needs of a harpist while performing were discussed, following a little prompting from the examiners.

Fail

The candidate had some understanding that memorization could be beneficial, but was unable to express exact ideas on how to memorize or, if not, how to manage a score.

Style and interpretation

Are there any specific aspects of the piano part that have influenced your performance?

Distinction

The candidate showed a thorough understanding of the nature of the work and the significance of the piano part and how, in general terms, this caused both players to approach their own parts. There was also an understanding of the historical context of the piano writing. The way the musical material was divided between the instruments had been carefully analysed and the candidate was able to explain how this influenced the performance, taking into account aspects such as balance, texture, harmony, motivic development and dynamic shaping.

Pass

The candidate showed a broadly convincing understanding of the nature of the work and the significance of the piano part. There was some understanding of the historical context of the piano writing. Some care had been taken to analyse the way in which the parts related to and supported each other and the candidate was able to describe and explain some particular aspects that had influenced the performance.

Fail

There was little evidence that the candidate had considered the significance of the piano part in any detail. The candidate was unable to discuss the historical context of the piano writing and there was no comment or explanation as to how the interrelation of the parts had influenced the interpretation.

LRSM

Repertoire and Programme Notes

For whom did Copland write his Clarinet Concerto? Do you think the dedicatee influenced the music in any way?

Distinction

The candidate gave an outstanding account of the influence of Benny Goodman on Copland's Clarinet Concerto and showed an excellent grasp of the work's idiom. Goodman's background as a classically-trained jazz clarinettist who had a significant influence on the classical music field through the commissioning of many important twentieth-century works, his importance as a figure in the swing period of jazz, as well as his own jazz compositions and manner of playing, had all been thoroughly researched by the candidate. The jazz elements in the Concerto were pointed out in the score and attention was drawn to rhythmic patterns and syncopation, to the quasi-improvisatory cadenza and to the extensive use of the high register of the clarinet. The candidate also explained how performance conventions (especially rhythmic flexibility, dynamic inflection and variety of attack) affect an interpretation of the Concerto. Specific instrumental features were also highlighted. The candidate was aware of Copland's other jazz-inspired works and explained that there are also South-American influences in the Concerto, particularly in the second movement.

Pass

The candidate displayed a knowledge of Benny Goodman and was able to list a number of the works written for him by important twentieth-century composers. There was also an understanding of Goodman's significance as a central figure in the swing period of jazz and how some of the features of swing jazz (harmonic, thematic and other stylistic conventions) can be found in the Concerto. However, more attention could have been given to details in the scoring and to the extent that Goodman's own playing influenced features such as the extensive use of the higher register and the inclusion of the final glissando. The candidate's comment on how unusual it was for a performer, in an age before Previn and Kennedy, to be equally at home in jazz and classical music was well made.

Fail

The candidate knew of Benny Goodman's influence as a leading exponent of the swing style, but was unable to list many of the other important works written for him. There was some awareness of the jazzy effect of the syncopated rhythm patterns but the candidate was unable to identify or explain in sufficient detail particular aspects of Goodman's swing style in the Concerto, such as the harmonic, thematic or particular performance conventions that might affect an interpretation. The candidate was not sufficiently familiar with Copland's other music to comment in an informed way on how this Concerto differed from, or resembled, his other major scores.

Repertoire and Programme Notes

In your Programme Notes you write that the D minor Sonata belongs to Beethoven's 'middle period'. Describe some of the features of his works of this time.

Distinction

The candidate displayed a clear understanding of the features distinguishing the middle-period works, with confident reference made to a number of pieces in different genres. The importance of harmony and key choice was clearly explained and illustrated, with good examples of Neapolitan and mediant relationships. The adaptation of existing forms was well explored, with reference to sonata and variation forms for the instrument. The use of a broadening range of effects on the instrument was illustrated, and illuminatingly linked to the composer's exploration of a wider orchestral palette during the period. Some ideas were also offered on how some of these points differed from the composer's usage in his earlier works.

Pass

The candidate had a good grasp of the distinguishing features of the middle period in pieces for the instrument, with some areas, such as key relationships and the adaptation of forms, needing some prompting. Illustration was forthcoming on request, with points sometimes not quite matching the extracts played. However, some valid points were presented on the increased compression of ideas during the period, with some good examples of motifs which generated larger structures.

Fail

The candidate showed only a limited idea of the main features, and some works named did not belong to the period. Ideas of key relationships and harmonic usage were vague. While the stormy mood typical of many of the middle-period works was identified, more searching and analytical responses were lacking. Comments tended to focus to a great degree on biography, making too simplistic a link between the life and the works.

Style and interpretation | **Other than technical security and musical sensitivity, what factors contribute to a successful recital?**

Distinction

The candidate described an ample range of factors, with particular attention given to programming. The importance of variety of mood, style, key and length in the pieces chosen was highlighted, with good examples of programmes involving a selection of composers as well as single-composer recitals. Communication at all levels was mentioned, including stage presence, eye contact, an easy unstressed manner, a serious focus and an appreciative smile at applause. Other attributes of the performer – including the attitude towards management and hosts, appropriate dress and a willingness to meet people – were communicated with humour and verve. The candidate went on to give striking examples of performances that entered another dimension through the personality of the interpreter or the character of the venue.

Pass

The candidate had some good ideas about the importance of being able to communicate the spirit of the music. Points concerning programming took a little while to emerge, but a fair range of possibilities was explored, some more fruitful than others. Some good suggestions for the use of more modern repertoire were made, with an awareness of a potentially wary audience reaction and how to moderate it. Some attributes of the performer were described.

Fail

The candidate mentioned the importance of a good instrument to show off the performer's skill, but had few other ideas and was inclined to think that little more was required. The audience was not taken into account and, when the idea of the importance of communication was suggested, it was greeted blankly. When prompted about programming, the candidate showed a tendency to stick to conventional combinations of pieces and communicated little sense of the wider repertoire for the instrument.

Style and interpretation | **Which performers do you particularly admire? Do you find that listening to their live performances or recordings helps you in matters of interpretation and style? Explain how, or why not?**

Distinction

The candidate discussed in an authoritative way a number of performers, some contemporary and some from the past (referring to their recorded legacy). The candidate was able to express detailed opinions on particular performers' strengths and weaknesses. The knowledge and understanding was such that real insight into the music was made through comparing performances of the same work by different artists. There were considerably probing and intelligent comments on matters concerning style and interpretation and how these, in different ways, may have affected the candidate's own interpretation.

Pass

The candidate named a number of artists and expressed, in a broadly convincing way, knowledge of their performances. There was some understanding of the chosen performers' particular areas of expertise. To some degree the candidate was able to discuss the style and interpretation of one or two performances familiar to him/her and how far these had influenced his/her own interpretation.

Fail

The candidate was able to name a few performers but was not sufficiently knowledgeable about their particular style or their interpretations. There was little evidence of any thought having been given to whether any performers had influenced the candidate's own interpretation.

FRSM

Repertoire and Written Submission

In the chamber music repertoire, the voice has been used by a number of composers. Tell us about some examples and any that you consider to be important in the historical context of the voice.

Distinction

The candidate began by explaining that prior to the twentieth century, the use of the voice within a chamber ensemble was a rarity, and he/she cited a few examples. It was pointed out that in such works the third instrument was generally used in an obbligato capacity to the duo protagonists of piano and voice. Discussion of the twentieth-century repertoire, including works by Butterworth and Vaughan Williams, was detailed and perceptive. The way in which Copland's *As it fell upon a day* and Barber's *Dover Beach* inspired other works of this kind was clearly articulated. The candidate considered that in all these compositions the voice was the dominant participant within the ensemble, but another work – *Notturno* by Othmar Schoeck – was significant in that it carried the description 'Five movements for string quartet and voice', thus suggesting a more balanced integration of the roles.

Pass

The candidate argued that, although we consider chamber music to be an invention of the eighteenth century, the meaning of the term was formerly interpreted as music which was not performed publicly in a church or theatre but was presented by small forces in a private setting. Consequently, there was some justification in suggesting that Bach's secular cantatas, such as the 'Peasant Cantata', were chamber music. The definition of chamber music for the voice was then established. The candidate explained that an early example was Schubert's *Der Hirt auf dem Felsen*. It was claimed, however, that the genre was not seriously developed during the nineteenth century but in the early part of the twentieth, with Vaughan Williams's *On Wenlock Edge*, which inspired other composers such as Barber to emulate it. The candidate suggested that contemporary composers had experimented with using the voice in an instrumental way (i.e. without text) within a chamber grouping, but was unable to give an example.

Fail

The candidate maintained that from the time of the Elizabethan composers the voice had been used in combination with other small-scale forces, such as lute and viols, which could be considered chamber music. It was stated that over the course of time keyboard instruments had become the norm as the partner of the singer, although composers had sometimes introduced additional instruments to the ensemble – a song by Schubert was recalled which required an obbligato woodwind instrument, although more precise details were not forthcoming. The candidate surmised that other chamber-group combinations have been employed alongside the voice since then, but was unable to give more than one example from the twentieth century.

Musical language and form

How does the composer achieve unity within this series of varied pieces?

Distinction

The candidate had an excellent grasp of the overall structure of this cycle of character pieces. The significance of the core motif, and many examples of its different uses and treatments, were cited. The sharing of thematic material and the linking of some movements were also suggested as ways in which the composer achieves a sense of unity, as was the use of closely related keys. At all times the candidate demonstrated a clear analytical understanding of the music and a readiness to draw attention to examples in the score. Also impressive was an ability to cross-refer to other pieces, showing an all-round familiarity with the composer's output and style.

Pass

The candidate displayed a grasp of the significance of the core motif and an awareness of its varied employment throughout the cycle. Detail was occasionally a little limited, but several examples of the motif's different treatments were cited with reference to the score, while some other aspects of how the composer achieves unity were touched upon, such as the sharing of thematic material. A generally good grasp of analytical detail was demonstrated.

Fail

Although the idea of the unifying motif was understood, the ways in which the composer varies its treatment throughout the cycle were not clearly explained. A much firmer analytical grasp was needed, as was an ability to draw examples from the music performed. No other suggestions as to how the composer achieves unity were put forward and there was little evidence of a real understanding of the structural aspects of the score.

Style and interpretation

What do you know of the composer's own performances? To what extent should a performer be influenced by them?

Distinction

The candidate explained that, despite having been present at a live performance of this work given by the composer, a recently issued recording – also by the composer – had been more beneficial in the preparation of the recital. The live performance had been notable for its billing as an 'event', but it was evident that the composer lacked the temperament to perform the work with sufficient technical assurance in a live context. In particular, the tempi had often appeared hurried, which limited the range of tonal expression in the performance. By comparison, the recording was much more instructive in displaying the intentions of the composer, since it had been recorded in the less pressured environment of the studio. Here the tempi were more controlled and the ideas within the music more clearly expressed. The candidate gave the view, however, that the recording was no more than a guide to the work, and that it was necessary to develop one's own individual interpretation rather than merely create a clone of the composer's performance. Correspondence with the composer had elucidated the images and ideas that had inspired the composition, and these, together with the programme notes from the concert and the sleeve notes from the CD, had helped shape the candidate's distinctive interpretation.

Pass

The candidate stated that, although he/she had attended a live performance given by the composer, this work had not featured on the programme. A recent recording of the work by the composer had been acquired and this had provided the interpretative basis for today's performance. The candidate stated that the recording had been useful in terms of developing the overall structure of the work – both for the tempo relationships and in suggesting tonal colours – but conceded that this was not an ideal means of developing an individual interpretation, as the composer's musical mannerisms might subconsciously be assumed. The CD had, however, offered the opportunity of a secure base from which the performance might mature.

Fail

The candidate was not aware that the composer had performed and recorded this work, and its place in today's recital programme had been suggested by the candidate's teacher. The candidate felt that, where a composer had performed or recorded his/her own work, it was perfectly valid to use the performance as an example of how the work should be played, as this gave it authenticity.

Style and interpretation

What criteria did you use when selecting your edition? How do the main editions of this piece differ?

Distinction

The candidate presented a clear overview of the published editions, from the first (available in facsimile) to the most recent. The significance of the lack of the autograph was clearly explained, as was the effect of this on all subsequent editions. The varying schools of editorial approach were outlined, with good examples from the nineteenth century in particular. Editorial practice and its effects on performance were well explained. The candidate proceeded to elaborate on criteria for choosing an edition, emphasizing the need both to check details against the earliest available sources and to guard against disguised editorial intervention.

Pass

The candidate gave a broad picture of the editions of the work, with some detail about how they differed. A little thought was required to proceed further, but eventually the significant fact of the absence of the autograph was mentioned. In choosing an edition the candidate was somewhat inclined to lean heavily on the most recent scholarship, but clearly identified and illustrated the value of earlier editions in terms of performance practice history.

Fail

The candidate showed little knowledge of editions other than the one chosen, and was dismissive of earlier editions, presenting them simply as inaccurate. The problems raised by the initial publishing history of the piece and its impact on performance were not mentioned. The candidate recognized the need to establish the composer's indications as a basis for interpretation, but was unable to view his/her own performance as itself forming part of, and being influenced by, performance practice history.

Marking criteria

The tables below outline the **marking criteria** for the Music Performance Diplomas. The demands of the criteria are carefully structured, not only between the levels of Diploma, as you move up from DipABRSM to LRSM and FRSM level, but also between the marking bands: Distinction, Pass and Fail. They are used by the examiners when coming to a decision about the way your performance measures up against the Associated Board's standards, and they also explain to you, the candidate, what qualities are required at each level and for each exam component, thus helping you to prepare for your exam with confidence. The attainment descriptions given on pp. 122–124 and the selected indicative responses to specimen Viva Voce questions on pp. 105–111 provide a further mechanism for showing the expectations at each level.

Section 1: Recital

	DipABRSM	LRSM	FRSM
42–60 **Distinction** Excellent. Candidate has demonstrated exemplary standards in most areas examined.	Assured, persuasive and effectively communicated performance, demonstrating both artistic awareness and a secure technique in a range of styles.	Authoritative and intuitive performance, demonstrating both artistic integrity and technical command in a range of styles.	Outstanding, completely assured and authoritative performance, demonstrating mature artistry and consummate technical ease.
36–41 **A high pass** Very good. Candidate has demonstrated commendable standards in most areas examined and may have shown excellence in some.	Confident performance, demonstrating some sensitivity and good technique in a range of styles.	Assured, persuasive and effectively communicated performance, demonstrating both artistic awareness and a secure technique in a range of styles.	**24–41** **Pass** Authoritative, persuasively communicated performance, demonstrating artistic integrity and technical command.
30–35 **A clear pass** Good. Candidate has demonstrated a good overall standard in most areas examined.	Good performance, showing technical competence and a broad range of musical understanding.	Confident performance, demonstrating some sensitivity and good technique in a range of styles.	
24–29 **Pass** Candidate has shown competence in most areas examined and has satisfied the requirements for the award.	Solid performance in a range of styles, showing technical competence and some musical understanding at a level beyond ABRSM Grade 8.	Solid performance, showing technical competence and a broad musical understanding in a range of styles.	
0–23 **Fail** Candidate has not satisfied the basic requirements for the award.	Despite evidence of some competence, technical and musical grasp not equal to the demands of the programme at this level.	Despite evidence of some competence, technical and musical grasp not equal to the demands of the programme at this level.	Insufficient evidence that the candidate has advanced significantly beyond LRSM level.

Programme Notes (DipABRSM and LRSM)/Written Submission (FRSM)

	DipABRSM	LRSM	FRSM
Distinction Excellent. Candidate has demonstrated exemplary standards in most areas examined.	Notes are pertinent and persuasively written, with thoroughly researched and well-balanced commentary.	Notes are highly perceptive and persuasively written, with a high level of research and excellent organization of material.	Submission is highly perceptive and convincing, clearly structured and expressed, with excellent organization and control of materials. Very advanced research skills, personal insight and critical evaluation of sources. A comprehensive survey of relevant source material. Excellent use of musical and literary quotations.
A high pass Very good. Candidate has demonstrated commendable standards in most areas examined and may have shown excellence in some.	Notes provide an interesting and relevant commentary on the items performed. The material is well-organized and logically researched.	Notes are pertinent and persuasively written. The material is well-organized and logically researched.	**Pass** Submission is pertinent and comprehensively argued, with good overall shape, use of language and organization.
A clear pass Good. Candidate has demonstrated a good overall standard in most areas examined.	Notes provide well-chosen detail on items performed, and firm evidence of helpful analysis based on sound research. Good presentation, structure, level of literacy and grammatical accuracy.	Notes provide well-chosen detail on items performed, and firm evidence of helpful analysis based on sound research. Good presentation, structure, level of literacy and grammatical accuracy.	A rigorous survey of relevant source material, with a high level of research, personal insight and critical evaluation. Apposite use of musical and literary quotations.
Pass Candidate has shown competence in most areas examined and has satisfied the requirements for the award.	Notes give background on items performed with some evidence of appropriate analysis and research. Acceptable level of presentation, literacy and accuracy, avoiding unexplained technical language.	Notes give background on items performed with some evidence of appropriate analysis and research. Acceptable level of presentation, literacy and accuracy, avoiding unexplained technical language.	
Fail Candidate has not satisfied the basic requirements for the award.	Notes fail to give background on items performed or sufficient evidence of appropriate analysis and research. Inadequate presentation and grammatically weak.	Notes fail to give background on items performed or sufficient evidence of appropriate analysis and research. Inadequate presentation and grammatically weak.	Submission shows limited understanding, is poorly argued, lacks appropriate examples and quotations, and demonstrates little evidence of appropriately advanced research. Grammatically weak.

APPENDICES

Section 2.1: Viva Voce

	DipABRSM	LRSM	FRSM
19–25 Distinction Excellent. Candidate has demonstrated exemplary standards in most areas examined.	Outstanding communication skills. A commanding knowledge of the instrument, its idiom and repertoire. Mastery of the issues raised in the Programme Notes.	Outstanding communication skills. A commanding knowledge of the instrument, its idiom and repertoire. Mastery of the issues raised in the Programme Notes.	Outstanding communication skills. An expert knowledge of the instrument, its idiom and repertoire. Mastery of the issues raised in the Written Submission.
16–18 A high pass Very good. Candidate has demonstrated commendable standards in most areas examined and may have shown excellence in some.	Impressive communication skills. A comprehensive knowledge of the instrument, its idiom and repertoire. A firm grasp of the issues raised in the Programme Notes.	Impressive communication skills. A comprehensive knowledge of the instrument, its idiom and repertoire. A firm grasp of the issues raised in the Programme Notes.	**10–18 Pass** Impressive communication skills. A commanding knowledge of the instrument, its idiom and repertoire. A full understanding of the issues raised in the Written Submission.
13–15 A clear pass Good. Candidate has demonstrated a good overall standard in most areas examined.	Good communication skills. A sound working knowledge of the instrument, its idiom and repertoire. A broad grasp of the issues raised in the Programme Notes.	Good communication skills. A sound working knowledge of the instrument, its idiom and repertoire. A broad grasp of the issues raised in the Programme Notes.	
10–12 Pass Candidate has shown competence in most areas examined and has satisfied the requirements for the award.	Competent communication skills. A broad working knowledge of the instrument, its idiom and repertoire. A grasp of the issues raised in the Programme Notes.	Competent communication skills. A broad working knowledge of the instrument, its idiom and repertoire. A grasp of the issues raised in the Programme Notes.	
0–9 Fail Candidate has not satisfied the basic requirements for the award.	Weak communication skills. Patchy knowledge of the instrument, its idiom and repertoire. Unconvincing grasp of the issues raised in the Programme Notes.	Weak communication skills. Patchy knowledge of the instrument, its idiom and repertoire. Unconvincing grasp of the issues raised in the Programme Notes.	Insufficient communication skills. Insufficient knowledge of the instrument, its idiom and repertoire. Unconvincing grasp of the issues raised in the Written Submission.

Section 2.2: Quick Study

	DipABRSM	LRSM	FRSM
12–15 **Distinction** Excellent. Candidate has demonstrated exemplary standards in most areas examined.	An excellent performance, demonstrating artistry and full technical security. An instinctive approach.	An excellent performance, demonstrating artistry and full technical security. An instinctive approach.	An excellent performance, demonstrating artistry and full technical security. An instinctive approach.
10–11 **A high pass** Very good. Candidate has demonstrated commendable standards in most areas examined and may have shown excellence in some.	Well performed and idiomatic, with attention to all or most points of detail. An assured approach.	Well performed and idiomatic, with attention to all or most points of detail. An assured approach.	**6–11** **Pass** An idiomatic performance despite technical imperfections and some missing points of detail. An assured approach.
8–9 **A clear pass** Good. Candidate has demonstrated a good overall standard in most areas examined.	A good performance despite technical imperfections and some missing points of detail. Clear evidence of a systematic approach.	A good performance despite technical imperfections and some missing points of detail. Clear evidence of a systematic approach.	
6–7 **Pass** Candidate has shown competence in most areas examined and has satisfied the requirements for the award.	Sufficiently competent to merit a pass despite some errors and missed points of detail. Few fundamental misreadings. Evidence of a systematic approach.	Sufficiently competent to merit a pass despite some errors and missed points of detail. Few fundamental misreadings. Evidence of a systematic approach.	
0–5 **Fail** Candidate has not satisfied the basic requirements for the award.	Did not meet the basic requirements of the test. Some fundamental errors and little or no attention to matters of detail. A flawed methodology and/or insufficient technique (including continuity).	Did not meet the basic requirements of the test. Some fundamental errors and little or no attention to matters of detail. A flawed methodology and/or insufficient technique (including continuity).	Did not meet the basic requirements of the test. Some fundamental errors and little or no attention to matters of detail. A flawed methodology and/or insufficient technique (including continuity).

Application form for appropriate professional experience approval

Please photocopy this form as necessary

Name _____

Address _____

_____

_____

Telephone/Fax _____

E-mail _____

Level of Music Performance
Diploma you wish to enter for   ☐ DipABRSM   ☐ LRSM   ☐ FRSM

Instrument _____

Prerequisite for which substitution is sought (see pp. 20–21)

_____

With reference to the guidelines given on p. 22, please detail the professional experience you wish to be considered by the Associated Board (continue on a separate sheet, if necessary)

_____

_____

_____

_____

_____

_____

_____

_____

_____

I confirm that the information detailed above is accurate and true.

Candidate's signature _____ Date _____

Please complete this form (or a photocopy of it) and send it to the Director of Examinations, The Associated Board of the Royal Schools of Music, 24 Portland Place, London W1B 1LU, United Kingdom. The form must reach the Board at least six weeks before the published closing date for the session in which you wish to be examined. Please remember that you must enclose supporting documentation verifying your application, as well as a signed declaration from an independent person of appropriate standing (see p. 22) – suggested standard wording for this declaration is given on p. 117. It is important that you do not send your Entry Form to the Associated Board until *after* you have received confirmation that your application for appropriate professional experience approval has been successful.

Suggested standard wording

In my capacity as < title & organization > I confirm that < full candidate name > has gained appropriate professional experience as a performer in connection with < give details of course/qualification/performing group, etc. >.

I have read the relevant syllabus regulations and am therefore able to confirm that < candidate name > has studied/demonstrated skills and understanding equivalent to or in excess of the prerequisite for which substitution is sought.

< signature & date >

NB *Signed declarations must be written in English and submitted on official headed paper. In the case of qualifications/courses, the Associated Board may request samples of relevant course work or certification from the institution concerned.*

Music publishers

The music listed in this syllabus should be available from good music retailers worldwide, who should always be contacted in the first instance.

The Associated Board ensures that its own publications remain in print for the duration of each syllabus. In case of difficulty obtaining Associated Board titles, please use our online ordering facility (www.abrsmpublishing.com) – available in most countries – or contact ABRSM Publishing (*telephone* +44 (0)20 7636 5400; *e-mail* publishing@abrsm.ac.uk).

Every effort has been made to ascertain that the set music from other publishers was available when the repertoire lists were compiled for this syllabus. In case of difficulty obtaining any such titles, please contact the publisher concerned or their UK distributor, as detailed in the list below. Candidates outside the UK should note that many publishers have local distributors around the world who may be able to supply their music more quickly. Details of these distributors may be obtained from the original publisher. Please note that the Associated Board does not supply any music from the publishers listed below.

Adlais
P.O. Box 28, Abergavenny,
Gwent, NP7 5YJ
telephone +44 (0)1291 690517
fax +44 (0)1291 691009
e-mail adlais@btinternet.com

Allegro Music
82 Suffolk Street, Queensway,
Birmingham B1 1TA
telephone +44 (0)1216 437553
fax +44 (0)1216 334773
e-mail sales@allegro.co.uk
www.allegro.co.uk

Ashley Mark Publishing Co.
1 & 2 Vance Court,
Trans Britannia Enterprise Park,
Bladon on Tyne, NE21 5NH
telephone +44 (0)191 4149000
fax +44 (0)191 4149001
e-mail mail@ashleymark.co.uk
www.ashleymark.co.uk

Banks Music Publications
The Old Forge, Sand Hutton,
York, YO41 1LB
telephone +44 (0)1904 468472
fax +44 (0)1904 468679
e-mail banksramsay@boltblue.com
www.banksmusicpublications.cwc.net

Bärenreiter Ltd
Burnt Mill, Elizabeth Way,
Harlow, Essex, CM20 2HX
telephone +44 (0)1279 828930
fax +44 (0)1279 828931
e-mail baerenreiter@dial.pipex.com
www.baerenreiter.com

Boosey & Hawkes Music Publishers Ltd
Aldwych House, 71–91 Aldwych,
London WC2B 4HN
telephone +44 (0)20 7054 7200
fax +44 (0)20 7054 7290
www.boosey.com

Brass Wind Publications
4 St Mary's Road, Manton, Oakham,
Rutland, LE15 8SU
telephone/fax +44 (0)1572 737409
e-mail brasswnd@globalnet.co.uk

Breitkopf & Härtel
Broome Cottage, The Street, Suffield,
Norwich, Norfolk, NR11 7EQ
telephone +44 (0)1263 768732
fax +44 (0)1263 768733
or Sales Dept, P.O. Box 1103,
D-65219 Taunusstein, Germany
e-mail info@breitkopf.com
www.breitkopf.com

Broadbent & Dunn Ltd
66 Nursery Lane, Dover,
Kent, CT16 3EX
telephone +44 (0)1304 825604
fax +44 (0)870 1353567
e-mail bd.music@broadbent-dunn.com
www.broadbent-dunn.com

Chester Music
see Music Sales

Comus Edition
Leach Cottage, Heirs House Lane,
Colne, Lancs., BB8 9TA
telephone +44 (0)1282 864985
fax +44 (0)1282 860770
e-mail wmd@comusic.demon.co.uk

Cramer Music Ltd
23 Garrick Street, London WC2E 9RY
telephone +44 (0)20 7240 1612
fax +44 (0)20 7240 2639
e-mail general@cramermusic.co.uk

De Haske Music (UK) Ltd
Fleming Road, Earlstrees, Corby,
Northants., NN17 2SN
telephone +44 (0)1536 260981
fax +44 (0)1536 401075
e-mail music@dehaske.co.uk
www.dehaske.com

William Elkin Music Services
Station Road Industrial Estate,
Salhouse, Norwich, Norfolk, NR13 6NS
telephone +44 (0)1603 721302
fax +44 (0)1603 721801
e-mail sales@elkinmusic.co.uk
www.elkinmusic.co.uk

Emerson Edition Ltd
Windmill Farm, Ampleforth,
York, YO62 4HF
telephone +44 (0)1439 788324
fax +44 (0)1439 788715
e-mail juneemerson@compuserve.com
www.juneemerson.co.uk

Faber Music Ltd
3 Queen Square, London WC1N 3AU
telephone +44 (0)20 7833 7900
fax +44 (0)20 7833 7939
e-mail sales@fabermusic.com
www.fabermusic.com

Forsyth Brothers Ltd
126 Deansgate, Manchester M3 2GR
telephone +44 (0)161 8343281
fax +44 (0)161 8340630
e-mail info@forsyths.co.uk
www.forsyths.co.uk

Goodmusic
P.O. Box 100, Tewkesbury,
Glos., GL20 7YQ
telephone +44 (0)1684 773883
fax +44 (0)1684 773884
e-mail Sales@Goodmusic-uk.com
www.goodmusicpublishing.co.uk

Griffiths Edition
21 Cefn Coed, Bridgend,
Mid Glamorgan, CF31 4PH
telephone +44 (0)1656 649351

Guitarnotes
Spanish Guitar Centre,
44 Nottingham Road, New Basford,
Nottingham NG7 7AE
telephone +44 (0)115 9622709
fax +44 (0)115 9625368
e-mail sales@spanishguitar.com
www.guitarnotes.co.uk *or*
www.spanishguitar.com

Hallamshire Music
Bank End, North Somercotes, Louth,
Lincs., LN11 7LN
telephone +44 (0)1507 358141
fax +44 (0)1507 358034
www.hallamshiremusic.co.uk

G. Henle Verlag
Forstenrieder Allee 122,
D-81476 München, Germany
e-mail info@henle.de
www.henle.de *or see* M.D.S.

Highbridge Music
Flat 6, 18 Kensington Court Place,
London W8 5BJ
telephone +44 (0)20 7388 6178
fax +44 (0)20 7938 1969

**I.M.P. – International Music
Publications Ltd (Warner/Chappell)**
Griffin House, 161 Hammersmith Road,
London W6 8BS
telephone +44 (0)20 8222 9200
fax +44 (0)20 8222 9260
e-mail imp.sales@warnerchappell.com
www.wbpdealers.com

Kerr Music Corp. Ltd
65 Berkeley Street, Glasgow G3 7DZ

Kirklees Music
609 Bradford Road, Bailiff Bridge,
Brighouse, West Yorkshire, HD6 4DN
telephone +44 (0)1484 722855
fax +44 (0)1484 723591
e-mail sales@kirkleesmusic.co.uk
www.kirkleesmusic.co.uk

London Pro Musica Edition
38 Manningham Lane,
Bradford BD1 3EA
telephone +44 (0)1274 393753
fax +44 (0)1274 393516
e-mail sales@earlyms.demon.co.uk
www.e-m-s.com

Maecenas Europe
5 Bushey Close, Old Barn Lane,
Kenley, Surrey, CR8 5AU
telephone +44 (0)20 8660 3914
fax +44 (0)20 8668 5273
e-mail maecenasmusicltd@aol.com

McGinnis & Marx
236 West 26th Street, Suite 11S,
New York, NY 10001-6736, USA
telephone +1 (212) 2435233
fax +1 (212) 6751630

M.D.S. International
5–6 Raywood Office Complex,
Leacon Lane, Charing, Ashford,
Kent, TN27 OEN
telephone +44 (0)1233 712233
fax +44 (0)1233 714948
e-mail orders@mdsmusic.co.uk

Moeck UK Ltd
38 Manningham Lane, Bradford BD1
3EA *telephone* +44 (0)1274 721646
fax +44 (0)1274 393516
e-mail sales@earlyms.demon.co.uk

Mostyn Music
8 Milvil Court, Milvil Road,
Lee-On-Solent, Hampshire, PO13 9LY
telephone 02392 550566
e-mail enquiries@mostynmusic.com
www.mostynmusic.com

Munson & Harbour
Old Station Works,
119–123 Sandycombe Road, Kew,
Surrey, TW9 2ER
telephone/fax +44 (0)20 8334 9990

Music Exchange (Manchester) Ltd
Claverton Road, Wythenshawe,
Manchester M23 9ZA
telephone +44 (0)161 9461234
fax +44 (0)161 9461195
e-mail sales@musicx.co.uk
www.musicx.co.uk

Music Sales Ltd
Newmarket Road, Bury St Edmunds,
Suffolk, IP33 3YB
telephone +44 (0)1284 702600
fax +44 (0)1284 768301
e-mail music@musicsales.co.uk
www.musicsales.com

MusT
P.O. Box 45004, London N4 4XZ
telephone/fax +44 (0)20 8341 4088
e-mail info@music-trading.co.uk

Novello & Co. Ltd
see Music Sales

O.U.P. – Oxford University Press
Music Department,
Great Clarendon Street,
Oxford OX2 6DP
telephone +44 (0)1865 556767
fax +44 (0)1865 353749
e-mail music.enquiry.uk@oup.com
www.oup.com

Peacock Press
Scout Bottom Farm, Mytholmroyd,
Hebden Bridge, West Yorkshire, HX7
5JS *telephone* +44 (0)1422 882751
fax +44 (0)1422 886157
e-mail ruth@recordermail.demon.co.uk
www.recordermail.demon.co.uk

Peters Edition Ltd
10–12 Baches Street, London N1 6DN
telephone +44 (0)20 7553 4000
fax +44 (0)20 7490 4921
e-mail info@uk.edition-peters.com
www.edition-peters.com

Phylloscopus Publications
92 Aldcliffe Road, Lancaster LA1 5BE
telephone +44 (0)1524 67498
e-mail enquiries@phylloscopus.co.uk
www.phylloscopus.co.uk

Primavera
11 Langham Place, Highwoods,
Colchester, Essex, CO4 4GB
telephone +44 (0)1206 751522
e-mail enidluff@globalnet.co.uk
www.impulse-music.co.uk/
primavera.htm

Recital Music
Studio Ten, Farnham Maltings,
Farnham, Surrey, GU9 7QR
telephone/fax +44 (0)1252 319610

G. Ricordi & Co. (London) Ltd
see U.M.P.

Roberton Publications
see Goodmusic

Rosehill Music
Winwood Music, Unit 7, Fieldside
Farm, Quainton, Bucks., HP22 4DQ
telephone +44 (0)1296 655777
fax +44 (0)1296 655778
e-mail info@winwoodmusic.com

Salvi, Lyon & Healy
Holywell Music Ltd, 58 Hopton Street,
London SE1 9JH
telephone +44 (0)20 7928 8451
fax +44 (0)20 7928 8284
e-mail holywell@holywell.co.uk
www.holywellmusic.co.uk

Saxtet Publications 63 Witherford Way,
Selly Oak, Birmingham B29 4AJ
telephone/fax +44 (0)121 4722122
e-mail info@saxtetpublications.com
www.saxtetpublications.com

G. Schirmer Ltd
see Music Sales

Schott & Co. Ltd
see M.D.S.

R. Smith & Co. Ltd
P.O. Box 367, Aylesbury,
Bucks., HP22 4LJ
telephone +44 (0)1296 682220
fax +44 (0)1296 681989
e-mail info@rsmith.co.uk
www.rsmith.co.uk

Southern Percussion
'Rossella', 194 Howeth Road,
Ensbury Park, Bournemouth,
Dorset, BH10 5NX
telephone +44 (0)1202 389793
fax +44 (0)1202 574968
e-mail sales@southernperc.demon.co.uk
www.southernperc.demon.co.uk

Spartan Press Music Publishers Ltd
Strathmashie House, Laggan Bridge,
Scottish Highlands, PH20 1BU
telephone +44 (0)1528 544770
fax +44 (0)1528 544771
e-mail mail@SpartanPress.co.uk
www.SpartanPress.co.uk

Stainer & Bell Ltd
P.O. Box 110, Victoria House,
23 Gruneisen Road, London N3 1DZ
telephone +44 (0)20 8343 3303
fax +44 (0)20 8343 3024
e-mail post@stainer.co.uk
www.stainer.co.uk

Studio Music Co.
P.O. Box 19292, London NW10 9WP
telephone +44 (0)20 8459 6194
fax +44 (0)20 8451 6470
e-mail sales@studio-music.co.uk

Suite Music
16 Oakwood Avenue, North Gosforth,
Newcastle upon Tyne NE13 6QE
telephone +44 (0)191 2362553

U.M.P. United Music Publishers Ltd
33 Lea Road, Waltham Abbey,
Essex EN9 1ES
telephone +44 (0)1992 703110
fax +44 (0)1992 703189
e-mail info@ump.co.uk
www.ump.co.uk

Universal Edition (London) Ltd
see M.D.S.

Vanderbeek & Imrie Ltd
15 Marvig, Lochs,
Isle of Lewis, HS2 9QP
telephone/fax +44 (0)1851 880216
e-mail mapamundi@aol.com

Wright & Round Ltd
The Cornet Office, P.O. Box 157,
Gloucester GL1 1LW
telephone +44 (0)1452 523438
fax +44 (0)1452 385631
e-mail inquire@wrightandround.com
www.wrightandround.com

The National Qualifications Framework (UK)

The Associated Board's Diplomas are accredited by the regulatory authorities in England, Wales and Northern Ireland and are part of the revised National Qualifications Framework (NQF). The number of levels in the revised NQF has been increased from five to nine (Entry Level to Level 8). The upper levels have been brought into line with the Framework for Higher Education in order to clarify the progression between NQF qualifications, such as the Associated Board's Diplomas, and university-awarded qualifications. The revised NQF is also more in line with the Scottish and Irish qualifications frameworks and is more compatible with developments in Europe.

The broad higher education comparisons given below are shown in terms of level of demand and not volume of study:

ABRSM Diploma	Higher education
DipABRSM	Certificate of higher education
LRSM	Bachelor degree with honours
FRSM	Master's degree

The Associated Board's Music Performance Diplomas have been provisionally placed at the following NQF levels, scheduled to come into effect from January 2006:

ABRSM Diploma	NQF level	NQF title	Accreditation no.
DipABRSM	4	Diploma in Music Performance	100/2799/3
LRSM	6	Licentiate in Music Performance	100/2800/6
FRSM	7	Fellowship in Music Performance	100/2801/8

Up-to-date information on the revised NQF levels is available on the openQUALS database: www.qca.org.uk/openquals.

Attainment descriptions

The attainment descriptions below have been created to give a general indication of the levels of attainment likely to be shown by candidates with results at two distinct levels within each qualification (Distinction and Pass for DipABRSM and LRSM; Pass and Fail for FRSM). These descriptions must be read in relation to the examination content as described for each level of Diploma on pp. 7–18 of this syllabus. The mark awarded will depend in practice upon the extent to which the candidate has demonstrated the skills, knowledge and understanding required at the level. Weakness in some aspects of the exam may be balanced by better performance in others, bearing in mind the marking scheme found on pp. 112–115.

DipABRSM (Music Performance)

Distinction Candidates are able to give an assured, persuasive and effectively communicated recital performance of a generalist programme that presents a wide-ranging yet coherent mixture of style, mood and tempo. Their playing/singing shows both artistic awareness and a secure technique at a level beyond ABRSM Grade 8. They can write programme notes that give a well-balanced commentary on the items performed, and that are pertinent, persuasively written and thoroughly researched. Their communication skills are outstanding and they have a commanding knowledge of their instrument/voice, its idiom and repertoire. They also have a mastery of the issues raised in their programme notes, including the idiom, form and style of the works performed, their historical position, and how these factors influence interpretation. They have a theoretical understanding of music at a minimum level of ABRSM Grade 5. They are able to perform a piece of previously unseen music of ABRSM Grade 6 repertoire level with excellence, demonstrating artistry, full technical security and an instinctive approach.

Pass   Candidates are able to give a solid recital performance of a generalist programme that presents a mixture of style, mood and tempo. Their playing/singing shows technical competence and some musical understanding at a level beyond ABRSM Grade 8. They can write programme notes that give background information on the items performed, with some evidence of appropriate analysis and research. Their communication skills are competent and they have a broad working knowledge of their instrument/voice, its idiom and repertoire. They also have a grasp of the issues raised in their programme notes, including the idiom, form and style of the works performed, their historical position, and how these factors influence interpretation. They have a theoretical understanding of music at a minimum level of ABRSM Grade 5. They are able to perform a piece of previously unseen music of ABRSM Grade 6 repertoire level with competence, taking a systematic approach which, despite some errors or missed points of detail, contains few fundamental misreadings.

LRSM (Music Performance)

Distinction   Candidates are able to give an authoritative and intuitive recital performance of a balanced programme that presents a contrast of repertoire from a minimum of two distinct musical eras. Their playing/singing shows both artistic integrity and technical command in a range of styles. They can write programme notes that are highly perceptive and persuasively written, with a high level of research and excellent organization of material. Their communication skills are outstanding and they have a commanding knowledge of their instrument/voice, its idiom and repertoire. They also have a mastery of the issues raised in their programme notes, including the idiom, form and style of the works performed, their historical position, and how these factors influence interpretation. They have a theoretical understanding of music at a minimum level of ABRSM Grade 5. They are able to perform a piece of previously unseen music of ABRSM Grade 7 repertoire level with excellence, demonstrating artistry, full technical security, and an instinctive approach.

Pass   Candidates are able to give a solid recital performance of a balanced programme that presents a contrast of repertoire from a minimum of two distinct musical eras. Their playing/singing shows technical competence and a broad musical understanding in a range of styles. They can write programme notes that give background information on the items performed, with some evidence of appropriate analysis and research. Their communication skills are competent and they have a broad working knowledge of their instrument/voice, its idiom and repertoire. They also have a grasp of the issues raised in their programme notes, including the idiom, form and style of the works performed, their historical position, and how these factors influence interpretation. They have a theoretical understanding of music at a minimum level of ABRSM Grade 5. They are able to perform a piece of previously unseen music of ABRSM Grade 7 repertoire level with competence, taking a systematic approach which, despite some errors or missed points of detail, contains few fundamental misreadings.

FRSM (Music Performance)

Pass   Candidates are able to give an authoritative, persuasively communicated recital performance of a specialist programme that is internally balanced and contains a contrast of mood and style. Their playing/singing shows both artistic integrity and technical command. They can write about the idiomatic features and performance issues of the recital programme in a written submission that is pertinently and comprehensively argued, with good overall shape, organization and use of language. They demonstrate an ability to survey relevant source materials rigorously, with high-level research skills, personal insight and critical evaluation. Their communication skills are impressive and they have a commanding knowledge of the instrument, its idiom and repertoire. They also have a full understanding of the issues raised in their written submission. They are able to give an idiomatic performance of a piece of previously unseen music of ABRSM Grade 8 repertoire level, demonstrating an assured approach.

Fail Candidates are able to give a recital performance of a specialist programme that is internally balanced and contains a contrast of mood and style, but there is insufficient evidence that they have advanced significantly beyond LRSM level. They can write about the idiomatic features and performance issues of the programme, but the argument may be disjointed or lacking in perception, or there may be an insufficient depth of research. Their communication skills are insufficient for the level and while they have knowledge of the instrument/voice, its idiom and repertoire, this is patchy. Their grasp of the issues raised by the written submission, including the idiom, form and style of the works performed, their historical position, and how these factors influence interpretation, is unconvincing. Their performance of a piece of previously unseen music of ABRSM Grade 8 repertoire level does not meet the basic requirements of the test as it contains some fundamental errors, with little or no attention being given to matters of detail, and with a flawed methodology and/or insufficient technique, including continuity.

The National Occupational Standards (UK)

The National and Scottish Vocational Qualifications entitled 'Music Practice' and 'Arts Development and Teaching', both at NQF Level 4 and offered by Edexcel, contain statements of competence that are known as 'national occupational standards'. These standards describe the functions and responsibilities within a range of job roles and can be used as benchmarks for measuring achievement in a vocational context. In preparing for the Associated Board Diplomas, candidates will be developing many of the competences described by these standards. Units 1–4 and 10 of 'Music Practice' are of particular relevance to performers.

INDEX